CANADIANS BEHIND ENEMY LINES, 1939–1945

By the same author

Canadians in Russia, 1918–1919

Canadians on the Nile, 1882–1898

ROY MACLAREN

Canadians Behind Enemy Lines, 1939–1945

UNIVERSITY OF BRITISH COLUMBIA PRESS
Vancouver and London

CANADIANS BEHIND ENEMY LINES, 1939–1945

This book has been published with the assistance of the
Canada Council.

Canadian Cataloguing in Publication Data

MacLaren, Roy, 1934 –
Canadians behind enemy lines, 1939-1945

Bibliography: p.
Includes index.
ISBN 0-7748-0147-6

1. World War, 1939-1945 – Secret service – Great Britain.
2. World War, 1939-1945 – Personal narratives, Canadian.
3. World War, 1939-1945 – Prisoners and prisons. 4. Escapes.
5. Spies – Canada – Biography. 6. Great Britain. Special
Operations Executive. I. Title.
D810.S7M24   940.54'86'71   C81-091300-3

International Standard Book Number 0-7748-0147-6

Printed in Canada

For Vanessa and Malcolm

in the hope that they may see
the courage but never the horror
described herein

Contents

Illustrations   ix
Preface   xi

PART ONE: Two Clandestine Organizations
  1 The Beginnings   1
  2 Recruitment of Canadians   11

PART TWO: Special Operations Executive
  3 The First Canadian Agents into France   27
  4 Victims   44
  5 Playing the Radio Game   57
  6 The Executions   65
  7 Survivors   75
  8 The Triumph of the Aged and Redundant   86
  9 D-Day   105
10 Assignments from Algiers   116
11 Yugoslavia   129
12 The Balkans and Italy   155
13 Asia   177
14 Sarawak   192
15 Burma   201
16 Malaya   221

PART THREE: M.I.9

17 Escape and Evasion 245
18 Dieppe and Beyond 261
19 The Cross-Channel Ferry 272
20 The Mediterranean and Asia 287

Epilogue 300
Appendix: Frogmen in Burma 302

Notes 309
Bibliography 317
Index 321

Illustrations

Maps

Western Europe   32
Central Europe   142
South-East Asia   181

Plates   *following p. 78*

Plate   1. Canadian Trainee at Ringway Parachute School, 1944
        2. R.A.F. daylight drop of cannisters, Prairie d'Echallons,
           1944
        3. Ray Wooler, S.O.E., near Ringway, 1941
        4. Gustave Bieler, first Canadian with S.O.E.
        5. Forged identity card of Al Sirois
        6. Two German soldiers taken by *maquis*
        7. German munitions train sabotaged by French
           underground
        8. Frank Pickersgill on his escape from prison camp,
           Vichy, 1942
        9. John Macalister, wireless operator for Pickersgill
       10. "Gaby" Chartrand, Chateau-du-Loir, 1943
       11. Pierre Meunier with Walter Stuki, Swiss minister to
           Vichy government, 1944
       12. Roger Caza's forged *Carte d'Identité* as Roger Marc Pilon
       13. Steve Mate, Canadian Armoured Corps
       14. Mate's tombstone, with both real and cover names
       15. Canadians who served with S.O.E. in Hungary

16. William Stuart, one of the first Allied officers to parachute to Tito

17. William Jones with his team sent to aid Tito, 1943

18. French-Canadian veterans of clandestine service, Montreal

following p. 206

Plate 19. Training site for Operation "Oblivion," Lake Okanagan, B.C.

20. Members of Operation "Oblivion" team, Lake Okanagan

21. Chinese-Canadian volunteers training near Melbourne, 1944–45

22. Team members before departure for Borneo and Sarawak, 1945

23. Dakotas of No. 436 Squadron, R.C.A.F., on supply drop

24. Charlie Chung, who served with S.O.E. team in Malaya

25. Henry Fung, first Chinese-Canadian to parachute into Malaya

26. Bing Lee and Bill Lee, who served in Malaya

27. Parade marking contribution of M.P.A.J.A., Kuala Lumpur

28. Harry Ho and Victor Louie, Meerut, 1946

29. French-Canadian veterans of France who served in Asia

30. Motor Gunboat 503, used for evacuation from Brittany

31. Robert Vanier with Canadian prisoners at Dieppe

32. French-Canadian escapees, Montmorillon, 1942

33. Forged identity cards of Ray LaBrosse, M.I.9, showing two false identities

34. Ray LaBrosse with German prisoner, Brittany

35. Arthur Stewart with M.I.9 in hills of Burma

36. Arthur Stewart and Bill Lee in Malaya

37. Emaciated Allied prisoners in Changi prison, Singapore

Preface

This account of Canadians who operated behind enemy lines in Europe and Asia between 1939 and 1945 has not been easy to write. The discovery that there were, to my surprise, so many Canadians who served in this way confronted me with the omnipresent problem that the book would become little more than a catalogue of vignettes. Yet equally, there were not so many Canadians that individual acts of courage and ingenuity could be subsumed in a broad narrative. It will be for the reader to decide whether a satisfactory balance has been achieved between acknowledging the role of each individual and setting his or her service in the wider context of the course of the Second World War.

This would have been a much longer book had I included the story of those brave Canadian soldiers and airmen who, having been shot down over enemy-occupied territory and having evaded or escaped from captivity, joined the local resistance in its war against the Germans or Japanese. I have followed the self-imposed rule of including only those who were intentionally sent behind enemy lines.

A further problem in writing this book arose from the remarkably uneven nature of the material upon which it is based.

First, the memory of survivors, after as long as forty years, is naturally faulty and selective. This would be so in any account of wartime service. Clandestine operations are, however, particularly susceptible to misunderstanding and misinterpretation. What an agent saw from his individual vantage point may well have been distorted by the contradictions of political and military goals, inter-service rivalries, and the differing policies of Britain and of Allied governments-in-exile. More fundamentally, simple, inevitable distortions arise when an individual agent has of necessity been given only limited information.

One test of memory can be to compare personal recollections with documents of the period. Unfortunately, the records of both the Special Operations Executive and M.I.9, the two principal British secret organizations with which Canadians served, are in many cases so scant or remain so restricted as to render difficult any intelligent survey of either the acts of individuals or the sweep of the policies and practices of the two secret organizations. One reason why records are limited is a human one: overwork.

> When considering, after the war, a complaint that the records of [the French] Section were somewhat incomplete, its wartime head commented that those who finished work at any time between three and five in the morning felt "little desire to tabulate the events of the day in order to earn the gratitude of some hypothetical historian of the future."[1]

An official history of the whole Special Operations Executive was written by Professor W. J. M. Mackenzie, but it has not been published. Professor M.R.D. Foot's *S.O.E. in France*, a volume in the British Official History of the Second World War, is a sagacious, perceptive, and measured account of S.O.E.'s operations in one occupied country. Yet, as its author is the first to acknowledge, it too is incomplete.

Another problem arises from restrictions placed on the use of official documents. These restrictions were rightly lamented by the late Lord Louis Mountbatten: "All books on S.O.E. activities [have] had to be written without full access to all relevant documents. Now that the thirty-year limitation on the publication of most wartime documents has been lifted, I personally feel that it is a tremendous pity that those relating to S.O.E. as a purely wartime organization have not yet been released."[2] The problem is compounded in the case of records relating to S.O.E. in the Mediterranean and Asia. During 1945-46, when files were being packed for shipment to Britain, many were destroyed to reduce space. The greatest damage, however, was done in London in 1948. Apparently nobody realized that S.O.E. records would be of historical interest. Indiscriminate destruction took place.

Despite the problems caused by lack of records and the confidentiality of those remaining, two historians have made noteworthy efforts to ferret out and evaluate material on S.O.E. from the now more open records of the British regular military services and of the public service. David Stafford's *Britain and European Resistance* and Elizabeth Barker's *British Policy in South-East Europe in the Second World War* are, in the circumstances, notable achievements. They are useful introductions for anyone seeking to understand the activities of S.O.E. in the broader context of British strategy as a whole.

Otherwise, one must rely largely upon the memoirs of those who served. These are, fortunately, numerous. They range from the stimulating and informative recollections of a senior S.O.E. staff officer, Bickham Sweet-Escott, to a multitude of books and articles written by survivors. A selection will be found in the bibliography.

About M.I.9, the escape and evasion organization with which several Canadians served, little has been written. The best survey is *M.I.9* by J.M. Langley and the same knowledgeable Michael Foot.

Lord Leverhulme, the soap manufacturer, once avowed that half the vast sums he spent on advertising was wasted; the problem was that he did not know which half. There are probably some inaccuracies in this book; the difficulty is that I do not know where they are. This account of Canadians who volunteered to go behind enemy lines is as comprehensive and accurate as I can make it, given the limitations noted above. Yet it is clearly incomplete. For example, there is an abundance of information about Frank Pickersgill, but much less about Romeo Sabourin or Al Beauregard. And very little is now known about the service and death in Burma of Paul Archambault. There is, to take another example, much still to be clarified about the work of Canadians of central European or Italian origin. In this account of service behind enemy lines, therefore, some volunteers emerge as vivid and colourful while others remain shadowy and blurred. Although I could not learn enough about the latter to do more than record their work in a general way, I did not want to omit anyone. Perhaps this book will serve to bring forward people who know something more about the agents or incidents described or indeed about other Canadians who may have served in a clandestine capacity.

In writing this book I have had the help, advice, and encouragement of many, but the responsibility for inaccuracies or misinterpretations is mine.

The Honourable Donald Macdonald, a former Minister of National Defence, first drew my attention to the fact that there had been Canadians who went willingly behind the lines of the enemy during the Second World War. I am grateful to my erstwhile Cambridge colleague for his suggestion about this book.

I am particularly indebted to Lieutenant-Colonel E.G. Boxshall of the Foreign and Commonwealth Office, London, for his great patience, indefatigable assistance, and unfailing courtesy in identifying and providing information. Professor Foot has been similarly resourceful and his wisdom and wit no less helpful. If nothing more comes from the writing of this book than the friendship of Colonel Boxshall and Professor Foot, I shall consider myself amply rewarded.

Others in Britain for whose assistance I am most grateful include Joan Astley, Vera Atkins, Peter Boughey, Sir William Deakin, Lady Elton, Kay Moore Gimpel, Roger Landes, Sir Fitzroy Maclean, and the late Airey Neave.

Of the Canadian survivors, I was able to discuss their adventures with the following: Gaby Chartrand, Pierre Chassé, Roger Cheng, George Chin, Charlie Chung, Guy d'Artois, Cyril Dolly, Lucien Dumais, André Durovecz, Henry Fung, Harry Ho, Paul Labelle, Ray LaBrosse, the late Conrad LaFleur, Bill Lee, Bing Lee, Bob Lew, Victor Louie, Pierre Meunier, Colin Munro, Stevan Serdar, Al Sirois, Paul-Emile Thibeault, Robert Vanier, John Wickey, Ted Wong, and Ray Wooler. Although contacted, John Dehler declined to be interviewed.

The following siblings, spouses, or children of agents were also most helpful: Jacqueline Bieler-Briggs, John de Chastelaine, Louis Deniset, Olive Fournier, Jack Pickersgill, Leon and Claude Taschereau, Robert Stewart, Michael Dafoe, Mrs. W. M. Gilchrist, formerly Mrs. William Stuart, and Mrs. William Jones. I am also grateful for the assistance of Harry Avery, James Barros, Eric Curwain, the late Tommy Drew-Brook, Gustav Duclos, Robert Elliot, Derek Fowkes, Ben Greenhous, John Holmes, Alison Grant Ignatieff, Tom Lock, Guy MacLean, George McLennan, Donald Molison, Meribeth Morris, and John Starnes.

In typing and retyping the manuscript, Noreen King and Elizabeth Wightman were models of patience and good humour, as well as accuracy. Don Constable made the maps. Diane Mew was the most helpful and perceptive of creative editors. My wife, Lee, provided constant support and suggestion.

PART ONE

Two Clandestine Organizations

1

The Beginnings

The British Special Operations Executive (S.O.E.) was born in 1940 and lived its short life in controversy and conflict. Although it was ended in 1946, the debate about its practices and even its usefulness has continued. Its mandate was to encourage resistance in enemy-occupied Europe and Asia by sending agents to help organize and train local volunteers in sabotage, industrial demolition, ambush, disruption of communications and, in a few cases, to engage in the collection of specific intelligence. Its task in one of Churchill's grand phrases was to "set Europe" – and later Asia – "ablaze." Brave men and women fought, endured torture and foul confinement, and were maimed, killed, or executed while serving with S.O.E. Its pre-eminence as the largest and most colourful of the various clandestine Allied services in the Second World War is unchallenged.

Although S.O.E. was not formally established until July 1940, British intelligence (M.I.6) had been considering the possibilities of a sabotage and subversive organization even before the war. S.O.E. came into being from the amalgamation of three small organizations which had been established quietly shortly before the war: Section D of M.I.6, M.I.(R) of the War Office, and a small unit attached to the Foreign Office which was intended to influence German opinion (it later evolved into the autonomous Political Warfare Executive).* The new organization had not been formally established, however, before the advent of Churchill's coalition government in May 1940 and the Dunkirk evacuation and the fall of France the following month. These events forced the British Chiefs of Staff to recognize the urgent need to encourage, in their words, "widespread revolt within [Germany's] conquered territories."[1] France, Poland, the Netherlands, Belgium, Denmark, and Norway were now occupied by German forces. Spain and Italy were in league with Germany with whom the Soviet Union had recently concluded a non-aggression pact. Britain stood virtually alone, her forces expelled from all of Europe except Gibraltar. In the absence of any other effective means of retaliation, emphasis was placed on the economic blockade of Germany, including the denial of petroleum and other raw materials from the Balkans. The need for a strategic bombing offensive was also much discussed in the wake of the French collapse, but bombers were still in short supply and night bombing techniques inchoate.

Having reviewed these and several other unpromising alternatives, the British Chiefs of Staff concluded that "the only other method of bringing about the downfall of Germany is by stimulating the seeds of revolt within the conquered territories."[2] Exaggerated hopes of underground armies and vast populations in general revolt began to proliferate. The provision of a "detonator" was seen as the most immediate contribution Britain could make to ignite local resistance against the Germans and, more broadly, hit back at the enemy. The Joint Planning Staff concurred: "The attack from within is the basic conception. Subversive action and propaganda will be at least as important as the operations of our normal armed forces."[3]

---

*This propaganda unit, briefly a part of S.O.E., was originally under the direction of a vulpine Canadian, Sir Campbell Stuart of Montreal, a director of *The Times* for most of the interwar years and an active partisan of the Conservative party. See Sir Campbell Stuart, *Opportunity Knocks Once* (London: Collins, 1952).

Hugh Dalton, the Minister for Economic Warfare, wrote enthusiastically to the Foreign Secretary in 1940:

> We have got to organize movements in enemy-occupied territory comparable to the Sinn Fein movement in Ireland, to the Chinese Guerillas now operating against Japan, to the Spanish Irregulars who played a notable part in Wellington's campaign or – one might as well admit it – to the organizations which the nazis themselves have developed so remarkably in almost every country in the world. This "democratic international" must use many different methods, including industrial and military sabotage, labour agitation and strikes, continuous propaganda, terrorist acts against traitors and German leaders, boycotts and riots.
>
> An organization on this scale and of this character is not something which can be handled by the ordinary departmental machinery of either the British Civil Service or the British military machine. What is needed is a new organization to co-ordinate, inspire, control and assist the nationals of the oppressed countries who must themselves be the direct participants. We need absolute secrecy, a certain fanatical enthusiasm, willingness to work with people of different nationalities, complete political reliability.[4]

And so it was that on 19 July 1940, Neville Chamberlain, in one of his last acts as Lord President of Council before his death, issued a "most secret" paper by which an autonomous organization, S.O.E., was launched on its unchartered, hazardous course of encouraging "fifth columns" in occupied countries.

The first year of its existence was to be an uncertain infancy, halting and occasionally marked by incompetence. Unlike the British M.I.5 (counter-intelligence) or M.I.6, S.O.E. had no immediate prewar antecedents, no peacetime staff, no traditions. Even at its peak in 1944 when it numbered almost fourteen thousand, it never completely lost its amateur status, its air of improvisation and occasional eccentricity so appealing to the many romantics it attracted. Gradually it became more proficient, but it certainly never achieved the global reputation – warranted or unwarranted – which M.I.6 enjoyed.

Michael Foot, the official historian of S.O.E. in France, has written of it:

Tales of derring-do fit for the reading of a schoolboy are entangled with tales of intrigue and treachery of a Proustian complexity; high strategy and low tactics are frequently hand in hand. The truth is that S.O.E. was an essentially unorthodox formation, created to wage war by unorthodox means in unorthodox places. Nothing quite like it had been seen before; probably nothing quite like it will be seen again, for the circumstances of Hitler's war were unique, and called out this among other unique responses.

S.O.E.'s work was true to the tradition of English eccentricity ... the sort of thing that looks odd at the time, and eminently sensible later.[5]

British intelligence services, especially the influential M.I.6, were not as enthusiastic as Churchill about S.O.E. They were not pleased that S.O.E. should have been given such a broad mandate, and certainly not autonomy to carry it out. The methods of M.I.6 were almost the antithesis of those of S.O.E. Sabotage and ambush brought immediate enemy response, heightened surveillance and suspicion, increased roadblocks and additional security checks, and even savage reprisal – everything, in short, a covert collector of intelligence wants to avoid. The quieter it was, the better M.I.6 liked it. S.O.E., on the other hand, was happiest when there were loud bangs. In the view of M.I.6, the introduction of yet another clandestine organization into occupied Europe would likely mean crossed lines – agents of one organization getting in the way of, confounding, unwittingly exposing or otherwise placing in hazard the activities of others. As we shall see, M.I.6 did succeed in having the operations of another new secret organization, M.I.9, placed under its control, but in the case of the much larger S.O.E., it failed. Although M.I.6 did control S.O.E.'s wireless services until May 1942, it was not given ultimate authority over S.O.E.'s wide-ranging activities, and for the remainder of the war there was no love lost between the two secret organizations.

Nor were the British Chiefs of Staff entirely easy in their minds about how best to co-operate with yet unidentified indigenous undergrounds. This was, to them, a novel, untested, and for some even unwelcome method of warfare, with the onus on its advocates to prove that it was a more effective way of damaging the enemy than conventional methods – even when the opportunities for conventional methods were few. All three regular services had their orthodox sceptics, but it was the R.A.F. that was most directly involved. It would be called upon to provide the aircraft and aircrew for the hazardous task of parachuting or landing agents, ammunition, money, medicines, arms, and other supplies in occupied Europe and Asia. But were not skilled aircrew and scarce bombers better employed on nightly raids? Only late in the war did tentative questions begin to be asked about the value of mass bombing. To this day, there is little analysis of the relative impact of resistance versus mass bombing; but for the most part, bombing always had priority over S.O.E. drops. Secret assignments were looked upon by many senior air force officers as a tiresome diversion of resources at a time when it was imperative to concentrate all resources upon night bombing raids. In the contest for air support, S.O.E. almost always came last. What Air Marshal Portal once said to a senior S.O.E. officer neatly summarized the conventional R.A.F. attitude: "Your work is a gamble which may give us a valuable dividend or may produce nothing .... My bombing offensive is not a gamble .... I cannot divert aircraft from a certainty to a gamble which may be a gold-mine or may be completely worthless."[6] The validity of this facile assumption was never tested; the shortage of aircraft was almost always a fatal obstacle to the full realization of the potential of S.O.E.

Controversy about the role of S.O.E. also arose from the nature of local resistance in Europe and Asia. In several occupied countries, civil wars were played out at the same time as the fight against the German, Italian, or Japanese invaders was pursued. This was most obvious in the Balkans and southeast Asia, but the struggle for the future between resistance movements of the right and left, between liberal and communist, monarchist and republican, was also evident in much of western Europe. Peter Cavelcoressi has caught the essence of the challenge facing S.O.E. as it attempted to balance political and military goals:

Prizing variety and unconventionality for their own sake, and stirred perhaps by the historical recollections of chouans, carbonari and klephts, Churchill welcomed the chance to revive the fighting spirit and fighting forces of Europe's nations. He wanted to summon them to make life hell for the Germans and, ultimately, to cooperate with the allies' regular armies when the time should come to return to the continent. But this part of the programme raised unforeseen political complications. S.O.E.'s emissaries became charged with diplomatic tasks: persuading Resistance groups to adopt certain policies or tactics, reconciling them with one another for the good of the common cause, reporting on them and advising which were more worthy of support than others. Supplying one organization with arms in preference to another was a political act. The British tried to operate on the principle that the only thing that mattered was harassing the Germans and the only touchstone for deciding between competing groups was this anti-German fervour. But this simple rule of thumb ignored the facts. The Resistance movements were not simply, sometimes not primarily, anti-German. They represented for the time being the domestic politics of their countries. Some of them were fighting against the pre-war order and distrusted or opposed their governments in exile with which the British government was in alliance; and they became more definitely left-wing after Hitler's invasion of the U.S.S.R. unshackled the communists and set them free to join and try to dominate the Resistance.[7]

Introduce S.O.E. and M.I.9 agents into such a kaleidoscope of mixed allegiances, deadly political rivalries, armed confrontations, and personal vendettas, and it was inevitable that they would become involved in much more complex matters than simple death and destruction of the enemy. To what degree did S.O.E. further the interests of the communist Tito against the royalist Mihailović in Yugoslavia? The monarchists over the communists in Greece? What roles did S.O.E. and M.I.9 agents play in the Malayan, Burmese, Thai, Indonesian, or Indochinese civil wars? These and a multitude of other essentially political questions asked about an avowedly apolitical organization – asked repeatedly by the British Foreign Office – added to the confusion that attended S.O.E. throughout its six years of controversial existence. As a senior S.O.E. officer later noted:

The people inside the occupied countries . . . on whom we had to
rely for action . . . were not necessarily, or even mainly, the people
who hoped that when the war was won things would go back to
being just what they were when it began. . . . They were risking their
lives for war aims of their own, which differed in many important
respects from ours.[8]

In enemy-occupied territories, all national resistance movements were fighting in their own homeland; their goal was the
expulsion of the enemy. To achieve that goal, co-operation
sometimes strengthened among local underground groups
within each national resistance, at least among those of similar
broad political persuasion. The national movement then became
the embodiment of the national spirit. The instigators of such
movements could not, however, be outsiders; what the Allies
could do was to assist the evolution toward national resistance.
From the summer of 1940 to the autumn of 1942, Britain was, in
effect, the sole arsenal, the banker, and in several cases, the
headquarters of European resistance movements.

After the entry of the Soviet Union and the United States into
the war, British strategic thinking gradually changed. More
confidence grew in the possibilities of direct confrontation of
army with army. "The grandiose theories of the detonator
concept, of the secret armies in Europe, of left-wing revolution,
of a combined programme of subversive propaganda and action,
had all dissolved. There remained the more limited (but no less
problematic or controversial) tasks of persuading resistance
movements to co-ordinate with, but be subordinated to, Allied
strategy, and of carrying out specific tasks of sabotage."[9] As the
war moved into additional areas and as a few more long-range
aircraft became available to S.O.E., new opportunities for the
encouragement of subversion opened up, causing changes in
emphasis. From 1942 the aim was increasingly to develop underground units to support the large land forces forming for eventual major amphibious operations in both Europe and Asia.

At first, only the most elementary contact existed between
London and local resistance movements. Gradually, as the war

progressed, S.O.E. consolidated its relations with them and with the secret services of other Allied nations. But from first to last, S.O.E. remained the prime outside support of resistance movements in occupied countries.

The other British clandestine organization in which several Canadians served was M.I.9, intended to help escaped prisoners of war and Allied servicemen in occupied territory who had evaded capture. When the Second World War began, the British were not new to the escape business. During the First World War, secret communications had been established with some P.O.W. camps in Germany and several British prisoners of courage and ingenuity had managed to escape from heavily guarded German and Turkish camps. Twenty years later, in 1938, War Office records were resurrected and the advice of First World War escapers sought. It is embroidering a truism to say that the person best qualified to help an escaper through enemy-occupied territory is one who himself has evaded capture or escaped.

When the "phoney war" ended in 1940 with the unleashing of Hitler's *Blitzkrieg* on the Lowlands and France, lessons of the past had been digested. A new secret agency, M.I.9, was set up by the War Office to help prisoners escape, instructing British and Commonwealth aircrew about the best ways to avoid capture and providing them with compact "escape kits."* In Europe, if they did evade capture or subsequently escaped, it was M.I.9 who debriefed them when they reached neutral territory – Spain, Sweden, and Switzerland – or Britain. Evaders frequently returned with useful and occasionally valuable information about conditions in occupied territories or about potential targets. A small section of M.I.9 began the more active clandestine task of

*The kits, which became increasingly sophisticated, varied a little according to the war theatre, but generally they contained a water bottle, water-purifying tablets, a razor, soap, fish hooks, concentrated food for three days, maps printed on silk, a small compass, a file, and a knife for cutting away parachute harness (if the landing was in a tree).

contacting, organizing, and assisting local individuals or groups in enemy-occupied countries who showed themselves willing to help Allied escapers or evaders.

M.I.9's first challenge was in France, to assist British soldiers left behind on the beaches of Dunkirk, survivors of the bitter fighting around Calais, or those who had been cut off from their regiments in the confused withdrawals from Brittany and Bordeaux. During the summer of 1940, several hundred made their way across France, some still in uniform, many simply walking. (One handsome Guards officer was safely passed across France from brothel to brothel.) The Germans had occupied northern France, so most men headed south, frequently aided by Frenchmen humiliated and angered by their country's sudden defeat. Until the Germans occupied the whole of France in November 1942, if British servicemen could once cross the demarcation line into Vichy France, they had a better chance of reaching Marseille, the principal staging point on the escape route to the frontier with neutral Spain.

By early 1941, few British soldiers remained on the run in France. It was becoming evident, however, that the number of R.A.F. airmen successfully evading capture after baling out from their damaged aircraft was rapidly increasing. A much more extensive M.I.9 was needed, along with a more professional approach to replace the somewhat amateur improvisations of the "phoney war." The formation of a yet more specialized group to take an active role in the work of the escape lines now seemed essential. M.I.6 remained sceptical; in its view, there were already too many Allied secret organizations spoiling the broth. Nevertheless, M.I.9 and its supporters in the War Office appeared to win the day. A new section of M.I.9–"Intelligence School 9" to give its cover name, or I.S.9 as it was subsequently known–was given the assignment of assisting prisoners of war to escape or evaders to regain Allied lines. More specifically, I.S.9 became responsible for identifying and supporting those in occupied Europe already operating or willing to organize escape lines. However, M.I.6, while reluctantly agreeing to the creation of yet another clandestine organization in occupied Europe–it had only recently been forced to accept the much larger S.O.E.–successfully insisted that all messages between M.I.9 and its agents should pass through M.I.6 wireless stations in Britain. It equally insisted that Brigadier Norman Crockatt, M.I.9's chief, and his senior colleagues, including James Langley, himself a successful and determined escaper who headed the new clandestine unit, should be guided by M.I.6 in operating escape networks.

The head of M.I.6, Major-General Sir Stewart Menzies, assigned one of his two deputies, Colonel Claude Marjoribanks Dansey, an old friend of Churchill, the task of ensuring that M.I.9 knew its place. As Langley later recalled:

> Appreciating that there was a very real chance that M.I.9 might try and go it alone on the lines of S.O.E. [Dansey] approached . . . Crockatt with an offer to help with the work of recruiting guides to conduct evaders over the Pyrenees and through Spain to either the consulate at Barcelona or . . . the British Mission in Madrid . . . .
>
> As M.I.9 were totally ill-equipped to undertake such work . . . Crockatt had little alternative but to accept the offer, . . . but the price was very high. [Dansey] had achieved his object and for the next four years M.I.6 were to control all M.I.9's clandestine operations in Holland, Belgium, France, Spain and Portugal.[10]

I.S.9 was in turn kept separate from other, less confidential activities of M.I.9 and was not to engage in the collection of intelligence or to attempt sabotage; those were assignments of M.I.6 and S.O.E. Crossed lines in the intelligence business would only cause trouble – including infiltration by the enemy – and probably deaths. With the question of ultimate control thus decided, Crockatt and his remarkably imaginative staff set about establishing in London the new organization for the co-ordination and direction of the growing number of escape lines which were being formed in Asia as well as Europe.

It was with S.O.E. and M.I.9, those two vital agents of clandestine warfare, with all their foibles and shortcomings and all their ingenuity, courage, and perseverance, that Canadians volunteered to go behind enemy lines.

2

Recruitment of Canadians

The Canadians who volunteered to go behind enemy lines came chiefly from three groups: French-Canadians; immigrants from Italy and eastern Europe; and Chinese-Canadians.* They would serve in France, Yugoslavia, Hungary, Italy, Burma, Malaya, and Sarawak. In the earlier days of S.O.E. most went about in disguise (roughly in accordance with the traditional cinema

*Any reader who wishes to pursue the subject of Canadians who were behind enemy lines unintentionally might begin with the adventures of Jack Fairweather and Jack Veness, two infantry officers who escaped in Normandy from German captivity and served with a *maquis* for several months (Will R. Byrd, *The Two Jacks* [Toronto: Ryerson, 1954]) or of Hubert Brooks, who was shot down over Poland and spent almost three years with the Polish underground (Hubert Brooks, "Escape to Danger," *Weekend Magazine*, vol. 7 nos. 40 and 41, 1957).

concept of a spy). By 1944-1945, most either served more like soldiers in civilian clothes or even remained in their uniforms, instructing and fighting with underground units.*

Recruiting for both S.O.E. and M.I.9 was a somewhat extemporaneous, haphazard affair – although in the case of M.I.9 there was, ideally, a successful escape amongst the qualifications of the candidate. Volunteers were sought first from the British armed forces, and soon after from among qualified civilians in Britain, "for tasks of great danger." Maurice Buckmaster, a tall, gentle, bilingual former Ford employee in France and eventually the dedicated head of S.O.E.'s French section, later stated in a peculiarly English fashion, "I have always held...that a good 'amateur' is worth more than a good 'professional'....Our officers were, without exception, 'amateurs' in the true sense of the word."[1] At the London headquarters that durable English institution, the "old boy network," produced much of S.O.E.'s senior and colourful staff. (Buckmaster noted candidly, "We were aided in our recruiting by the advent of men and women vouched for and recommended by existing members of the service."[2]) As S.O.E. became more methodical in its recruiting, military intelligence helped by undertaking to identify those already in uniform who spoke, for example, faultless Albanian or Thai. Their background was investigated before they themselves were sounded as to whether (and subsequently why) they were willing to volunteer for highly dangerous, frequently solitary work. The demand always exceeded the supply, especially given the small percentage of candidates accepted for training after their initial interviews. Felix Walter, the senior intelligence officer at Canadian Military Headquarters (C.M.H.Q.) in London, later recalled:

---

*Canadians went behind enemy lines in a variety of roles during the Second World War but although in numbers they exceeded those who undertook clandestine assignments in earlier wars, their heterogeneity was at least matched by Ismail Me'ereh ("Mike Merry"), the Druze grocer from Winnipeg who, employed by the Eastern Mediterranean Special Intelligence Bureau, served with Lawrence of Arabia in 1918 in the Arab uprising against the Turks (Sir Alec Kirkbride, *An Awakening; The Arab Campaign 1917-18* [University Press of Arabia, 1971]).

By the end of 1941 and the beginning of 1942, British secret organizations were becoming hard pressed for lack of personnel. Expert linguists, always at a premium in Great Britain, were urgently required for a great variety of duties in other fields and it proved very difficult to find men and women who were not only thoroughly acquainted with the countries to which they were to be sent, but possessed courage and physical stamina of a degree sufficient to enable them to live the lives of hunted outcasts with the threat of torture and death constantly in the offing.[3]

In Britain there were, of course, more prospective recruits who spoke French fluently and who knew France more intimately than, say, those with comparable knowledge of Bulgaria or Borneo. British citizens with a French parent; natives of the Channel Islands; long-time bank employees; travel agents; representatives of Imperial Chemicals, Dunlop, Ford, or other British-based companies active in prewar France – all were canvassed. (French refugees or citizens resident in Britain were expected to serve in the Free French forces.) They were a diverse lot, ranging from "pimps to princesses."[4]

It was soon recognized, however, that the limited supply in Britain of those who might be able to pass as Frenchmen in France could not meet the growing demand for agents capable of evading increasingly strict German controls. Further, those with relatives in France or those from the Channel Islands, at that time occupied by the Germans, were especially vulnerable if captured, since the lives of their families might be threatened. Yet others were unsuitable in light of their strong views about internal political struggles in France. Therefore it was thought that problems might be fewer if French-speaking volunteers could be found from other than France or the Channel Islands. Within the Commonwealth, it was not long before the potential which Mauritius and Canada offered as fields of recruitment for the "F" Section of S.O.E. began to be explored actively. Fluent French and an intimate knowledge of France were among the ideal qualifications. Although French-Canadians had the former, few had much experience of the latter. But the pressing need justified the risk: French-Canadians, who were North Americans in so much, might be taught enough about the strange practices of Frenchmen to enable them to pass unremarked.

In the event, it seemed that no Canadians would serve in clandestine warfare. As early as 12 March 1940, four months before S.O.E. itself was initiated, its War Office predecessor approached Canadian Military Headquarters in London to inquire whether Canada would want to recommend personnel for "irregular leaders or guerilla warfare jobs." The War Office specified "social and political" training about particular occupied countries, intending to create a pool of trained men for political missions, "especially at the end of the war when conditions may be somewhat chaotic"[5] – a far-seeing, optimistic statement for the War Office to make during the dismal days of 1940. General Andrew McNaughton, commanding the Canadians in Britain, had reservations about such clandestine service, but he did finally agree, a year later, to permit volunteers from among the twenty-three thousand Canadian soldiers then in Britain.

By late 1942, following the termination of the link with M.I.6, S.O.E.'s needs for trained, French-speaking wireless operators had become acute. One British officer summarized S.O.E.'s communication challenge succinctly. "There were three problems," he wrote:

> how to confirm that worthwhile resistance movements existed (and, if they did, how to establish contact); how to maintain contact when established; and, this having been done, how to provide the sinews of war to those in occupied territories prepared to fight. The first and third postulated the establishment of physical means of communication, the second the ability to transmit and receive – at an acceptable speed – messages, information and orders.[6]

Broadcasting brief, innocuous messages on the European services of the B.B.C., understandable only to agents who had been instructed in their real meaning before departure, reduced the need to receive wireless transmissions from Britain, but S.O.E. radio operators were nevertheless being captured or killed at an appalling rate. Competent radio operators were essential to the success of an agent, who necessarily depended on continuing and rapid contact with Britain for air drops, targets, and co-ordination with other underground circuits. In its increasingly urgent search for operators, the War Office asked the chief signals officer of the Canadian army in Britain to identify likely candidates. Thereafter, Canadian wireless operator volunteers – and they became the majority of Canadian agents – were nominated by the chief signals officer while the identification of other volunteers was more the responsibility of the senior intelligence officer at C.M.H.Q.*

From the beginning, the training of all agents was made as rigorous, systematic, and thorough as the pressing need for such agents on the one hand and accumulated experience on the other permitted. For those going to occupied Europe, the commando base at Arisaig in a rugged, remote part of western Scotland offered seclusion from unwanted attention. Before encountering the rigours of Scotland, however, a first assessment and screening was provided by constant surveillance during basic training. What were the prospective agent's attitudes and foibles? How would she or he meet the strains of clandestine warfare? What evidence of resourcefulness was there? Of endurance? Of self-reliance? During this initial phase, some of the more obvious misfits were weeded out and returned to other duties. A week of leave for the agent allowed staff time to review carefully who should go on to the commando base in Scotland. There much more exacting and strenuous training followed: knife, rope, map, and boat work; "silent killing"; instruction in small arms (both Allied and enemy); elementary Morse; maximum demolition with a minimum of explosive; field craft and living off the country.

The experiences of a Canadian infantry officer, Guy d'Artois, and Sonia Butt, his English fellow agent and bride-to-be, were typical of many who trained for clandestine warfare:

---

*The files of C.M.H.Q. should be a fecund source of information about Canadians who served behind enemy lines, but unfortunately several of the principal volumes were found to be missing when the C.M.H.Q. files were transferred from the Department of National Defence to the Public Archives of Canada in 1968 and 1972.

Within a few hours they were calling their new quarters the Looney Bin. They had to unravel puzzles for a psychiatrist.... Officials asked them snap questions like "How many windows in the east wing of this house?" Both men and girls climbed trees, jumped from high walls, crossed rivers on ropes and wriggled through obstacle courses. They were all, women included, taught how to slaughter a sheep, gut a rabbit and break a man's neck before he could scream.

In the mess they were encouraged to drink and knew that great interest was taken in their capacity. After one heavy session Sonia woke up to find an officer sitting at her bedside. He was there to hear whether she talked in her dreams and, if so, in what language. At mealtimes all conversation was in French. Those who made bad slips soon vanished. Anybody who left his knife and fork resting together on the plate English style, instead of apart, French style, was rebuked. They were not allowed to leave the grounds or make a telephone call. All their mail was censored.

Still in the same squad, Sonia and Guy went to another camp in the Midlands nicknamed the Cookery School. They mixed explosives from household acids and demolished bits of railroad track and trees. They learned the niceties of putting abrasives in piston housings and axle boxes.[7]

But before agents could put all this arduously acquired expertise to work, they had to get to their theatre of war. To infiltrate agents into enemy-occupied territory, both submarines and various types of surface vessels were occasionally used, especially in the Mediterranean and southeast Asia. But submarines were scarce and much too valuable to risk often. Agents could be landed by trawlers or fast naval craft, but they were noisy and could be detected by surface vessels and radar, a major problem especially along the heavily guarded English Channel. In Europe the silent parachute was the preferred method of penetration; indeed, in much of Europe, the parachute was the *only* way. This required a higher degree of physical fitness on the part of the agents than had at first been anticipated.

Some older or infirm agents had to be landed – and removed – by aircraft. For these surreptitious comings and goings, the aircraft most commonly used was the Lysander, a single-engined, high-wing monoplane with a maximum speed of 260 k.p.h. and a range of about 720 kilometres. Originally designed for artillery and other army support work, it could carry only two passengers (its pilot had to double as navigator), although three could somehow be squeezed in or a few high-priority packages added. The Lysander's greatest virtue was its ability to take off from an exceedingly short runway: 150 metres was sufficient. By 1942, the U.S.-designed, two-engined Hudson began to supplement the Lysanders.* With its squat, rotund fuselage, the Hudson could carry more than a dozen passengers. But it was too slow and it required a kilometre of clear field to take off. Later in the war, DC-3 Dakotas, into which as many as forty passengers could be crowded, were on occasion used.

For parachute drops, Whitleys, Wellingtons, Stirlings and, later, Liberators were employed, the last especially on the long hauls to Poland and throughout Asia, where amphibious Catalinas as well as Dakotas were also used for shorter trips. In England, flights originated first from a secluded part of the R.A.F. station at Newmarket in Cambridgeshire, then at Stradishall in Suffolk, and finally at Tempsford in Surrey and, for Lysanders, from Tangmere in Sussex. For the Mediterranean and the Balkans, drops were made from airfields near Algiers, Protville in Tunisia, and Derna in Libya. From Italy, Bari in the south was generally used.

It was to these various bases that agents were taken to be parachuted or to be landed in enemy territory. As part of their training, almost all agents had to complete a brief parachute course at Ringway near Manchester or, later, in Palestine, Algeria, Italy, Australia, or India. Infiltrating agents by parachute was something new in warfare; until the Second World War, there were no parachutes capable of fulfilling the various tasks demanded of them by subversive operations. Much pioneering development work had to be done before the parachuting of agents began to approach a routine.

---

*The initial Special Duty squadrons, as was frequently the case in the R.A.F. generally, had some Canadian air and ground crew. Most supply drops were at night, but later in the war there were special drops in daylight by Mosquitoes of 418 Squadron, R.C.A.F., and massive drops by Flying Fortresses of the U.S.A.A.F.

The first parachuters who risked their lives were dropped "blind"; as best he could the pilot found the point selected, frequently on the basis of sketchy information; the aperture opened and the man was swallowed by the empty blackness. Navigational errors were numerous and accidents frequent. Even if the operation was successful, the agent was then alone in a country perhaps unfamiliar to him; at the outset he did not even know which door to knock at; some old friend, on whom he thought he could rely, might well be only too eager to denounce him . . . .

The early agents, if lucky enough to reach their destination, recruited "reception committees" for the more fortunate ones who followed. Dropping areas were carefully chosen; they had to be adequately flat and completely open, at a sufficient distance, therefore, from houses, forests, roads or high-tension lines; their minimum dimensions (400-500 square yards) and their coordinates were transmitted to London by radio. At the same time the agents signalled the types of weapons and explosives they required and the number of containers they could receive. Each dropping area was given a code-name and the day of the operation was announced by broadcasting over the radio a pre-arranged sentence, incomprehensible to all but the initiated.

As soon as the sentence was heard the reception committee, some ten men, moved to the dropping zone; this they marked with four electric torches or four bonfires laid out on a pre-arranged pattern indicating the direction of the wind; torches and fires were lit as soon as the aircraft's engines were heard. The pilot circled above the markers for a moment to get into the best position and then dropped his cargo of men and/or containers. The former were quickly taken to the hideout prepared for them, while the reception committee, with some of its members on guard, set about burying the parachutes and concealing the containers (they weighed 225 lbs) in some safe place pending distribution of their contents.

The main risk in this system was that the lights might attract the attention of some German aircraft flying in the vicinity – and it would not hesitate to machine-gun any suspect area. This danger was eliminated by the 'S-phone', which provided direct communication between aircraft and the ground at a range of several thousand yards. Once contact was established recognition signals were exchanged fearlessly. Other problems remained such as the transport, maintenance and employment of the equipment dropped, but all were solved in time.[8]

That all such problems were eventually solved and, more fundamentally, that agents were adequately instructed in the fundamentals of parachuting was due in part to the courage of John Raymond Wooler. A stocky young man with bright eyes, a saturnine complexion and the quick, decisive movements of an athlete, Wooler was supremely confident and determined. Born in Toronto in 1917, he had been educated in Montreal, France, and the Channel Islands. After an unsuccessful debut in the business world as a seventeen-year-old truck salesman in London, Wooler invested in a citrus plantation near the Argentine-Paraguay border. From there, during the Munich crisis, he worked his passage back to Europe on a Belgian steamer to enlist as a private in the British army. Within a year, Wooler had been commissioned, become an instructor in the Royal Artillery, and been given skiing training in the Alps with the French *Chasseurs alpins.*

In early 1940, he had volunteered for the "Independent Companies" (later renamed the Commandos) which briefly served in northern Norway following the German invasion. The Independent Companies were commanded by Colin Gubbins, later to become head of S.O.E.[9] On a destroyer taking them back to Britain from their somewhat ignominious debut, Gubbins had outlined to the young gunner subaltern the type of clandestine organization he wanted to create to help strike back at the victorious enemy. Wooler promptly volunteered. Having assured Gubbins that he already knew how to parachute (a claim he hastily made good upon their return to England), Wooler soon found himself developing parachute equipment and techniques for "the Firm" and training Czechs, Poles, and Free French for some of its first operations into occupied Europe. He became a highly skilled parachute instructor and an expert on supply drops and container packing. But, as he later recounted, he first had to learn to jump himself:

Ringway at the beginning of the '40s was where the first British paratroops were trained and where I self-instructed myself after posing as an old hand and made several jumps with them until I felt I was sufficiently competent to train others. S.O.E...acquired two country mansions within a 12 mile radius of the airport–Dunham

House at Altrincham and Wilmslow Manor at Wilmslow – where agents were housed and where, behind the walls, . . . I gave them their basic ground training and taught them aircraft exit procedures using two simulated aircraft fuselages. When ready to jump, the "lambs" [agents] were sped to a waiting aircraft at Ringway – in those days old Mk. 2 & 3 Whitleys – with as little exposure to curious eyes as possible . . . and dropped in Tatton Park, a ten minute flight away. I would jump alone on the first pass and then from the ground, with electric megaphone, instruct each as he or she came down. Their dropping altitude was 800'. Everyone's first jump is the worst, but once completed turns you into an excited kid. No less the agents and they would jump around hugging each other – and me – and shouting in whatever was their native language, another source of worry to the security people who always feared that a civilian or two might have penetrated Tatton Park and would be spilling the beans in local pubs . . . . To cool off many of the lambs, I would rush them back to Ringway for a second and on occasion even a third jump. This was also dictated by weather conditions as fog was prevalent in that part of Lancashire even in summer months. We would wait sometimes two or three days for it to clear enough to fly. It was hard on a first jump agent. Partly to overcome this, the R.A.F. rigged a balloon in Tatton Park with a cage and aperture from which drops could be made from approximately 800'. This balloon was also used for night drops if the weather closed in. I insisted that every agent did a night drop as this simulated more accurately the operational drop by moonlight or part moon. The balloon drop was the most unpopular type of jump as there was no engine slipstream to help open the "statichute" – chutes operated by an attached static line – and often times the chute took its time to crack open from the upward air generated by the speed of bodily descent. However, it was quite a safe practice if a little unnerving to the novice.[10]

Among Wooler's three hundred jumps during the war were many to test new equipment, a dangerous job which nearly killed him on several occasions. Agents of both British clandestine organizations and, later, of the Office of Strategic Services of the United States (O.S.S.) had reason to be grateful to Wooler, not only for the many risks he took in helping to improve their equipment, but for the unfailing encouragement which he gave to the usually frightened and sometimes terrified novice jumpers. Wooler went as despatcher on more than twenty drops of agents into Europe and Asia, occasionally doubling as front gunner in Whitley bombers. We shall meet Wooler again in North Africa, Italy, and eventually even Sarawak.

Upon completion of their parachute training at Ringway, agents were generally returned to country houses in the south of England. Indeed, the proclivity of S.O.E. to use large, secluded country houses for training purposes soon gave rise to the explanation that S.O.E. was an abbreviation of "Stately 'Omes of England." There they received final instruction in security, codes, and clandestine techniques: what to do if trailed, how to move safely from house to house, what to do if captured and interrogated. They were also drilled extensively about the country to which they were going – some had never been there – and about the specific region in which they would operate. For many, there followed more specialized instruction in wireless, aircraft reception, or industrial sabotage. Most training concluded with a four-day exercise directed at a specific industrial target somewhere in Britain. Surveillance by unknown observers and, occasionally, attempted seduction were part of these final exercises, the last testing before the agent was finally approved. Throughout their several months of training, the agents were accompanied by "conducting officers," who at any stage, including the final exercise, could recommend their removal at any sign of an excessive love of liquor, a failure of nerve, or a serious lack of discretion or judgment. If the agent survived all the tests and met all the rigorous mental and physical requirements, he or she was finally cleared to go into enemy territory.

The greatest care was taken to establish viable alibis for agents. Cover stories were concocted which provided the agent with the details of parents, grandparents, and other relatives. Buckmaster of "F" Section and his staff worked to ensure that every agent had an impeccable alibi.

If a slight Canadian accent, for instance, had to be accounted for, the cover-story provided for a residence in Canada between the wars. Each officer, male or female, had to be given an occupation which would assure them immunity from liability to service in a factory working on war contracts. In this, naturally, we had to have assistance from inhabitants of France who had businesses of their own and who would therefore engage an extra traveller or an accountant without suspicion being aroused. In many cases (with the connivance of the head of the firm), we portrayed our officer as a distant relative who had been driven by Allied bombing to relinquish his house and had taken sanctuary with friends outside the region of aerial warfare.[11]

False documents had to correspond in the minutest detail with the agent's cover story. The problem of providing authentic-looking papers became more difficult as the war in Europe continued. Police and ration regulations changed and multiplied, increasing the problems of supplying agents with current versions of such documents as identity cards, ration cards, and coupons; special passes for any restricted areas; demobilization certificates (for those passing themselves as having served in the local army); and work and travel permits. One French resister later described how false papers had been prepared in his occupied homeland:

It is best to keep the real Christian name since the user is then less likely to make a blunder. One or two other Christian names should be added since the single Christian name is a rarity in France. For the surname one takes the initial letter of the real name and, starting from this, chooses some French-sounding name in sufficiently common use not to attract attention but not one so overworked as "Durand" or "Dupont" which are too frequently used as cover. One should avoid using a name which might indicate Jewish origin and so one cuts out names like David or Simon. One must also take account of current usage in mayors' offices; the name is written larger than other entries on the card but not in block capitals. For date of birth it is advisable to keep to the real date. Place of birth must never be Paris or a major city since immediate verification would be too easy; it is better to choose a village or locality where the records have been destroyed during the invasion or by bombing. For residence one chooses a street which actually exists, consulting the street guide or telephone directory. As far as description is concerned, this must obviously be accurate and care must be taken to use only the terms currently employed in mayors' or police offices; colour of hair, for instance, must be either black, auburn, average or dark and for these colours clearly defined abbreviations must be used; eyes can be chestnut or green or blue or grey-green or blue-grey; black eyes do not exist under civil service rules. A whole range of descriptions is available for shape and width of nose, facial characteristics and complexion. The attestation of signature is productive of the most serious risk run by the forger. In the smaller places attestations are always carried out by the mayor; if a specimen is available, therefore, one forges his signature and if not uses an illegible signature with "p.p." added. The date is one of the most important entries. Under all circumstances it must be later than May 1940 since this was the time at which an identity card was made compulsory. Care must be taken not to use a date which was a Sunday or holiday since no mayor deals with papers on those days. Even after all this there is still much work to be done. The stamp, for instance, must be a 13-franc stamp but these are very difficult to come by since they were withdrawn from circulation to stop the production of false papers; in April 1943 they were replaced by 15-franc stamps. The 13-franc stamp can still be found in solicitors' offices.[12]

After a few days' leave the fledgling agent received a final briefing, local contacts and a code name, forged identity and ration cards and work permits and European-style clothing, and then, weather permitting, was despatched from one of the aerodromes from which the R.A.F. special duty squadrons operated.

Initially, Canadian volunteers were discharged from the Canadian army and re-enlisted in the British. This soon proved unsatisfactory. In the interest of security, all clandestine agencies operated with a minimum of paper work and several early Canadian volunteers for both S.O.E. and M.I.9 were engaged on an oral rather than written basis. The later confusion that this caused may be imagined. By the end of 1942, this casual practice was replaced by a "loan" (a convenient euphemism) to the War

Office for six months, to be extended as required. A variety of pay arrangements remained until May 1944, when the Canadian army finally assumed responsibility for the pay of Canadians (while continuing to deny them the special allowances granted British agents).*

In any discussion of Canadians who served in S.O.E. and M.I.9 the question of how a French-Canadian accent was explained away invariably arises. A common assumption is that a French-Canadian must have been in constant danger of being spotted as such. In fact, this was not so. Few Frenchmen in the 1940s had ever heard a Canadian accent. When they did, most simply assumed that it was from another region and rarely gave it another thought. Wartime France was, moreover, full of transient workers who spoke something other than the accustomed local variety of French. Certainly no French-Canadian volunteer was ever betrayed by his accent. As Ray LaBrosse, a French-Canadian who long served on escape lines, noted, "In France you may have many accents. East, north, west, south, you have people who sound very much like French-speaking Canadians. What one had to be very careful about was not to use French-Canadian slang or idiomatic expressions. If you spoke correct French but had an accent, that didn't tell anyone you were Canadian."[13]

---

*Eventually, in August 1946, an Act of Parliament (10 George VI, chapter 64), the Special Operators War Service Act, extended the benefits of various veterans' acts to "a person...having been enrolled...by United Kingdom authorities for special duty." The bill passed with little comment other than from a loquacious nationalist, Jean-François Pouliot, the member for Témiscouata, who observed:

I know very well that the press will come out with headlines: "Quebec Member opposes grants for heroes who were picked out by the United Kingdom to serve in most difficult jobs during the war."
...I protest against the principle of always doing more and more for other countries – not only for the United Kingdom but for other countries. Canada should be symbolized by a squeezed lemon on a white square. (Debates of the House of Commons, 1946, vol. IV, p. 4461.)

PART TWO

Special Operations Executive

3

The First Canadian Agents into France

On the night of 18 November 1942, Gustave Bieler, the first of the Canadian volunteers with S.O.E., parachuted into France. The date of his parachuting had a particular signifiance: the same month the Germans promptly responded to the Anglo-American landings in North Africa by occupying the remainder of France (until then the Vichy regime had nominally governed southern France). Now there were no longer the escape possibilities offered by Vichy, possibilities always hazardous but never so difficult as the routes through German-occupied France. By November 1942, S.O.E. had been sending agents into France – by parachute, Lysander, small boat or submarine – for eighteen months. As a result, much had been learned about the imperative need for security and for prompt and reliable wireless contact with London; about German anti-subversion and counter-intelligence methods and the nature and extent of French resistance; about the possibilities and difficulties of sabotage and the chances of escape through Spain, Switzerland or Sweden or across the Channel. But even as S.O.E. had steadily enlarged its knowledge and techniques, so had German counter-intelligence.

Bieler was dropped from a Whitley bomber with Michael Trotobas, one of S.O.E.'s best organizers, and Trotobas' radio operator. Trotobas, an Anglo-French solicitor ten years younger than Bieler, had lived in northeastern France before the war. Having been trained and commissioned in the British army, he was returning to Lille where he had already served as one of S.O.E.'s original agents in France.

Both Bieler and Trotobas were to recruit workers for new networks in northeastern France, in the areas of Lille and St. Quentin, in preparation for the eventual Allied invasion of France. In the northeast, French memories of battles against the German invaders twenty-five years before were still fresh. Further, the industrialized northeast offered prime targets for sabotage, with willing accomplices among both the growing local resistance and among Poles who, before the war, had come to work in its mines and factories. What had delayed the earlier despatch of trained agents to northeastern France was not merely their limited availability. Intensive German anti-aircraft defences made it a dangerous area for the low-flying aircraft from which agents were dropped. However, while the risks were high, so were the prizes. The main rail lines from Germany to the German armies in the west of France passed largely through the northeast. It was vital that these lines be cut at the time of any Allied invasion of France.

Gustave Daniel Alfred Bieler was born in France in 1904 of Swiss parents and educated at Lausanne and Geneva. His father and grandfather had been Huguenot pastors; it was partly to escape from this family vocation that Bieler, at the urging of an uncle who taught at McGill University, emigrated to Montreal at the age of twenty. He became a Canadian citizen ten years later. Completely bilingual, he was for four years a school teacher at Pointe-aux-Trembles near Montreal before joining the translation department at the head office of the Sun Life Assurance Company. An affable man, short and sturdy with dark hair and a thick, drooping moustache, Bieler had a strong, spontaneous sense of humour. He played the piano well and loved the abundant canoeing possibilities of Quebec. A volunteer in the Canadian Officers' Training Corps at the University of Montreal in 1939, Bieler was commissioned in the Régiment de Maisonneuve in June 1940. Within two months, he sailed with his regiment from Halifax to Scotland, leaving his wife and two small children in Montreal.

In southern England, the quiet, pipe-smoking Bieler became his battalion's intelligence officer, involved in the preparations for the expected German onslaught across the Channel. His work meant contacts at the War Office. These led to a chance meeting with Buckmaster during the spring of 1942. An interview by a board followed – the discussion centred on Proust – and as a result, Bieler joined S.O.E. for a trial period from 4 June 1942. First during a probationary month at Wanborough Manor in the Surrey countryside and subsequently in Arisaig in Scotland, he undertook the rigorous training course. At thirty-eight the oldest in his class, he was affectionately known to other aspiring agents as "Granddad." At Arisaig and on the parachute course at Ringway, Bieler's instructors and fellow students alike quickly recognized his remarkable courage and determination to excel in the secret service for which he had volunteered. Most clandestine organizations are chary of superlatives in describing their operatives, but one senior instructor felt no such restraint in Bieler's case: "Very conscientious, keen and intelligent...generations of stability behind him...sound judge of character; good-natured; even-tempered; absolutely reliable; outstandingly thorough and painstaking; a born organizer."[1] Sergeant Gabriel Chartrand, also of the Maisonneuve, had volunteered for S.O.E. shortly after Bieler. He began his training as Bieler was completing his, finding that his friend, now known as "Guy," had set a high standard:

> The C.O. at Wanborough told me, "if you're half as good as Guy, you'll be magnificent." Everywhere I was told, "Guy was here," and there was a sort of awe about the way they said it. "Guy," of course, was all they knew him by: he'd adopted his nickname as his code name....He was a fatalist, the kind who says, "I'm going to die the

day I'm going to die." I told him once, "Guy, we're way on in our 30's; we could have stayed home." He looked at me and said very simply, "You *cannot* permit what these Germans are doing to spread." Then he said something more: "I have people in France, don't forget – my brother and others. I'm a soldier and I'm here because I want to help save people from being pushed around."...
To his wife Marguerite, in Montreal, he wrote, "It will be very great fortune and privilege, I think, to see the very best in men."[2]

After the war, Felix Walter stated flatly, "Major Bieler was the most brilliant of all the Canadians to be employed....Again and again in reports prepared by his superior officers phrases are used which underline his extraordinary qualities of leadership and the enthusiasm which he was able to communicate to others."[3]

By early November, after having completed four months' training, Bieler dined with his sister, Madelaine Dale, in her home in the London suburb of Ewell. He had visited Madelaine and her husband regularly since his arrival in England. His sister recalled:

> This time, however, instead of being in the uniform of a captain of the Maisonneuve, he was in a dark civilian suit. He wasn't allowed to talk and my husband and I knew it, so we didn't ask any questions. But I'd guessed, even when he was in uniform. That night he wore civilian clothes. I looked in his overcoat and there was no identification of where it had been made. That was the kind of thing that happened when people went to occupied France, and [we] guessed this was his last visit.

It was. When Bieler departed, he simply said, "See you soon."[4] Madelaine never saw her brother again.

Eight days later, on the evening of 18 November 1942, Bieler took off from Tempsford aerodrome to parachute southwest of Paris. His final briefings had included sessions with Vera Atkins, the intelligence head of "F" Section, who possessed an encyclopaedic knowledge about life in occupied France. She reviewed with him everything S.O.E. knew about the everyday conditions he would probably encounter: curfews, rationing, travel restrictions, documents, surveillance, and security checks.* Vera Atkins always remembered Bieler from among the many hundreds of agents whom she briefed. She recalled "his mature outlook, his calm, kindness and poise and beautiful voice." He was "a man among boys."[5]

Within days of their landing in a woods near Montargis (about one hundred kilometres southwest of Paris), Trotobas and his radio operator were able to begin their work of recruiting saboteurs in the Lille region. Bieler had, however, to wait several months before he could do so. He landed heavily on rocky ground, severely injuring his back. For several hours he lay more or less helpless in the dark, but Trotobas and his radio operator somehow managed to get him several kilometres south to the village of Auxy-Iuranville from where they took him by train to Paris. There, from the "safe house" of an elderly Frenchwoman on the Boulevard de Suffren, Bieler contacted his younger brother, René-Maurice, a French army veteran who, with his Czech-born wife, was active in the resistance.† Bieler's spine had been so severely injured that he had to spend six weeks in a Paris hospital under his assumed identity of Guy Morin, followed by three months recuperation in a resistance flat near the Eiffel Tower. He rejected an offer from London to be flown out, determined as he was to take up his original assignment in St. Quentin as soon as he could walk again.

At St. Quentin station, Bieler was met by a small, slim land surveyor, Eugène Cordelette, a leader of the local underground.

---

*S.O.E. accumulated and employed every possible source of information about what an agent might expect to encounter in an enemy-occupied country: railway timetables, newspaper announcements, refugee testimony – anything that might reduce the possibility of an agent being caught through ignorance of a local or recent requirement. Xan Fielding has provided a harrowing account of the consequences of omitting a stamp on a document (a single demobilization certificate required as many as twenty) in *Hide and Seek* (London; Secker and Warburg, 1954).

†René-Maurice Bieler died in a concentration camp in February 1945. His wife was imprisoned.

Cordelette had been told by London that an Allied officer would soon arrive to assist them. Still in precarious health and limping badly, for the first week Bieler did not have sufficient strength to leave the surveyor's house in the village of Fonsomme. Sitting in the pale April sunshine under a tree behind the house, disguised in the universal blue smock and trousers of a worker, Bieler interviewed and recruited agents for his incipient circuit which was to receive arms and train others for an uprising whenever the Allies invaded France. Finally, in April 1943 – a full five months after his landing – Bieler was to be seen hobbling painfully about St. Quentin, beginning to instruct his sabotage network (known as "Musician"). He could still stand only a few hours a day and moved with his head to one side, one shoulder hunched from pain.

Bieler chose his workers carefully and well; they were mostly railway men with an expert knowledge of the local target lines. Eventually twenty-five separate armed teams were operating in the Lille–St. Quentin region. In May 1943 alone, the various resistance groups cut the main Cologne-Paris rail line thirteen times, blowing up signal boxes, switching gear, or the rails themselves, destroying a troop train and derailing twenty others. By the second half of 1943, they were disrupting the important Lille–St. Quentin line about every fortnight. By the end of the year, the resistance had received in the fields around St. Quentin a total of sixteen drops of money, arms, and explosives, despite the fact that during Bieler's first six months of operations he had no radio operator and had to risk passing his coded wireless messages to London through two other nets, "Butler" and "Prosper," of necessity violating the rule of not crossing circuit lines. (As we shall see, both "Prosper" and "Butler" were later penetrated by the Gestapo.)

But before that time, fortuitously, Bieler had received his own radio operator. Yolande Unternährer Beekman was a slim, unassuming thirty-two-year-old Anglo-Swiss in the W.A.A.F. who had been educated in both Paris and London. She had landed in a Lysander northeast of Angers on 17 September and, carrying her heavy transmitter disguised as a suitcase, had made her way alone across northern France to Lille to join Trotobas. There a signal from London awaited her, ordering her to work instead with Bieler in St. Quentin. Beekman proved an excellent match for Bieler: cheerful, methodical, determined, unflappable. In early October, she began transmitting from an attic in St. Quentin, sending and receiving the messages which Bieler alone coded and decoded.

Using parachuted supplies, Bieler and various resistance groups systematically blew up rail equipment and line after line, which the Germans in turn repaired with disconcerting rapidity. In disrupting the railways, they also employed a special abrasive material invented by S.O.E. which looked like ordinary grease but in fact had the opposite effect on parts on which it was smeared: it rapidly wore them away rather than lubricated them. Members of the underground who were employed by the French railways put twenty locomotives out of action by this untraceable method, in addition to destroying an engine repair shop and eleven other locomotives at Tourcoing. Railways were not, however, the only targets; occasionally Bieler permitted his teams to diversify their experience by destroying a bridge or petroleum storage tanks.

St. Quentin, a city of about sixty thousand, is also an important link in the canal system which stretches from northeast France south to the Mediterranean. Amongst the vital German supplies carried on canal barges were submarine components made in Rouen. The R.A.F. had bombed the canal locks, but had caused little lasting damage. In another effort to destroy the locks, the R.A.F. dropped to Bieler underwater limpet time bombs, which could be attached readily to a vessel or canal lock. Lying flat in the bottom of a drifting and apparently unoccupied punt, Bieler and two assistants placed three below the waterline of a principal lock gate. The devices were triumphantly successful. They used them again to destroy forty loaded barges, accurately timing the explosions, with the help of a resistance member who was a junior clerk in the canal's administration, when the most damage would be done, thus blocking the canal for several weeks.

The favourable impression which Bieler had made during his training had been clearly justified. Despite crippling pain, he had proven himself conscientious, keen, intelligent, even-tempered, and absolutely reliable. His French colleagues had complete faith in him; he became deeply loved. One of the many reasons why Bieler was so highly regarded was the result of the extreme care which he took of civilian life in his operations; he regretted greatly the indiscriminate damage that bombing entailed. Cordelette later described how, "on one occasion, to avoid a loss of civilian lives, he refused to blow up an important munitions train on a siding near many houses. He made up for this by having another munitions convoy blown up in the uninhabited countryside."[6] On another occasion, to provide both the underground and fugitives with food, he organized a burglary of the town hall of Vaux-en-Digny. The stolen food ration coupons were quickly distributed to those needing them most.

No one, not even those working most closely with him, knew who Bieler was, although several were aware that he was a Canadian. The only other fact that they knew about the man pursuing his intensely lonely tasks was that he was married: he occasionally showed them a photograph of a wife and two small children. Details of Bieler's activities are unfortunately limited, since all copies of his wireless messages were destroyed in 1947. But Henri Michel, the leading historian of the French resistance, has graphically described the difficulties facing saboteurs such as Bieler as they pursued their hazardous assignments:

S.O.E. set up special workshops manufacturing sabotage equipment of increasing perfection and ingenuity – "sausages" to be placed on German aircraft and adjusted to explode at the right moment, magnetised boxes to be attached to a tank or armoured car, explosive "horse-droppings" and pebbles to burst the tyres of a vehicle, plastic explosive of all shapes and size .... The art of sabotage was taught in the training schools for agents. For their part the resisters obtained such explosives as they could from quarries or mine depots ....

The resisters gradually discovered that sabotage meant learning difficult techniques demanding psychological, professional and economic knowledge. If it inconvenienced the population too much, it became counter-productive – a power cut might be more effective than a costly explosion. Inventiveness and ingenuity were their stock in trade. To be fully effective sabotage had to be supported by propaganda; it accordingly had a part to play in psychological warfare and for this reason the clandestine press reported, magnified and sometimes even invented it. It was important that operations should be numerous and continuous to keep the enemy on guard, play on his nerves and compel him to disperse his forces. Care had to be taken to avoid ill-considered destruction which might even be harmful; if a lift was to be blown up in a coal mine, for instance, it was essential to choose a moment when it was untenanted since, if a miner were killed, the psychological effect might be the opposite of that intended. In general terms, if the main object was to lower or even stop production, too many workers must not be thrown out of work for too long or they would be taken to work in Germany. All this was frequently difficult to appreciate. In fact resisters attacked everything within their capabilities – factories, stocks, warehouses and businesses of all sorts; transport and communication facilities such as bridges, canals, telephone lines and railways were favourite targets; owing to their length they were poorly guarded and therefore easy to attack with only minor risk.[7]

As Bieler was leading his teams on their increasingly complex sabotage career, the second and third Canadians sent into France by S.O.E. landed within a few days of each other.

Sergeant Charles Joseph Duchalard of Quebec was in and out of France quickly. A tall, thin, dark-haired young man of about twenty-five, Duchalard was self-confident, even cocky, but he did speak good French. He had joined S.O.E. from the British army in 1942 (where it seems he was briefly in the Commandos), received the standard S.O.E. training, additional instruction as a radio operator, was commissioned and, as "Charles Deniset," was assigned a specific job for which he was given yet more training.

Duchalard's prime assignment was to establish in the Gascony region of southwest France an "Eureka" beacon transmitter whose signals could be received by an aircraft as much as one hundred kilometres distant. These transmitters, properly sited, could remove much of the chance involved in the dangerous R.A.F. night landings or parachute drops to tiny, ill-lighted, obscure targets. But even when available, they had not always been correctly placed by sceptical or slapdash agents. The need for greater accuracy was especially apparent in those areas of southern France where some aircraft neared the limit of their range and where many valleys look identical from the air. Here conditions for both pilots and those receiving the drops were especially difficult. A few flashlights or other small lamps alone indicated to the pilot the target and wind direction. Reception committees – who were breaking the German curfew – "were instructed to choose sites for their dropping grounds which could easily be seen from the air; but for many reasons this was often not possible for them, and the aircraft, after having found its target area, might have to search for sometime before discovering lights half-hidden by a wood, or obscured in a valley…the navigator nearly always had to rely on map-reading and D[ead] R[eckoning]. In order to enable him to do this, the pilot would take his aircraft across enemy-occupied Europe at a low altitude."[8] Eureka beacons could remove much of the hazardous guesswork from such operations, homing in the aircraft accurately on its target.

It was near Gers in southern France, in the area of Toulouse, that Duchalard was parachuted on 12 April 1943 to establish a dependable Eureka beacon and to join the "Prunus" circuit as a radio operator and demolitions expert. London had placed high hopes on "Prunus" for the sabotage of several prime targets, especially a former French army munitions factory in Toulouse now operated by the Germans. Unfortunately for Duchalard, the circuit was reckless in its disregard of security. Its young French leader, Pertschuk, installed Duchalard in a safe house in Toulouse before dawn on the morning of his arrival, then spent the day on his circuit business. When Pertschuk returned to his own Toulouse lodgings that evening, he was arrested by the Germans who had obtained his address from a talkative sub-agent. Within a week, all the "Prunus" agents except Duchalard had been rounded up. Having just arrived, Duchalard's whereabouts were known only to a few, and they did not give him away. It had been a close thing.

What exactly Duchalard did during the next six months remains unclear. He claims to have joined an escape line helping Allied airmen reach the Pyrenees after being shot down. However, Duchalard's behaviour was reported to London as drunken and dangerously indiscreet (he was always noted as talkative); it seems that he had learned nothing from observing at first hand the results of the sloppy security of "Prunus." His carelessness, extending to using American cigarettes, speaking English, boasting about being a parachuted British agent, and drinking in bars with Germans, clearly endangered others. Before the local resistance carried out its decision to kill him, he was ordered to return to England. Disguised as an R.C.A.F. evader, "Charles Deniset of Lethbridge, Alberta," Duchalard was guided across the Pyrenees, avoiding both German and Spanish border patrols and making his way by bus from the Spanish frontier to Barcelona. There the British consulate arranged for him to be taken by car to Madrid and by train to Gibraltar. He arrived back in London on 5 October 1943 having, in a sense, served only one day with his circuit. Upon his return to England, Duchalard was posted to the Pioneer Corps, hardly a glamorous conclusion to a career in S.O.E., which had reported curtly to C.M.H.Q. that it had no further employment for him.

The third Canadian who went into France in 1943, only a few days after Duchalard, was Joseph Gabriel Chartrand, the short, effervescent insurance salesman who had known and admired Bieler in Montreal during the late 1930s. Upon the declaration of war, Chartrand had volunteered for the predominantly English-speaking Royal Montreal Regiment, but he was considered too old at thirty-two to be sent to an infantry officers' training school. Following his arrival in England with the First Division in December 1939, his quick intelligence and fluent bilingualism were put to good use as a sergeant clerk (eventually in the Judge Advocate's branch) at C.M.H.Q. in London.

Chartrand's older brother Paul was an officer with Bieler in the Régiment de Maisonneuve in the south of England. Soon Chartrand and Bieler had re-established their prewar friendship, Bieler occasionally spending leaves in London with Chartrand and his English fiancée. In 1942, after Bieler left the regiment and Chartrand was posted as a statistics clerk at C.M.H.Q., they would sometimes meet in London. Chartrand recalled:

> He'd spend the occasional weekend at a place I had in Bramham Gardens in Kensington....
>
> One day about the middle of 1942 Guy said to me, "Gaby, you're miserable, aren't you?" "Well," I said, "I am, dammit." I was in a dead-end job and I was bored stiff. Guy said, "I've got just the job for you. I'll recommend you." He said a lot of crazy things might happen, starting with a very strange interview.
>
> It was in a London hotel room bare but for one table and three chairs. Three men in civilian clothes sat.... They knew all about me and they asked a lot of things. Then one of them said, "Here, memorize this. Do *not* write it down. Be there at 10 on Monday morning, will you?" It was an address on Baker Street, the headquarters (as I later learned) of S.O.E.[9]

Training similar to Bieler's followed for Chartrand during the autumn and winter of 1942, culminating in visits to electricity-generating plants and various factories in the Midlands to become more familiar with the kind of machinery he might be called upon to sabotage. An exercise in Leeds as a final test of his resourcefulness in shaking pursuing police preceded his despatch to France in one of two Lysanders on the night of 14 April 1943. Chartrand had injured a leg in parachute training at Ringway, and his circuit chief, Charles Liewer, a former Paris journalist with whom Chartrand had trained, was unable to parachute. The two men were accordingly deposited in the meadows of the Loire, almost under the walls of Amboise.

Through a misunderstanding, only two resistance workers were on hand when the Lysanders landed and there were only two bicycles for the four agents and their several suitcases. Fortified by a small bottle of rum which had been given to them upon departure a little more than two hours before, Liewer and

Chartrand volunteered to walk eighteen kilometres through misty fields to a rail station, well away from the area of landing. A short rail journey to Tours in the early morning – the curfew ended at six o'clock – took them to the supposed safety of the Ecole Supérieure pour Jeunes Filles de Tours. While Chartrand was shaving there, a German commission arrived unannounced at the school to ensure that the girls were using only approved textbooks. Liewer and Chartrand were hastily hidden, escaping arrest by minutes.

Chartrand remained secluded in a safe house in Tours for a fortnight, while Liewer made the necessary contacts for them to move on to Rouen where they were to establish a new circuit. En route through Paris during Holy Week, Chartrand had his first shoulder-to-shoulder contact with German troops at mass in the Madeleine, on the Metro, and in bistros. Although it was Chartrand's first visit to the city, fortunately Liewer knew it intimately. Such useful friends as André Malraux and his two half-brothers, all active in the resistance, provided the two men with several contacts in Rouen.

A switchboard operator at a Paris insurance company had agreed to confirm that Chartrand was one of their salesmen. However, soon after Chartrand's arrival in Rouen, he was detained overnight by the police for an infraction of the local curfew regulations. This would have been a matter of no consequence had it not been for the requirement imposed on the police to hand over to the Germans details about anyone they had detained, even for the most trifling offence. Further, it was known to the police – who in turn warned Liewer – that the Germans had begun to suspect anyone claiming to be an insurance salesman. It was a disguise which could readily explain the need to travel, but its frequent use had made it a liability. The Germans would doubtless note the presence in Rouen of an insurance salesman named Gabriel Chartrand (he was one of a few agents allowed to use his own name). Since German security was especially tight in Rouen, being near the English Channel, Chartrand must move to a less heavily policed region. François Garel, another prewar French journalist (of heavy drinking and spending habits), was organizing the "Butler" circuit in the Departement of the Sarthe. Liewer arranged for Chartrand, who had met Garel during training in England, to return to the small town of Château-du-Loir, only forty kilometres from his initial hiding place of Tours. There Chartrand changed identities, becoming "Claude Carton," an inspector of pensions.

The "Butler" circuit under Garel was successful in its initial efforts to recruit and train workers, to arrange for supply drops, and to begin the sabotage of rail lines around Angers. From June 1943, Chartrand participated in the organization and reception of three supply drops, subsequently instructing the local resistance in the use of Sten guns and assisting in the sabotage of rail lines. But the circuit had little real sense of security.

Garel, his mistress, and Rousset, his Mauritian wireless operator, were arrested on 7 September in Paris where Garel was recovering from a broken ankle. Although S.O.E. was becoming increasingly expert in its clandestine activities, the Germans were also becoming more effective in their various counter-measures. "Prosper," another large circuit with which "Butler" was associated, had been penetrated as a result of its carelessness and bad security. The arrest of Garel and other "Butler" agents was not, however, the direct result of the downfall of the related "Prosper" circuit or even of the agents' own carelessness: it was largely the result of a routine German security check which had by chance picked up a "Butler" sub-agent in Nantes who had talked. Following interrogation, the captured agents were sent to Ravitsch (Rawicz) concentration camp in Poland.

Chartrand in Tours was fortunate not to have been caught with the free-wheeling Garel that fatal week in Paris; Garel was later executed at Buchenwald. Upon learning of the arrests, Chartrand immediately went into hiding, adopting yet another alias as "Georges Chenier," a clothing salesman. He was, however, far from safe. His help had been sought in moving an American pilot from the house of a woman in Tours active in the underground. He managed to move the hidden Missouri airman to a safe farmhouse as the next step in getting him out of France, but upon returning to Tours by bicycle, he was arrested by two Gestapo agents. Chartrand had been drilled on the need to attempt to escape during the first phase of arrest; once in prison, the process leading to a concentration camp and likely execution would be virtually irreversible. "Captif, votre sort est certain:

vous serez torturé et finalement exécuté. En vous évadant, vous risquez une balle dans le dos mais si la chance vous aide, vous aurez la vie sauvé."[10]

While Chartrand's mind was racing over all possible chances of escape from his two Gestapo captors, one stopped at a street corner for no apparent reason. Ordering his companion to continue on to the police station with Chartrand, he disappeared down a side street. About three hundred metres from the Gestapo headquarters, Chartrand saw his chance. A street ran off to the right; he was pushing his bicycle on his left, between himself and the German. He suddenly threw his bicycle at him and, in the momentary confusion, made his escape despite pistol fire. Chartrand remembered the repeated assurance of his instructors in England: if a fugitive had fifteen long strides on anyone chasing him, and if he kept dodging, he might well escape: "Prenez ma parole, j'ai sûrement battu le record de 500 mètres."[11]

As a result of Garel's arrest, the Gestapo were obviously now on Chartrand's trail. He later suspected that Garel's mistress was the informant, especially when a telephone call to Garel's flat in Paris was answered not by his mistress, but by a German-accented voice. In any event, Chartrand knew now that it was imperative for him to get out of France somehow. That, however, was no simple proposition: he was virtually penniless, on the run in an enemy-occupied city and, worst of all, his identity documents were now compromised.

At the very moment when even the incorrigibly cheerful Chartrand was becoming doubtful about his prospects, a chance encounter on the Champs Elysées with his old circuit chief, Charles Liewer, brought him to safety. Liewer immediately housed Chartrand – as a paying guest – with one of the Malraux brothers, while reporting to London on his plight. During the late autumn of 1943, Chartrand was moved to another Paris flat – where he helped an R.A.A.F. squadron leader to reach an escape line – before being placed himself in the hands of "Paul," a British agent heading an S.O.E. escape line across the Channel ("Paul" was, in fact, a Viennese Jew named Irving Dent). Chartrand, still as "Georges Chenier," was sent to Rennes where, with two Free

French agents and a young U.S. air force gunner, he was to await orders to proceed to the Brittany coast whenever a pick-up by the Royal Navy could be arranged. After several days in Rennes, Chartrand and the three other "packages" were moved to a defunct flour mill in Normandy, about thirty kilometres from the coast. After ten days at the mill disguised as workers ostensibly rebuilding it, "Paul" arranged for its owner to take the escapers to the coast where he joined them for the midnight descent to the heavily guarded, designated beach. There an R.N. motor gunboat from Dartmouth would collect them.

On the appointed night, however, while the prospective passengers clung to the cliffs, flares suddenly lit up the coast. Back to Rennes Chartrand and the others made their way, despondent and doubtful about their future chances.

A second pick-up was arranged for the night of 9 December 1943. Chartrand, the other three passengers, and their guides again went to the beach, sitting silently in the cold and darkness, straining to catch the first muffled sound of the M.G.B. Soon after hearing it, two small rubber boats appeared from the Channel blackness, landing in-coming agents and supplies and quickly taking off Chartrand and the others. The total turn-around time was thirty-five minutes. Chartrand returned to London, still dressed in little more than a woman's black sweater and dirty black trousers; he had given his other clothes to the underground. British intelligence decided, after interrogating him about conditions in occupied France, that there could be no question of his returning there: German security had much too graphic an impression of him for that.*

---

*The irrepressible Chartrand did, however, return to France about a year later. He entered Paris shortly after its liberation to assist French censors working with the Paris press and radio and later still did similar work in Brussels. Chartrand now lives in retirement near Montreal, as replete with a sense of humour and enthusiasm as he was when he first joined the army in 1939.

4

Victims

During the spring of 1943, as Gustave Bieler continued in St. Quentin his highly successful and increasingly dangerous career in sabotage, and as Duchalard and Chartrand passed in and out of France, Frank Pickersgill of Winnipeg and John Macalister of Guelph, Ontario, parachuted in. They were the fourth and fifth Canadians in – and the first to be captured.

What is there to say about Frank Pickersgill? His S.O.E. service in France was brief. He accomplished nothing before being arrested. Only a few lines, then, since the Germans picked him up almost on arrival? Or a whole chapter because he remains a haunting, appealing figure, *der ewige Student*, the boisterous, fun-loving intellectual, the questioning iconoclast, the young man of promise who was executed in the most cruel way the Gestapo could devise?

Frank Herbert Dedrick Pickersgill was born in 1915 in Winnipeg, the youngest child of a First World War veteran who died as a result of his war service when Frank was only five. A powerfully built, prematurely balding, blond intellectual, he did exceedingly well at the University of Manitoba. During the summer vacation of 1934, he fulfilled many a student's ambition by working his way to England on a cattle-boat and cycling through Britain, France, and Germany. The Pickersgill family had little money; when they moved from their farm to Winnipeg their mother worked as a nurse and the oldest brother, Jack, taught at the University of Manitoba after his return from Oxford in 1929. Frank worked on Manitoba roads during other summer vacations, but wherever he was, he was seldom without his literature textbooks: French, German, English, Latin, and Greek. As a graduate student on scholarship at the University of Toronto from 1936 to 1938, he earned an M.A. in classical history, a shift away from his previous study of literature toward religion and politics. Although money was always short in Toronto, there were

> gatherings for talk and beer and cards which constituted his principal form of an evening's entertainment. Another favourite diversion was hunting up double-billed moving pictures. They were usually at inexpensive little places in the remoter suburbs of Toronto. Having a part-time job as a reader [University of Toronto lecturer], he was economy-conscious, and therefore insisted that no matter how far he had to travel on the street-car, he saved money by attending these outlying theatres. Often, however, the double-bill would be so outrageously bad that he would be obliged to leave . . . vowing that he would never go again. But he always did.[1]

Somehow Jack Pickersgill put together enough money to offer his younger brother a year of post-graduate study in Europe, beginning in the summer of 1938. As a result, Frank was travelling in Europe throughout the Munich crisis, talking with everyone about just about everything and writing occasional articles for Canadian newspapers and periodicals from Belgium, Italy, France, Poland, Germany, Britain, and Romania, an experience which, among other things, deepened his abhorrence of the Nazi regime in Germany and confirmed him in his deep love of France.

He wrote to a Winnipeg girl friend, then living in London, about Germany:

> God what a country. It was an interesting three weeks but about as depressing as any I've ever spent. The thing is so much worse now

than four years ago that the place isn't recognisable–I heard the Nürnberg business–nearly all of it–over the radio. I'm glad I didn't see it in the flesh–I think I wouldn't have remained sane. It was bad enough over the radio. That was National-Socialism *en fete*. If it had been merely barbaric it wouldn't have been so bad. Honestly that nation is, I think, possessed by the devil–I see now what Dostoevsky meant in his novel. The inspiration behind their "culture" isn't merely subhuman or uncivilised. It's worse than that. In Munich I went to visit the exhibition of Nazi art at the New Museum of German Art–it is incredible the effect that stuff has on one. An absolutely unheard of unity of inspiration hangs over the place like a fog–and a sinister fog, because the pictures are really unpleasant. I felt an almost insane desire to grab an axe and go to work on the place. Of course the superficial objection to the exposition is that it reeks of sadism and homosexuality, but there's something lying behind that even which is much more sinister – maybe it's my imagination–but by Heavens I wish Dostoevsky were alive to look at the stuff. And not only there. The thing hangs in the air of the country. Honest to God I feel superstitious. I imagine Italian Fascism must look like the incarnation of sunny health and sanity by comparison. When I saw the sloppy dirty cheery French customs officers at Kehl I could have hugged them. And then at Strasbourg the train filled up and I never would have dreamed that the crowded noisy disorder could be so glorious. I just sat in the corner of the carriage and grinned and giggled like a loony for about an hour. No wonder these people love their country.[2]

Pickersgill was making a sort of pilgrim's progress. His father had been a victim of the First World War. He himself had lived as a student through the worst years of the Depression, reading everything–Hemingway, Maritain, John Dos Passos, Dostoevsky, St. Augustine, Pascal–questioning, debating, supporting the Spanish Republic, Anglo-Catholicism, China; utterly opposed to Nazism and cynical about Munich, yet deeply concerned about the global disaster a second world war would inevitably be. In 1938–39 he asked himself repeatedly what he should do: return to Canada or remain in Europe to fight the fascists? Along with many other young intellectuals in Paris during the dirty thirties, Pickersgill had regarded the possibility of another world war as the result of rivalry between two oppressive systems. Now he had seen enough to recognize where the real evil was – and to recognize that Canada would be a participant in the impending conflict.

The outbreak of war in September 1939 caught Pickersgill in Bucharest. Three days on a crowded train across an uncertain Europe finally returned him to his beloved Paris, a Paris where his now fluent French could be further improved. During the next ten months, during the uncertainties of the "phoney war," Pickersgill lived precariously on freelance journalism, writing occasional articles for newspapers such as the Vancouver *Sun*, the Winnipeg *Free Press*, *Le Devoir*, and for *Saturday Night* and the *University of Toronto Quarterly*. He spent happy hours with those French friends who had not yet been mobilized and with Kay Moore, a friend from undergraduate days at the University of Manitoba who was working in the office of the British military attaché. He intended to translate a novel by Sartre whom he knew. At the Canadian embassy he successfully wrote the Foreign Service Officer examinations for the Department of External Affairs (which his brother Jack had entered two years before), but he noted in one letter that "I should like, on returning to Canada, to do newspaper or radio work rather than anything else."[3]

In June 1940 Pickersgill remained in Paris as the German Panzer divisions approached still hoping, apparently, to be able to go to London for his External Affairs oral interview. There seems, however, an ambivalence in his attitude; he longed to become a Canadian diplomat, yet at the same time he wrote repeatedly, "Please God let me stay in France at least until this war is over."[4] With the entry of the German advance units into Paris on 11 June 1940, Pickersgill cycled to Tours, from where Major-General Georges Vanier, the Canadian minister, had hurriedly departed with his legation only a few hours before. By the time that Pickersgill, now penniless, pedalled into the city, there was no longer a Canadian legation in Tours to help him. Pickersgill should have followed it southward to safety; instead he turned westward to Brittany, apparently hoping to find there some way of crossing the Channel to England. On 3 August he was interned by the Germans when he was living quietly with a friendly French family near Quimper, giving English lessons in an attempt to earn enough money to pay his way southward. Following his arrest as an enemy alien, hard labour and near-starvation in a camp near Saumur on the Loire preceded somewhat less arduous internment with other civilians (including many from the British Commonwealth) at a former French army barracks at St. Denis, a workers' quarter of Paris. In all, Pickersgill was to be in German camps for almost two years. "What a lot of things I'll have to tell my grandchildren."[5]

The threat of brutal reprisals at first deterred Pickersgill and other civilian prisoners from attempting to escape from St. Denis. But in March 1942, he and a British prisoner finally made their way out by using a hacksaw smuggled into them – literally in a loaf of bread – by French friends. After escaping at night through the office of the German camp commandant (who usually slept in Paris with his French mistress), they eventually succeeded in crossing into Vichy France. "Then the relief of safety set in. My legs suddenly collapsed and I just faded out into the road and sat there trying to keep the tears back."[6]

Another six months were to pass, however, before Pickersgill was able to leave Vichy France. The problem again was an exit permit. Only in September 1942, after staying with French friends at Pau and with the assistance of the U.S. vice-consul at Lyon, did the Vichy authorities finally grant the necessary exit visa for him to go to neutral Portugal. By then he had been in France almost continuously for more than four years.

While Pickersgill awaited his exit permit, the U.S. vice-consul soon realized that "Pick's French was perfectly amazing. He not only spoke – but what is much rarer – wrote beautiful, accurate French."[7] She recruited him to help prepare a newsletter for clandestine distribution in Paris, and he may have travelled on resistance business as far afield as Marseille and Grenoble.

Upon reaching Lisbon in October 1942, Frank wrote his brother Jack (now a secretary to Mackenzie King, the Canadian prime minister):

I only got away thanks to an *idée fixe:* that I'd make my way to
England to fight, or at any rate to suitable work in the danger zone.
As I was waiting for my visa, I became more and more fanatical
about my *idée fixe* – and here in Lisbon I'd already seen the people

who were going to put me in touch with the right people in London.

As I say, I realize what a joy it would be to see you all, and would like nothing better than to come back to Canada, report as it were, and spend about a month with the family, then buzz off to England and the war. But I'm afraid such a prospect is a pipe-dream and that once in Canada I'd have the devil's own time getting back to Europe.

I do hope you'll understand what I mean. I've seen and done some things which have rather radically changed my outlook. After seeing a French soldier clubbed to death by German cops at Quimper, after starving in a gravel-pit at Montreuil-Bellay...and spending four months in Lyon doing illegal propaganda and not quite sure from one day to the next when I might be arrested – well I'm afraid I'd find it pretty difficult to settle down to pushing a pen in an Ottawa office for the duration of the war and trying to convince myself that it was "useful work"....

I'm convinced that as far as this war is concerned there are certain jobs I could do better than anybody, but about a handful of people – and surely that would be the most suitable thing for me to do. That such jobs would be dangerous is just one more thing in their favour. If any preparing the way can be done, do prepare the way so that I can see and talk to the right people. I'm sure I can convince them there as I've been able to do here – or seem to have. Remember, I kept my eyes wide open wherever I was.[8]

Gone now was the student of philosophy; here was the man of action – but a pronounced romantic still.

At the British legation in Lisbon, Pickersgill was put in touch with the local M.I.6 and S.O.E. representatives (neutral Portugal being a resort of all intelligence services, both Axis and Allied). Once in London in October, he pursued the contacts in S.O.E., was commissioned as a lieutenant in the Canadian Intelligence Corps in November, and loaned to S.O.E. the following month.

Why was Pickersgill so eager to return to France, when he could not be certain of being able to pass as a Frenchman or any other national likely to be found in occupied France? Although his brother Jack and friends have joined the U.S. vice-consul in Lyon in testifying to his remarkably good French,* it appears

---

*His friend Kay Moore (who after the war married Charles Gimpel, a French resistance leader) and his brother Jack considered his French so fluent that he could have been, and occasionally was, mistaken for a Frenchman.

unlikely that either he or fellow Canadian, John Macalister, who was to accompany him to France as a wireless operator, could have successfully impersonated Frenchmen. Yeo-Thomas, a British S.O.E. agent, believed upon first meeting Macalister and Pickersgill in France that they must be fugitive Canadian soldiers who had somehow evaded capture at Dieppe. Yeo-Thomas wrote in 1952:

> I can remember my first reaction when I heard them conversing in French with some of our group, and that was: "Why on earth were they sent out on such a dangerous job when their French was so faulty that they could never hope to pass themselves as Frenchmen?"
>
> It so happens that to-day, I met quite by accident, Squadron Leader Southgate, who was one of the officers among the 37 of us who went to Buchenwald together: I reminded him of the two Canadian boys, and asked him what he had thought of their French, to which he replied that it was bad; ... their French was not up to the required standard, and one was said not to speak French at all. That would be Macalister, who was certainly very weak in the language ....
>
> All this does not detract from their courage, which was to my mind outstanding. I liked them both immensely ... they were wasted and their qualities and courage could have found better and more profitable employment in every way, in another field.[9]

If so, why did S.O.E. send Macalister and Pickersgill into France? First, they themselves pressed to go at a time when there was an increasing demand for people who knew France intimately and who were also qualified radio operators. Secondly, Pickersgill not only knew France; he knew occupied France, a rarer knowledge, and he had, moreover, French friends who would presumably help him in his assigned tasks of sabotage and arms instruction. As for fluency in French, they might manage well enough to get through German controls which were every day dealing with Polish, Italian, and other foreign workers. It was clearly a gamble, but they were sent.

Pickersgill had first met John Kenneth Macalister during training. Macalister had been born in 1914, the only child of the publisher-editor of the Guelph *Mercury*. A short, "very dreamy, thoughtful guy,"[10] Macalister had so distinguished himself at the University of Toronto, both as an athlete and in law, that he was awarded a Rhodes scholarship in 1937, enabling him to study law at Oxford until 1939. In preparation for a year at the Institute of Comparative Law in Paris, Macalister decided in the spring of 1939 to improve his French by living with a family in Normandy. Macalister and Jeannine, the daughter of the family, soon married, and with the outbreak of war in September, Macalister volunteered for the French army. His eyesight was too poor, however, and he returned alone to New College, Oxford, to complete his degree in the summer of 1940. Jeannine, now pregnant and unhappy at the prospect of life in wartime England distant from her family, remained in France. A miscarriage followed and the Macalisters were never reunited.

At first, Macalister's weak eyesight excluded him from both the Canadian and British armies, but finally in February 1941 he was accepted as a private in field security in the British Intelligence Corps. During his work in various parts of Britain, he came in touch with S.O.E. and, on the first day of 1943, transferred to it. Near the end of his training, he was commissioned and for a brief period acted as an S.O.E. conducting officer, helping agents through their courses.

Many S.O.E. instructors or conducting officers sooner or later decided that they wanted to go into occupied areas themselves; Macalister was no exception. To what degree his decision was influenced by a desire to see his wife remains unclear, but he was junior enough to be allowed to go; more senior instructors knew too much to risk their capture. Both during training and on leave in London, Pickersgill and Macalister became good friends, Macalister deciding "that he couldn't go on sending other people and that Frank was a great fellow and that they could go together."[11] The two men spent as much time as possible at the Kensington flat of Kay Moore, back from Paris and now an officer in the S.O.E. liaison section working with the Free French intelligence service. Kay soon found herself the focus of Macalister's ardour, as Alison Grant of Toronto (working with M.I.5) did of Pickersgill's. "Frank brought a breath of new life into our home" where all sorts of military and government people gathered, eager for good talk and whatever limited food and drink wartime London afforded. And Pickersgill "had two years of cinemas to make up;...he was always disappearing into the distant suburbs to see some old film."

Before his S.O.E. training, C.M.H.Q. arranged for Pickersgill to visit several Canadian regiments in southern England, including the Maisonneuve ("all Gaulliste") from which Bieler and Chartrand had already gone to S.O.E. To the assembled soldiers he gave first-hand impressions of occupied France.

His subsequent S.O.E. training Pickersgill found wholly absorbing. "I'm enjoying it as I've never enjoyed anything in my life before. I've been in a permanent state of exhilaration since March 8 last (the date on which I made my get-away), on the crest of a wave which kept getting higher and higher as each frontier was crossed, and which now, instead of subsiding, seems to be going on up. I don't know where it's going to land me, but it's damned good while it lasts."[12] Pickersgill's final evaluation stated that he was "very sound and reliable, courageous, determined and showed qualities of a good organizer and leader. Has shown great interest in all matters appertaining to France and concentrated on reading French literature. Very sound on security. His morale and physical condition have improved considerably."[13] The only problem noted was that, during the early stages of his training, he had talked in English while asleep.

Much has been written about the painstaking efforts made to ensure that the clothing of secret agents resembled in the most minute detail that worn in their assigned country: foreign labels were removed (and local ones substituted) and styles and materials carefully scrutinized for their compatibility with those of the agent's destination. In the case of Macalister and Pickersgill, however, the selection of clothing seems to have been left largely to chance. Alison Grant accompanied them to the second-hand department of a large London clothier. "I went with them to Moss Bros. and we bought a coat. We ripped the lining out to help make all the clothes look older and more suitable to their supposed conditions. We rubbed them in dirt and tried to make them appear worn. It was all very amateurish, I suppose."[14] Kay Moore recalls the regret that she and Alison felt at making clothing look shabby when they were constantly repairing and attempting to improve the appearance of their own aging and rationed clothing.

In such a dubious disguise, Pickersgill and Macalister parachuted north of Valencay on the night of 15 June 1943, to help organize a sub-circuit of the much larger network "Prosper." Unknown to them and to London, "Prosper" was on the edge of catastrophe. One root of the impending disaster was the extraordinarily complicated double role which Henri Déricourt, a prewar French airline pilot, was playing. On behalf of S.O.E., he organized a series of successful landings of both Lysanders and Hudsons (Chartrand, for example, had travelled to France on a flight organized by Déricourt) which the Germans apparently condoned in return for Déricourt arranging for them to read agents' correspondence before he sent it on out-going flights to England.* Through this means and by their own intensified surveillance, German security gradually pieced together a fairly comprehensive picture of "Prosper."

However, even without the information supplied to the Germans by Déricourt, the overblown "Prosper" circuit would probably have been penetrated; it had grown too large with too many careless, incompetent agents. By mid-1943 the members of the circuit, including its energetic leader, Alfred Francis Suttill, an Anglo-French barrister, were convinced that an Allied invasion of France was planned for later that year. On 12 June 1943, Suttill had returned to France from briefings in London, apparently under the impression that he had been ordered both to place his circuit on the alert and to expand it to support an early invasion. Such expansion and increased activity, however, only

*Which side Déricourt was really on was hotly debated after the war and led to a sensational Paris trial at which he was finally acquitted, largely on the favourable testimony of senior S.O.E. staff officers. For as full a discussion as is probably now possible, see Foot, *S.O.E. in France*, p. 302.

increased the omnipresent danger of German penetration.

The growing vulnerability of "Prosper" should have become manifest to both Suttill and to S.O.E. headquarters when, in mid-May, two Germans broke into the network by passing themselves off as Allied airmen sent to "Prosper" by an escape line in the Netherlands. They knew the secret identification words and they stayed long enough to meet some of "Prosper's" Paris agents. This alone would have probably been enough to cause the collapse of the circuit.

Into this rapidly disintegrating situation, Pickersgill and Macalister had the misfortune to be parachuted with orders to help establish a new sub-circuit of "Prosper" north of Sedan. They parachuted without detection or serious injury near Romorantin, south of the Loire, and a few miles from where Chartrand had been landed two months before. As arranged, they were promptly collected by Pierre Culioli, a young, diminutive, former lieutenant in the French army and one of "Prosper's" more effective agents. He had with him Yvonne Rudellat, a cheerful, forty-seven-year-old former hotel receptionist in London and now a sabotage instructor in the circuit. Although Macalister's French seemed to them irreparable – and Culioli had been working with S.O.E. agents since 1941 – they hid him and Pickersgill in a safe house in the woods near Romorantin, pending their departure by train for Paris. During the next few days, Culioli had to collect other stores and agents, despite the fact that he had urged by wireless three days before that all such drops be suspended; the area of the Loire was on a full alert and thick with German police, partly as a result of a supply canister exploding upon landing. One of the agents dropped, a young French subaltern, hid with the two Canadians on 19 and 20 June, before making his way safely to Paris by train. Pickersgill and Macalister were to follow the next evening, their false papers having been improved and a rendezvous at the Gare d'Austerlitz arranged with Suttill.

On the warm, sunny morning of 21 June, while driving into the village of Dhuison with Culioli and Rudellat, they saw German troops everywhere. Both Suttill and the young French agent had reached Paris after having passed safely through one control near the village, but at a road block at its entrance, the two Canadians were suddenly taken out of the Citroen, two German soldiers took their places, and Culioli was ordered to drive to the town hall. There both his and Rudellat's papers were carefully examined. They seemed in order and accordingly they were released. Meanwhile, Pickersgill and Macalister, escorted by German police, arrived on foot at the town hall where Culioli and Rudellat had decided to await them in their car. The Germans soon became suspicious of Pickersgill and Macalister and ordered Culioli and Rudellat back into the building.

Now realizing that their cover was blown, Culioli and Rudellat drove away, but the Germans were ready. The two agents were pursued and when they were fired on, they crashed and were wounded, Culioli in the leg and Rudellat more severely in the head.*

There can be little doubt that, despite the increasing penetration of "Prosper," the arrest of the two Canadians was fortuitous. Whether they would have survived the now-imminent collapse of the network can only be a matter of conjecture; what is certain is that Pickersgill and Macalister brought with them two of the latest, more compact wireless sets, some radio crystals, and *en clair* messages. The messages were clearly addressed to agents, a highly questionable procedure. Although a surprised Culioli had taken the precaution of wrapping them in brown paper to make them look like a package addressed to a prisoner of war in Germany, the Germans had found the parcel in his car and soon realized what they had stumbled upon. They did not delay. They moved in on "Prosper" over the next few days, arresting most of its agents, including its leader, Suttill.

At first no one gave much away, despite the terror and torture

---

*The most graphic accounts of the capture of Macalister and Pickersgill are in Cookridge, *Inside S.O.E.*, pp. 228-30, based on post-war conversations with Culioli; and in Ford, *The Making of a Secret Agent*, pp. 246-53. After the war, Culioli was acquitted on charges that he had collaborated with the Germans following his capture. Rudellat died a few weeks after the liberation of the concentration camp at Belsen where she had been confined.

of which the Gestapo was so capable (agents were instructed to hold out for at least forty-eight hours to allow time for others to attempt to escape). Eventually, it seems that Suttill's radio operator cracked under torture and divulged addresses and later even assisted the Germans in arresting several of his fellow agents. In all, many hundreds of arrests were eventually made by the Germans and 470 tons of arms and explosives uncovered. It was the greatest success of German counter-intelligence against S.O.E. in France. Macalister and Pickersgill had the misfortune to be caught in it, dressed in their Moss Bros. clothes, speaking less-than-perfect French, using less-than-perfect identity papers, carrying instructions which incriminated not only them but other agents and resistance workers. It all seems, in the words of their devoted friend Alison Grant, "a little amateurish." The eventual price, however, was their lives.

Following their arrest in Dhuison, Pickersgill and Macalister were relentlessly and brutally interrogated, first in Blois and then, from 26 June, at the huge Fresnes prison near Paris. But they told nothing of value to the Germans and were soon sent by train to the concentration camp at Ravitsch, between the German border and Warsaw (to which Garel and his workers were to follow three months later). Postwar interrogation of prison personnel at Blois testified "to the outstanding fortitude and courage displayed by both these officers...neither revealed a scrap of information that was the slightest use to the Germans."[15]

5

Playing the Radio Game

The Germans had captured intact Macalister's wireless set and codes and had somehow learned where Pickersgill and Macalister were to establish their sub-circuit. They even had Macalister's correct security checks, presumably because he had, against standing orders, written them down. But none of this was known to "F" Section. Here was a golden opportunity for the Germans to play a *Funkspiel*, a wireless game, and they seized it eagerly. An S.S. officer, Josef Placke, a prewar salesman who, it seems, had once lived in Canada, travelled to Alsace. From there he began sending messages to London on Macalister's set. As a result, during the next ten months, London made many large drops of *matériel* which landed in the hands of the Germans. Placke, who spoke good French and a little English, moved about the area of the Franco-Belgian border, enjoying himself hugely while impersonating Pickersgill to members of the local resistance whom he organized in reception committees for the R.A.F. supply drops which he arranged by radio.* "Pickersgill" soon

---

*The stores were sent to the Satory barracks near Versailles where eventually they were recovered by the British army.

had a considerable reputation for being able to provide money, to travel freely about the countryside and to arrange arms drops. No one in the underground suspected that the drivers of the trucks which "Pickersgill" obligingly arranged to pick up stores were, in fact, German soldiers in civilian clothing.

During the winter of 1943–44, the Germans had an unbroken run of success in their French *Funkspiel*, not on the grand scale that they had concurrently in the Netherlands, but extensive enough to result in a substantial loss of valuable supplies and the capture of a number of S.O.E. agents, including several Canadians. In the Netherlands, the Germans ran the whole S.O.E. network from the spring of 1942. London blithely considered it secure and continued to send to it both agents and supplies.* In the case of the French *Funkspiel*, the Germans initially played back two wireless sets: Macalister's and that of another captured agent. Soon they added a third: the wireless set of the "Butler" circuit to which Chartrand had been assigned (and which had been operated by Rousset, the Mauritian who, following his capture, had been sent to Ravitsch with Pickersgill and Macalister). In October 1943, the Germans added a fourth wireless set, having penetrated yet another S.O.E. circuit, this one in the Chartres-Orleans region.

How the Germans managed to play back four sets and escape detection has never been adequately explained. The system of security checks, as a survivor of the Dutch *Funkspiel* explained, should have made such a fiasco impossible.

> This check was a means of indicating to my director in London that all was well with me. A lack of this check or any unexpected change in its nature would indicate that the agent concerned had fallen into the hands of the enemy. Any arrangment made for the purpose – even the simplest – will fulfil its object if it is rigidly laid down that normal use proves that the agent is working in freedom, and

---

*Several books have been written about the *Englandspiel*, the German radio game played from the Netherlands; among the more informative is the account by a German officer involved, H.J. Giskes, *London Calling North Pole* (London: Kimber, 1953); by a Dutch agent, Peter Dourlein, *Inside North Pole* (London: Kimber, 1953); and passages in E.H. Cookridge, *Inside S.O.E.*, (London: Barker, 1966).

absence or alteration of the check in use that he has fallen under enemy control. The check-indicator, furthermore, must be selected in such a way that it cannot be detected by an enemy operator listening in to the transmissions. It is quite obvious that headquarters must keep strictly to the prearranged plan, as otherwise it is better left altogether. The check, when properly used, will provide headquarters with complete and unbroken control, and its absence or alteration should result in a breaking-off of communication with the agent concerned, or at the very least in regarding the link with suspicion and in setting in train a searching investigation. The agent's duty, therefore, is to use his security check with the greatest care and to leave it out of his signals directly he is arrested. If the check is carefully chosen the enemy may think that he knows it, but will in fact never discover it. If pressure should be brought to bear on the agent, he must not reveal the correct check. The enemy will be bound to accept any statement which he may make up on the spur of the moment and will thus not be given the possibility of establishing control.[1]

Nevertheless, in both the Netherlands and France during the winter of 1943–44, the Germans managed to bring off their deception. Either the British ignored the absence of the assigned security checks or their faulty transmission or, even more incredibly, the Germans somehow gained full knowledge of them. The whole sorry episode became a major blot on S.O.E.'s developing competence.

The Germans arranged for no less than seven S.O.E. agents to be parachuted to them during February 1944 alone. On the night of 7 February, two Canadians were among four agents dropped near Chartres to an awaiting Gestapo "reception committee." One was Robert Bennett Byerly, a twenty-five-year-old American serving in the Canadian army who was a skilled radio operator. A graduate of the University of Chicago and a prewar journalist and school teacher with a lively intelligence and a marked aptitude for languages, "Bud" Byerly had volunteered for the Royal Canadian Corps of Signals in Ottawa in April 1941, eight months before the United States entered the war. Upon completing his S.O.E. training and intensive wireless instruction in England in late 1943, Byerly had been commissioned in the Canadian army before assuming his new identity of "Robert Antoine Brevil."

The other Canadian officer captured that fatal night of 7 February was François Adolphe Deniset from St. Boniface, the largely French-Canadian area of Winnipeg. Under the *nom de guerre* of "François Dussault," Deniset had been assigned as a small arms instructor to a circuit which, unknown to London, the Gestapo had in fact penetrated four months before.

Deniset had met and married an English girl in the summer of 1941 and the following year they had a daughter. Nevertheless, he had volunteered for S.O.E. in May 1943 and had proved to be an exceptionally able trainee. He spoke French fluently, using it at home, at the Jesuit College in St. Boniface, and at the University of Manitoba where he had studied history and economics in preparation for the Foreign Service Officer examinations of the Department of External Affairs. Two days before war was declared, the amiable, laconic Deniset had joined the Royal Canadian Artillery – one of two gunners among the Canadians who volunteered for S.O.E. in Europe.

Deniset, however, had no opportunity to use his French, his S.O.E. training or his acting ability (he had performed in college theatricals). Along with Byerly and the other two agents captured that night, he found himself being interrogated by the Gestapo within an hour of landing. Yet more severe interrogation awaited them in Paris at the notorious Gestapo prison at 3 bis, Place des Etats-Unis. However, having jumped into the arms of their captors, they knew almost nothing about local underground activities. In July 1944 they were crowded into the foetid box cars of a train that carried them half way across Europe to the Gross Rosen concentration camp in Poland.

Meanwhile, Placke's particular *Funkspiel* continued without interruption throughout the winter of 1943–44. Having impersonated Pickersgill with such gratifying results – fifteen large supply drops, including about $40,000 in francs, and several captured agents – Placke became even more ambitious. A full nine months after Macalister and Pickersgill had been dispatched to the concentration camp in Poland, Placke radioed London to send to him a total of six more agents. Incredibly,

S.O.E., still suspecting nothing, promptly complied.

Four more agents, two British and two Americans, were accordingly dropped to "Pickersgill" on 3 March 1944. Within a few hours of saying good-bye to the S.O.E. staff seeing them off, they were undergoing Gestapo interrogation. Again, having little to divulge that the Germans did not already know, they too were packed off to a concentration camp. That same night, the fifth and sixth agents Placke had requested were dropped to another of his reception areas: Alec Rabinowitch (whom another agent admiringly described as a "violent, difficult, devoted and heroic" Russo-Egyptian Jew) and his radio operator, Romeo Sabourin from the north end of Montreal, who had left his work as an apprentice mechanic in a shoe factory to join the army.

Sabourin had lied to the recruiting officer about his age; he was under the mandatory seventeen and a half years when he volunteered to join the Fusiliers Mont-Royal in April 1940. By mid-1943, as a French-speaking signalman in southern England, he had been interviewed and recruited by S.O.E. Upon completion of his training in February 1944, he was assigned as radio operator to Alphonse Defendini, a Corsican who crossed by R.N. motor gunboat to Brittany a few days before Sabourin parachuted. Defendini's instructions were to establish a new circuit at Verdun. He and Sabourin never kept their initial rendezvous in Paris since Rabinowitch and Sabourin were barely on French soil before they were arrested. Upon landing, Sabourin and his companion had freed themselves of their parachutes before Placke's "reception committee" approached. The two agents, hearing German voices, hid behind trees and opened fire. In the moonlight, they killed two Germans before being themselves wounded and captured. Neither had information of value. Soon they too were on their way to a concentration camp – in their case, eventually to Buchenwald.

By mid-April 1944, "F" Section had finally begun to suspect that several of their circuits – they remained uncertain how many – had been penetrated. With the Germans playing back so many captured radio sets, including Byerly's, the enemy's errors and omissions in sending the agreed security checks contributed to London's growing realization about how far the rot had spread.

With the suspected loss of six more agents, London finally concluded that something might be wrong with Pickersgill's and several other circuits. Weeks had passed, during which Sabourin had failed to send the test messages agreed upon, so S.O.E. headquarters decided that a conclusive effort should be made to speak with Pickersgill himself. One way of so doing was at hand, even if it was risky and cumbersome. The "S phone" was an early microwave voice radio with a maximum range of about eight to ten kilometres. "Pickersgill" was notified by wireless that voice contact would be attempted from an overhead aircraft in May. Unable to stall any longer, the Germans hurriedly brought Pickersgill, now emaciated and weak from almost six months in Ravitsch, to talk on a captured S phone to the S.O.E. staff officer who would be circling overhead in a low-flying aircraft. aircraft.

Pickersgill refused, despite repeated offers of improved treatment. Another S.O.E. agent who had already collaborated with the Germans was taken to the Sedan region to impersonate Pickersgill, but at the last minute he too declined. In desperation, a German officer attempted to deceive the S.O.E. staff officer overhead by speaking into the S phone with what he hoped was a Canadian accent. The staff officer was not fooled. He returned to London convinced that at least Pickersgill and Macalister were in German hands. All supply drops ceased. Placke's *Funkspiel* was finally over, although several harmless messages were sent by London to "Pickersgill" to keep the Germans guessing for a few weeks whether the British had fully understood what had happened.

Following his repeated refusals to co-operate, Pickersgill was held in an S.S. prison on the Avenue Foch in Paris from where he made a desperate attempt to escape. A French agent in the prison later described the episode:

> Pickersgill's courage was extraordinary. He came within an inch of freeing the whole prison . . . . One day, using a bottle as a weapon, he attacked one of the the S.S. guards, knocked him to the floor, and then descended the stairs where he came upon the guard post. The guards there had unfortunately heard the cries of the first man (who

had not been killed by the blows from the bottle) and were on the alert. Pickersgill nevertheless rushed into this group of guards, knocked them out of his way, and then leaped from the second storey window into the street. But he was exhausted from such a long period of inactivity and imprisonment; he was unable to run very quickly. The S.S. opened fire from the windows with their sub-machine guns; he was hit four times, fell, tried to run again but stopped from exhaustion and lost consciousness.[2]

Upon recovery in a Paris military hospital, Pickersgill was held in Place des Etats-Unis and again on Avenue Foch, where Macalister was also being held. There they learned of the Allied invasion of Normandy, which raised their hopes of early liberation. Instead, on 8 August, with the Allies only twelve days from Paris, they were herded into box cars with thirty-five other agents destined for Buchenwald.

While "F" Section had been slowly groping its way toward realization that what had appeared to be several of its best circuits were in fact controlled by Germans, brave agents were being captured, brutally treated, and eventually executed. As a result of this particular radio game, three Canadian as well as several French, American, and British agents died. Could this have been avoided?

One problem was simply the persistent overwork at both the S.O.E. wireless stations and at headquarters. Weary operators and supervisors, burdened with coding and decoding thousands of messages, occasionally failed to notice that the agreed security checks were missing from a message which, in any case, might well arrive so garbled as to make meaningless the rigid application of such tests. A second problem was that the Germans too were clever: they, as well as the British transmitting in the opposite direction, developed operators able to imitate the "hand" of an agent (all of whom had individual styles and idiosyncrasies in transmitting). The Germans also applied the lessons of observation and experience and became increasingly adept at penetrating S.O.E. networks. And finally, "some agents were braver, and some staff officers brighter, than others."[3] At several points the Germans clearly outwitted S.O.E.

If the *Funkspiel* in the Netherlands was S.O.E.'s worst debacle in Europe, the *Funkspiel* in France during the winter of 1943–44 was its second worst. It even caught the attention of Hitler. He had several discussions with Göring and Himmler about the most opportune time to reveal to London that several of its most important circuits in France were, in fact, being worked by Germans. They eventually decided to give London the bad news whenever D-day arrived, the day when the Allies would land on the beaches of France. Hitler evidently believed that the morale and hence the effectiveness of the invasion commanders would be reduced at such a critical moment by the realization that resistance networks upon whose support they had counted were, in fact, in enemy hands. Accordingly, at noon on 6 June 1944– D-day–the German security service radioed to S.O.E. head-quarters in London: "Many thanks large deliveries arms and ammunition...have greatly appreciated good tips concerning [Allied] intentions and plans." London by then was well informed about the penetration of several of its circuits and replied archly: "Sorry to see your patience is exhausted and your nerves not so good as ours...give us ground near Berlin for reception organizer and [wireless] operator."[4]

This staff banter between enemies may have been amusing, but it did not explain why errors had been made and assumptions had remained unquestioned. About all that can be said in explanation of the debacle is that the Allied invasion was fully expected by both sides during the spring of 1944; many had been convinced that it would come during 1943. The Germans redoubled their efforts to exterminate the resistance which they knew could seriously hinder their efforts to supply their front line. The Allies, for their part, did everything they could to encourage, train, supply, and otherwise assist the resistance, even if in the winter of 1943–44, as German counter-intelligence further improved, this involved yet greater risks of detection. The invasion had to succeed; Germany had to be defeated. If this involved the capture and death of yet more agents, the price had to be paid. The *Funkspiel* was one such price.

6

The Executions

The first two months of 1944 were disastrous for Canadians with S.O.E. in France. Bieler was captured in St. Quentin; Byerly, Deniset, and Sabourin were parachuted to awaiting Germans; and another Canadian, Alcide Beauregard of the Eastern Townships of Quebec, was also destined never to return.

Beauregard originally enlisted in the Régiment de Maisonneuve (he had arrived in Britain with Bieler and Chartrand) and later transferred to the Royal Canadian Corps of Signals. Dark, slight, and by prewar training an electrical and radio mechanic, the twenty-six-year-old Beauregard volunteered for S.O.E. in mid-1943, when there was an acute shortage of French-speaking wireless operators. The enemy had long realized that wireless operators were the most vulnerable link in the S.O.E. chain. If an operator could be eliminated, a whole circuit could be paralysed. The premium on operators was exceptionally high. As a result, many operators, including Beauregard, were given accelerated training. On his Ringway parachute course in late November, Beauregard sprained an ankle. Accordingly, on 8 February 1944, he was landed by Lysander east of Tours (on almost the same field where Chartrand had been deposited a year before) to journey across France to his assignment in Lyon. Beauregard was to be radio operator to a Frenchman in his fifties, J.E. Lesage, who had already worked with a circuit in Lyon and was returning from training in Britain to establish a new sub-circuit of the larger "Ditcher" circuit based on Lyon. Lesage, however, soon proved to be of no further use as an organizer. During his first tour, he had so alienated other resistance workers that he could find few still willing to co-operate with him. When Lesage retreated into bucolic inactivity, Beauregard was left without a circuit chief. What he did thereafter is not clear from the scant records in London and Ottawa, although it appears that he joined "Ditcher" in Lyon. A Canadian army record suggests that he operated his wireless set continually from the house of a schoolmaster. London apparently warned Beauregard of the growing danger from wireless detection equipment as he continued to transmit from the same place. With the Allied invasion rapidly approaching, Beauregard accepted the risks in view of the heavy volume of messages–which, by their numbers, also increased the chances of his detection. He was caught on 15 July, but only after he had destroyed his wireless set and codes with the help of the schoolmaster's son.

After being interrogated at the Gestapo headquarters in the Place Bellecoeur, Beauregard was imprisoned in Fort Monluc, a dark, gloomy fort in Lyon. A postwar Canadian army intelligence report noted tersely: "His reason is believed to have been unhinged by the tortures to which he was subjected. Lieut. Beauregard gave way no information."[1] With the approach of the Allied armies up the Rhône, the Gestapo in Lyon carried out Hitler's order to execute all resistance and "commando" prisoners. On 20 August, Beauregard and one hundred and twenty of the resistance were machine-gunned to death at St. Génie Laval. Hand grenades were thrown among their bodies to ensure that no one was still alive. Himmler had always intended that all such "terrorists" should be murdered, "but not before torture, indignity and interrogation had drained from them that last shred and scintilla of evidence which should lead to the arrest of others. Then, and only then, should the blessed release of death be granted them."[2] Having disclosed nothing, the time had come for Beauregard to be cast aside.

And so it was for all the captured Canadian agents. None survived the autumn of 1944; they were of no further use to the Germans. And neither the Gestapo nor the S.S. wanted surviving Allied agents to report to their liberators what had been done to them in captivity. In any case, many agents succumbed to the appalling day-to-day conditions of their camps. Of the remainder, most were murdered during the last quarter of 1944 or the first months of 1945. Hitler himself approved an order for some agents to be garrotted with nooses of piano wire; death would then come more slowly and more agonizingly. Beauregard escaped that final degradation by being machine-gunned. Gustave Bieler was also shot, but in a different way – if that is a distinction of any moment.

By Christmas 1943, time was running out for Bieler and Yolande Beekman. At an overnight meeting in Lille on 25 November, Trotobas had confided to Bieler his concern about the carelessness and incompetence of one of his workers. Two nights later, the agent, under torture, disclosed to the Germans his chief's hiding place. Trotobas fought it out with the Germans. He and several of his workers who were later captured were soon executed. Bieler, after reporting the disaster to London, did what he could from St. Quentin to help the crippled circuit in Lille to regroup.

Bieler was left too long in France. He should have been brought out after about six months – long enough for any agent, however dexterous, brave, and security-conscious. But Bieler stayed, since "F" Section, greatly pleased by his success, wanted to expand his circuit to help meet the increased needs for sabotage, both preceding and following the anticipated Allied invasion. In a sense, Bieler became a victim of the omnipresent tension arising from the long-term need to husband resources for the impending invasion and the immediate need to harass the enemy wherever and whenever possible.

Bieler's success was, in a sense, his own undoing. It attracted the intensified attention of the Germans. Having his own wireless operator contributed to his greater efficiency, but it also enabled German counter-intelligence to use its detection equipment to pinpoint the St. Quentin transmissions – an advantage they did not have earlier when Bieler was passing messages through other circuits. From October, Beekman had been transmitting from a secluded house. In December, a German automobile equipped with wireless-detection equipment was seen nearby. Beekman hurriedly moved her set to the house of Camille Boury, a pharmacist in the resistance. It was with the Bourys that Bieler and Beekman spent Christmas Eve of 1943, a Christmas that Mme. Boury never forgot:

> Guy arrived in his familiar garb (he was almost always dressed as a workman) carrying two Santa Clauses stuffed with candy for our children and under each arm a few good bottles. We listened to the [BBC] messages from London and then the wonderful Christmas music. We had arranged a good Christmas atmosphere with the traditional pine-tree and candles. Guy recited to us (as he could so well) the beautiful poetry of Victor Hugo. We also sang Canadian and French choruses.
>
> At midnight Guy held his head in both hands for a long time. When this . . . silence . . . was over, he was very serious and seemed completely overcome. He asked us for a pencil and wrote on the back of one of our photographs an address: "Chief, French Dept., Sun Life Assurance Company, Dominion Square, Montreal."
>
> He then said to us . . . "If misfortune overtakes me some day, write to this address. You will find my wife there. Tell her how I spent Christmas of 1943, describe this evening to her. Tell her of how I thought of them."
>
> He also used to speak to us often of his children . . . . His greatest pleasure was to go and look at my little boy and girl sleeping. They never saw him for he did not want them to be able to chatter. We had to take so many precautions against this accursed Gestapo but each time that he could, he went to see them asleep.[3]

Within three weeks, a stranger was seen in the Boury's street, his collar turned up apparently to conceal earphones. Three days later, on 15 January 1944, Bieler and Beekman were at the drab, red-brick Café du Moulin Brûlé on a lonely road near the St. Quentin Canal where they had spent many evenings. Suddenly a dozen armed Germans rushed in. The café owner and his wife, along with Bieler and Beekman, were included in the total of forty members of the network arrested that day and the days following. Among the few to escape arrest was a veteran Franco-Swiss agent who had parachuted to Bieler four days before to assist in the demolition of the gates of the canal locks.

The Germans had done their homework well. They had removed the copestone of Bieler's carefully constructed network. During the following days, they arrested more than a dozen agents in the area, but they were unable to destroy the network completely. Six months later, when the Allied invasion began, several of Bieler's sabotage and ambush teams were still intact, hindering the arrival of German reinforcements on the Normandy front.

Among those arrested with Bieler was Eugène Cordelette, the land surveyor who had housed him when he had first arrived in St. Quentin fourteen months before. On the night of their arrest, Cordelette saw Bieler in a corridor of the St. Quentin prison, being taken to a small cell after the first of many brutal Gestapo interrogations. "He was chained hand and foot. His face was horribly swollen, but I could read in his eyes this order: 'Whatever happens, don't talk!' ... In spite of all torments, he showed no weakness."[4] The horror of Bieler's treatment seeps through even the usually arid prose of his citation for a posthumous D.S.O.: "Despite the most barbarous forms of torture by the enemy over a period extending over at least eight days, he refused absolutely to divulge the names of any one of his associates, or the location of any arms dumps. Despite the intense pain that he was suffering from the injury to his back, he faced the Gestapo with the utmost determination and courage."

Following almost three months of interrogation during which his back injury was exacerbated and his kneecap broken, the now-emaciated Bieler was sent with fourteen British officers to narrow, windowless cells in the concentration camp which took its name from the nearby Bavarian town of Flossenbürg.

In their tiny concrete cells, Bieler and the British agents were cut off from each other as well as the outside world, aware of the passage from night to day only by the appearance of a watery soup and a dark, spongy substance that passed for bread. There was no exercise, no reading or writing, no news of the war – only solitary confinement, increasing debilitation from malnutrition, and the endless struggle to retain one's sanity. His anxious wife in Montreal knew only from a terse War Office message that he was missing following an operation "somewhere in Europe." Captain Lunding, a Danish army officer and one of the few survivors of Flossenbürg, was in an adjoining cell and later supplied a few details about Bieler's fate. By September 1944, Bieler had become a physical wreck as a result of his back and leg injuries, torture, and malnutrition. But his courage remained. According to a statement made to Lunding by a camp official the day after the execution, Bieler conducted himself with such courage and dignity to the last that even the camp guards themselves had paid a peculiar tribute to him: he had "made so powerful an impression on his captors that when the order for his execution came from Berlin... the S.S. at Flossenbürg mounted a guard of honour to escort him as he limped to his death."[5] For an Allied agent to be executed by a firing squad was in itself a rare, if dubious, honour. Most agents were hanged as terrorists. Buckmaster recorded, "This is the only instance known to us of an officer being executed in such circumstances by a firing squad with a Guard of Honour."[6]

Several of Bieler's French accomplices were also in prison. His radio operator, Yolande Beekman, was in Karlsruhe jail. Three days after Bieler was executed on 9 September 1944, Beekman, with three other female S.O.E. agents, was killed at Dachau concentration camp near Munich, shot through the back of the neck.

There is abundant material about Frank Pickersgill's short life. There is also much detail about his death, and that of Macalister and Sabourin. F.F.E. Yeo-Thomas, one of the most intrepid S.O.E. agents, provides in *The White Rabbit* a graphic account of his own experiences and the end of the three Canadians at Buchenwald.

On 8 August 1944, with the Allied vanguard twelve days from Paris, the Gestapo had hurriedly rounded up a total of thirty-seven male and female agents from several prisons in and near Paris and sent them by rail to Germany, most destined for the notorious Buchenwald. With Yeo-Thomas aboard that crowded and stifling train of death were Sabourin and Defendini, the Corsican to whom he had been assigned as a radio operator; Pickersgill, Macalister, and Culioli who had been arrested with them; Garel whom Chartrand had joined; and Garry to whom Deniset had been sent as wireless operator. The fortitude of Pickersgill shone through again; he attempted to tell jokes. Yeo-Thomas later recalled, "They weren't particularly funny jokes.... At first they weren't appreciated. Then suddenly everyone realized that Pickersgill was only trying to keep them from all going crazy. They cheered up a bit and took a grip on themselves."[7]

On the second day, near the German border, the agents almost died an unexpected death. They were left locked in their over-crowded box car while their guards took cover from a roof-top strafing by the R.A.F. After a total of eight days of foetid confinement, brutality, starvation, and agonizing thirst, all the prisoners were delivered on the night of 18 August to the gates of Buchenwald. Upon entering they had good reason to abandon hope.* During the following three weeks, the prisoners existed in a world which must have been close to Hieronymus Bosch's vision of souls writhing in the torments of hell.

> As they were marched across the camp the prisoners had their first glimpse of their fellow inmates, and it was anything but reassuring. The compound was filled with emaciated, hairless wretches shuffling wearily round and round in heavy wooden clogs. The eyes of those listless sub-human creatures were mean with terror. On the faces of many of them a sticky stream of yellow rot oozed from purulent sores set in the middle of purple weals. Others were so weak that they staggered as they walked. Even when their clothes

---

*Sabourin, Pickersgill, and Macalister would not have known it, but at least one other Canadian was in Buchenwald when they arrived. Signalman George Rodrigues of Montreal, an M.I.9 agent, was sent to Buchenwald in late 1943 or early 1944. He survived more than a year of its bestiality, but died shortly after liberation from the maltreatment which he had received (see page 301).

were too short for them, they were too wide because of the thinness of the frail bodies which they covered. The same grim question occurred simultaneously to all the thirty-seven as they beheld this gruesome spectacle: "How long is it going to be before we look like them?"

They were ... in the worst camp in Germany. Their chances of survival were practically nil: if they did not starve to death they would be worked to death; and if they were not worked to death they would be executed. Every single day more than three hundred prisoners died from starvation or from being beaten by their guards.... Each [working party] consisted of hundreds of prisoners quarrying stone, dragging logs or cleaning out latrines.... The S.S. guards were also there and so were their Alsatian hounds, and when enough amusement couldn't be derived from bludgeoning a man's brains out there was always the alternative of setting the dogs upon him to tear out his throat....

A squat black chimney just beyond the Block was pointed out to them. "That's the crematorium," they were told. "It's the surest of all escape routes; most of us will only get out of this camp by coming through that chimney as smoke."[8]

On 6 September, three weeks after their night arrival, the camp loudspeaker called for fifteen of the thirty-seven S.O.E. agents to report to the headquarters tower. They did not return to their hut. The following day a Polish prisoner with contacts in the crematorium squad told the remaining agents of their comrades' deaths. Now the surviving twenty-two could have no more doubt about what awaited them. Three days later, on 9 September – by coincidence the same day Bieler was shot in Flossenbürg – another sixteen prisoners were summoned, including the three Canadians.* According to one postwar account:

Some knew what it meant. Others suspected. All hoped for the best. Without a word they fell in, in threes, with Pickersgill at the head of one of the files. At Pickersgill's command they marched off ..., a threadbare, forlorn little band, trying to march like guardsmen. Up

*There is disagreement between Foot and George Ford, the editor of Pickersgill's letters, about the date of Macalister's and Pickersgill's deaths. Foot, drawing upon S.O.E. archives, puts it on 6 September; Ford places them in the first rather than second group, but gives 9 September as the date.

front they could see Pickersgill, limping and occasionally staggering as his unhealed wounds, malnutrition and slight deafness combined to unsteady him, a cracked husk of a man, but unbroken.

Pickersgill began flailing the air with his hands, just as he had done on the campus years before. But now he was no longer celebrating André Gide, passing judgment on Neville Chamberlain or analyzing St. Augustine. He was beating time . . . .

That night the marchers were thrashed and flung into a bunker. An emaciated French priest, Father Georges Stenger from Lorraine, stumbled a mile across the camp and pleaded for permission to administer the last sacrament to the Roman Catholics. He was refused. Stenger stayed all night outside the bunker praying and managed to slip into the captives, via a guard who began to show a sense of shame, wafers of the Sacred Host.

The following night the sixteen were taken to the crematorium and the doors were slammed. Once more Father Stenger knelt outside and prayed. Later he recalled that he'd heard scuffling noises and faint cries of "Vive la France!" "Vive l'Angleterre!" and "Vive le Canada!"[9]

Macalister, Sabourin, and Pickersgill died the cruellest death which Gestapo sadists could devise: they were hanged from meat hooks cemented in a wall, nooses of piano wire slowly strangling them. Theirs was not the quick death of hanging by breaking the neck; it was slow strangulation, garrotting. Hitler had a number of such executions filmed so that he might have the pleasure of seeing prisoners perish in agony.

The end of François Deniset and Robert Byerly is not so well documented. All that is known is that after a period of interrogation and torture at the Gestapo prison in Paris – they were seen there by other agents on 27 June 1944 – they were taken by train to the Gross Rosen concentration camp in Poland where they were executed in September. While varying perhaps in detail, their end cannot have differed so very much from that of their fellow Canadians at Lyon, Flossenbürg, and Buchenwald.

And so they died: Byerly, the American serving in the Canadian army, and six Canadians who had volunteered to serve with S.O.E. in France–Beauregard, Bieler, Deniset, Macalister, Pickersgill, and Sabourin.

7

Survivors

During the eight months from February to August 1944, a total of eighteen other Canadians (mainly French Canadians from the Royal Canadian Corps of Signals) parachuted into France with S.O.E. – and all survived. The year 1944, which had started so badly for the Canadians in S.O.E., ended in triumph.

With the approach of D-day, the Allies did everything possible to encourage, train, arm, and otherwise prepare the resistance to hinder the flow of German reinforcements and material to Normandy. In London, reorganization at headquarters eventually resulted in closer co-operation between British and Free French intelligence and subversive units. From 15 June 1944 the whole of the clandestine efforts of the Free French, the British and the Americans was placed under the overall command of the French General Koenig. S.O.E. detachments were assigned to Army and Army Group headquarters in an effort to relate resistance efforts to the operations of regular units. In the field, S.O.E. agents worked with resistance groups, frequently as staff officers in contact with London, keeping the *maquis* informed about local Allied intentions and arranging for drops of arms and other equipment. By D-day, S.O.E. alone had 145 agents in France, operating in forty-five separate circuits.

As early as mid-1943, S.O.E., together with other services and Allied representatives, had accelerated the planning of what the underground could best do both before and after the invasion. Sabotage of locomotives, power stations, petroleum dumps, and fighter aircraft would be especially valuable before the Allied assault. Once the invasion was underway, disruption of roads, railways, and telephones would be intensified, particularly of those leading to Normandy; troop movements would be harassed everywhere and by any means; and local German headquarters would be attacked wherever feasible.

This was offensive warfare, not the clandestine work that Bieler, Chartrand, Pickersgill, and Deniset had been sent to do. The summer of 1944 promised S.O.E. agents more overt action, including even being parachuted in uniform. Felix Walter made the point – albeit in an exaggerated way – when he wrote immediately after the war: "The successes of 1944...were the fruit of bitter years of effort and partial failure and it is clear from a perusal of the reports of...agents...that the life of an Allied agent in [France] in the summer of 1944 was almost a picnic compared to the existence of those of his colleagues 'dropped' a few years or even a few months previously."[1] Several of the "class of 1944" lived at least intermittently the fugitive life of Bieler, Duchalard, and Chartrand, but there remains a pronounced difference between the experiences of the earlier and the later volunteers, many of whom were specialized radio operators from the Royal Canadian Corps of Signals. Whatever their role, the agents who were dropped into France either shortly before or following the Normandy invasion of June 1944 served more like soldiers and less like secret operatives. By then the Germans were on the defensive, the resistance more an offensive underground army than pockets of saboteurs working stealthily in the shadows. The risks of clandestine warfare were still high, but they were less than in 1942 and 1943.

Let us pause here for a moment to review briefly the nature of the resistance. First, it was highly dangerous to be in the underground. And it was difficult. Success, as in so many things, depended upon careful preparation. But it also depended upon the availability of food, arms, and money, and the self-discipline of its members.

> The circuits produced some sensational incidents in the "spy war" and a whole series of bestsellers have recounted them. In fact, however, the great innovation of clandestine resistance was that it relied on patriotic volunteers rather than on professional agents or mercenaries; the volunteers made up for their lack of experience by knowledge of the problems with which they had to deal and of the human environment in which they worked. The few brilliant successes were counterbalanced by the tiny modest efforts of hundreds of men. The shadow war was a war of self-denial and self-sacrifice rather than one of spectacular exploits.[2]

In the beginning, to have any chance of surviving, an active resister, whatever his or her country or background, had to observe the same inescapable discipline: to live in perpetual fear and loneliness, using a false identity, trusting none, suspecting everyone, even old friends and relatives. All this had to be accepted in addition to the daily difficulties facing those living in any enemy-occupied country: the increasing regulation and surveillance of everyday life and the growing shortages of even the most basic goods and services so familiar in peacetime that they pass almost unnoticed. Life in the underground was not easy; most found it a severe test of their physical and above all mental endurance, especially as enemy retaliation became more foul and frantic.

The members of the resistance were, not surprisingly, a mixed lot, engaged in activities ranging from the most trivial of acts such as mimicry of Germans to the most ambitious acts of sabotage and ambush that available supplies and numbers would allow. Women and men of the greatest patriotism and courage and of the most reckless gallantry were mixed with cowards, incompetents, and traitors. Some were near saints; some no more than common criminals. Some were apolitical; others were deeply committed to social change by civil war or revolution. And the early hard core of idealism and devotion was to a degree diluted by the rapid increase in less motivated volunteers who joined the underground following the German introduction of widespread forced labour into France during the latter half of 1942. Rather than be caught up in such a *corveé,* young men fled to rural and mountainous areas to join the resistance. Generally living in the woods with little food, the groups varied greatly in quality and organization. Christopher Sykes provides a memorable sketch of the *maquis* his S.A.S. unit parachuted to support in 1944:

> We were greeted by a host of untrained, unarmed, expectant, and physically exhausted young men, whose only idea of military formation was to assemble in large masses, whose strategy consisted of firing what few weapons they possessed at every rustle of a rabbit, or in shouting their passwords from wood to wood, and into whose ranks traitors had been introduced.[3]

With the invasion of France only months away, we have now entered that period of "F" Section's activities when the floodgates were opened, agents went in by the dozen, massive supply drops (some now by daylight) multiplied, and *maquis* surged out of their hiding places to confront German units–occasionally sometimes so boldly, carelessly, or prematurely as to invite disaster–as well as to ambush them. It was a time when most able-bodied Frenchmen were eager to join in (or to be seen as joining in) the fight against the enemy. During the few weeks around D-day, more Canadians went into France with S.O.E. than during the whole of the nineteen months since Bieler had first landed on French soil.

> By this time the whole business of sending clandestine agents into France had developed qualities of routine . . . . [Staff] continued to treat every agent they saw off as an individual, but this too had become part of the drill. In all 1941, "F" Section had only sent 24 operational agents into the field; by the [spring of 1944] over 40 separate "F" circuits, most of them with several British-trained agents, were at work.[4]

The nature of S.O.E.'s operations in France also changed, be-

A 1944 Canadian trainee
at the Ringway Parachute
School near Manchester,
England braces in the
approved fashion, head
back to avoid hitting the
cowling of the floor hatch in
a Whitley bomber, while
awaiting the signal to jump.
(Public Archives Canada)

1.

A rare daylight drop by the R.A.F. of supply cannisters at Prairie d'Echallons,
France, 1944. Generally drops were under the cover of night, but following
D-day, daylight drops multiplied especially in areas where the resistance
could guarantee security. *(Public Archives Canada)*

2.

3.

The irrepressible Ray Wooler of Montreal, one of S.O.E.'s most skilled and experienced parachute experts who, after service in Britain, North Africa and Italy, volunteered in 1945 to parachute into Sarawak. The photograph was taken in 1941 near the Ringway parachute school. Wooler is surrounded by several Polish trainees (later to be executed by the Germans). *(Courtesy Ray Wooler)*

The forged identity card of the boyish Al Sirois of Saskatchewan who celebrated his twenty-first birthday with a *maquis* in the Cognac area of occupied France. *(Courtesy Allyre Sirois)*

4.

5.

The first Canadian into France with S.O.E. was Gustave Bieler of Montreal, seen here in London with his sister and niece shortly before he parachuted to the French underground. *(Courtesy Jacqueline Bieler-Briggs) Opposite:* Two German soldiers, taken prisoners by a *maquis*, glance at a dead comrade whose corpse has already been stripped of his boots. Arms drops arranged by S.O.E. were the main source of supply for the French underground. *(Public Archives Canada)*

7. A German munitions train sabotaged by the French underground near Abbeville in September 1944. In the period around D-day, the underground, supported by S.O.E., made its most sustained effort to disrupt enemy communications. *(Public Archives Canada)*

8.

Prematurely aging and emaciated, Frank Pickersgill had spent almost two years in a German camp in a suburb of Paris before his escape to Britain through Vichy France and Portugal. He nevertheless returned with S.O.E. to occupied France in June 1943 only to be arrested almost upon landing. This photograph was taken in September 1942 for his Vichy exit permit. *(Courtesy Jack Pickersgill)*

9.

John Macalister of Guelph, a graduate of the University of Toronto studying law at Oxford when the war began, volunteered for S.O.E. and accompanied Frank Pickersgill as wireless operator on their ill-fated mission to France which was to end in the furnaces of Buchenwald. *(Courtesy George Penfold)*

10.

"Gaby" Chartrand on his thirty-sixth birthday, 14 August 1943, at Château-du-Loir. The third Canadian into occupied France with S.O.E., he managed to break away from his captors upon being arrested while helping an American airman to safety. (*Courtesy Gabriel Chartrand*)

Pierre Meunier of Montreal arm-in-arm with Walter Stuki, the Swiss minister to the Vichy government of France. Meunier, in September 1944, was sent to Vichy to encourage the few remaining diplomats there to accept his offer of safe passage to Paris. (*Courtesy Pierre Meunier*)

11.

12.

Roger Caza, the graduate of the University of Ottawa who had been a pre-war journalist with *Le Droit*, was disguised as Roger Marc Pilon, a travelling salesman. Caza's radio work ranged from Toulouse to Lyon in 1944. *(Canadian War Museum)*

Steve Mate of Thunder Bay in his uniform of corporal in the Canadian Armoured Corps, at the time of his recruitment to parachute into Hungary from Italy. Mate was killed in an air crash in the English Channel. His tombstone in Cornwall is unusual in recording both his real and cover names. *(Courtesy André Durovecz and Derek Fowkes)*

13.

14.

Hungary was one of S.O.E's less successful areas of operation. The Canadians who served there encountered constant dangers and obstacles, despite intensive training in Egypt and Italy. At San Vito dei Normanni in southern Italy; left to right *(front row)*: Adam Herter; Alexander Vass; an unknown British captain; Joe Gelleny; *(back row)*: Adam Magyar; John Coates; Mike Turk; and André Durovecz. *(Courtesy André Durovecz)*

William Stuart, the prewar C.P.R. immigration official who, having been born in the Austro-Hungarian Empire, spoke several central European languages. One of the first Allied officers to parachute to Tito, he was killed in June 1943 by the same German bomb which wounded Tito. The photograph is from early 1943. *(Courtesy Didi Gilchrist)*

17.

William Jones, a veteran of the First World War from Nova Scotia, was one of the first Allied officers to parachute to Tito's Partisans in Yugoslavia. Shortly after his team's night drop in April 1943, Jones stands in the centre, Black Watch tam o'shanter still firmly in place; his R.A.F. wireless operator, Ronald Jephson, is on his right and a British captain, Anthony Hunter, on his left. (*Courtesy Mrs. William Jones*)

Seven of the Canadians who, after service in occupied France, volunteered for more secret warfare in Asia. Upon their arrival in Montreal for Christmas leave in 1944 before going to Burma and Malaya were (*front row* left to right) "Rocky" Fournier, Paul Thibeault, and "Ben" Benoit; (*rear row*) Paul Labelle, Jacques Taschereau, Guy d'Artois and Paul Archambault (who was to die in Burma). (*La Presse* 16 December 1944)

18.

coming more overt and mobile, taking on something of the character of open warfare. As we have noted, agents were no longer primarily saboteurs; increasingly they became liaison officers with resistance groups operating in the field.

The first of these "1944" Canadians – and the first other than Duchalard and Chartrand to survive their service with S.O.E. – was Roger Marc Caza of Ottawa, who had joined the Royal Canadian Corps of Signals a few days before Canada declared war. Following graduation from the University of Ottawa in 1937, Caza had been a reporter for Ottawa's Le Droit until enlistment in August 1939; by the end of the same year he was a signalman in southern England. When Caza completed his S.O.E. training in January 1944 and was commissioned, he was fortunate to be assigned to "Pimento," one of the more extensive but also one of the more secure circuits which stretched from Lyon to Toulouse. "Pimento" was under the direction of a highly skilful agent, Tony Brooks, an Englishman only twenty-one years old and six years younger than Caza. Brooks, born in Switzerland, had earlier in the war helped several British soldiers escape through Marseille. He had thereby come to the attention of S.O.E. As a result of his experience as an S.O.E. agent in 1942, Brooks ran a taut ship in 1944, maintaining strict security which was never compromised (he survived several near arrests). Probably Caza owed his own survival to Brooks' admirable sense of security and to his own practice of moving constantly. Although such activity increased the risk of being arrested with his wireless suitcase in hand in sudden and random security checks at rail stations or road-blocks, it greatly reduced the possibilities of being pinpointed by German wireless detection, as had befallen both Beekman and Beauregard.

Despite what was later described as his poor French, Caza was supplied with false identification papers as "Roger Marcel Pilon," a businessman from Limoges whose work took him across France. So disguised, Caza parachuted near Toulouse on 4 February 1944 (three days before Beauregard landed near Tours). From Toulouse, he began at once transmitting to London, arranging for supply drops and reporting the successes of local sabotage teams in blowing up railyards and tracks. So effective did Caza prove to be – he was one of the better wireless operators in S.O.E. – that Brooks entrusted him with the leadership of his circuit while in England for three weeks of consultation (in total, Brooks spent almost three years with S.O.E. in France). When the Allies landed in Normandy, disguised messages on the B.B.C. ordered Brooks' circuit, along with all other circuits, to redouble efforts to disrupt German communications. This was a speciality of "Pimento," which had been formed largely to support the railway workers in the south of France who constantly cut the lines between Toulouse and Montauban and between Lyon and Marseille.

For both Brooks and Caza, the summer of 1944 was one of sabotage and harassment of the retreating enemy. In Toulouse, Caza was involved in part of a massive effort to delay the move of a crack S.S. armoured division northward to Normandy. Eventually, on 25 and 26 September 1944, Brooks led units which he had earlier trained and equipped at Lyon in bitter street fighting in the suburb of Villeurbanne, helping to liberate the city before the arrival of the U.S. Fourth Army. With France passing rapidly into Allied hands, Caza returned safely to Britain in late September 1944.

Allyre Louis Joseph Sirois of Vonda, near Saskatoon, one of two Saskatchewanians in S.O.E., was sent into southern France a month after Caza. Along with Sabourin the youngest amongst the Canadian volunteers, Sirois was a diffident, self-effacing radio student in Toronto before he joined the Royal Canadian Corps of Signals there in December 1941 at the age of nineteen. His less-than-perfect French was readily overlooked (as in the case of Caza) in "F" Section's eagerness to find capable wireless operators during the autumn and winter of 1943. As Buckmaster later recalled, S.O.E. relaxed its language requirements for France during 1943 – 44. "We modified these strict requirements in certain cases where an officer could be sent to a maquis group in which he was unlikely to come into contact with German or, worse, French officials."[6] Sirois himself acknowledged his less than complete fluency:

> Although I had spoken French since I was a child (it was my mother tongue), I fully recognized the fact that I was born and raised in

Saskatchewan, not even in Quebec, so my French was certainly not up to the standard of a French native. But I talked as little as possible and worked at perfecting myself as much as I could. Some people in France confided that I could pass for a native of Lorraine; since I worked in southwestern France, in the Charente, this served me in good stead at times. But other more worldwise and well-travelled French people were not so easily fooled. They had me spotted immediately as a [North] American . . . and they worked that much harder to keep me under cover.[7]

The young, blond, and very boyish Sirois had first been interviewed for S.O.E. near Cobham, Surrey, in May 1943. Buckmaster and Georges Bégué, the S.O.E. staff officer in charge of communications, briefly questioned him and several other Canadian signalmen. Nothing happened for the next two and a half months. Finally, in August, Sirois learned from the War Office that he had been interviewed as a potential clandestine radio operator in occupied France. For such work Sirois was already partly qualified by his army training. The standard instruction in sabotage and other commando-type warfare in Scotland and parachute training at Ringway preceded final specialized wireless training at the S.O.E. station at Thame in Oxfordshire. On 2 March 1944, after one abortive flight the night before, Sirois and Roger Landes, a skilled and experienced Anglo-French agent, dropped from a hatch of a Halifax bomber near Auch, in southwest France. Almost a year had passed since Sirois had first been interviewed by Buckmaster. D-day was only three months away.

Both Landes and Sirois were sheltered briefly in the minute village of Marsan before Sirois caught a train to nearby Toulouse. While Landes went to Bordeaux where he had already served, Sirois' orders were to join Charles Rechenmann, a former French police officer who would be returning to France by sea in three weeks to establish a new circuit based on the picturesque walled city of Angoulême.

We took [off] at 8.22 p.m. exactly, rolled ourselves in our blankets and tried to sleep, but the cold made sleep impossible.

Around 11.30 p.m., the despatcher warned us to get ready. His face was pale as he attached our static lines. He seemed just as nervous as we were. He asked which of us wished to jump first. I said I would.... The green light appeared; I dropped into the void. The wind caught me. I kept my eyes open, and saw the plane pass overhead. The parachute opened, I adjusted the lines, took the prescribed position and watched the ground.

I caught sight of the three red lamps of the reception committee. The moon threw a yellow light through the clouds, and I saw two houses below me, at some distance, but in the grip of the breeze I was drifting rapidly towards them. They neared and, instinctively, I raised my feet to avoid hitting the closer, just in time. I grazed the rooftop and drifted towards the other. An oak tree loomed up and, protecting my face with my hands, I crossed my legs and, plonck! I hit earth at the foot of the tree. I retrieved my parachute, rolled it, and then heard voices of two women. They came forward, grasped my arms for a moment; they were so overcome with emotion they could scarcely speak. They took my equipment and I left them saying that I must find my comrade and "Arthur," the man designated by London with whom I was to stay until the arrival of my organizer, Charles [Rechenmann].[8]

When Rechenmann arrived in Angoulême in late March, he immediately put the training he had received in Britain to good use. During April and early May, he and other members of the resistance seriously disrupted production at a major aero-engine factory and arsenal in the Haut Pyrenees, using in part explosives Sirois arranged for the R.A.F. to drop. In mid-May, however, Rechenmann was seized by the Gestapo in a café in Angoulême, the first stage in a journey which was to end in Buchenwald. Only gradually did it become evident that Rechenmann had been betrayed by René Bochereau, a resistance worker who had been successfully bribed by the Gestapo. Sirois, having recently made a brief bus journey with Bochereau, was known to the traitor, but he managed to elude arrest and find refuge in Cognac, about forty kilometres distant.

Had times been normal, as soon as my sector was "smoked out" I would have saved myself by going to Spain with the object of getting back to London. However, we had been strictly warned before leaving England that it was a case of do-or-die now that D-day was so near, and that we should not return until the liberation was achieved. Then, too, the Colonel [Buckmaster] had given stern injunctions that, in such a contingency, certain security precautions should be taken: (1) that we should not communicate with H.Q. for two weeks; (2) that another radio transmitter should be found immediately, and (3) that we should get to work in another sector.[9]

Pending the arrival of another experienced resistance leader, Sirois was ordered by London to remain in the area of Cognac. At the age of twenty, Sirois was now on his own in an enemy-occupied foreign country. For almost three months, from the arrest of Rechenmann until the arrival of Charles Corbin, his new chief and also a former police inspector, Sirois was hidden by the resistance in several towns and villages near Tarbes and Angoulême. While carefully avoiding any casual contact that might lead to questions about his accent, he was anything but inactive. He radioed London information about German troop movements and, beginning in early June, his transmissions resulted in a series of successful drops of arms.

With irrefutable evidence of Bochereau's duplicity, the resistance, with London's approval, executed both the traitor and his wife following D-day. Free from the threat of Bochereau, Sirois was more secure than he had been since his arrival, but arranging parachute drops brought him perilously close to capture. Following one drop,

we were within a kilometre of the village, in a farm road, talking in undertones, when the click-clack of weapons stopped us in our tracks. I whispered "Boches." It was lucky we had heard ... or they would have taken us by surprise. We plunged into a vineyard alongside the road and, taking advantage of the cover afforded by the rows of vines which ran at right angles to the road, we ran as fast as we could to the other end of the field, a distance of a hundred yards. A hedge blocked us from the road on that side of the field, but we managed to find a low spot and got through. Then we dropped to the ground to catch our breath. For a brief moment we thought we were safe; but the hope was vain. Some seconds later, we heard the voices of three Germans who came from the rows of vines, arguing. One said: "Drei, drei!" another stubbornly insisted, "Nein, zwei, zwei!"

I glanced at Sorin. He looked pale, distraught. "Our number's up," he whispered. "Not yet," I said in my turn. "We've got to take an all-out risk and run for it along the edge of that cornfield." A field of wheat, short but ripe, lay behind us.

We ran crouching, like lost souls, the two hundred yards to the end of the field, jumped the fence, crossed the road and slunk into another vineyard. The Boches had followed us at top speed but when they came to the end of the field they could not make up their minds which direction we had taken on the road. They thought we were hiding in a coppice near the vineyard, and opened fire into it with all they had to mow us down if we were there. We lay thirty yards away, trembling in every limb. The Boches then continued along the road firing into the trees alongside as they went.

Sorin, who knew every inch of the ground, led on silently to the far side of the field where some sixty paces separated us from a wood leading to the village. We took the interval at a bound and reached the wood without incident. Once in the obscurity of the wood we stopped running; we had still a good bit of road to cover before reaching home, and the Boches would soon be patrolling the whole countryside. We reached the verge of the wood, but had still the railway to cross and we feared the Germans would be manning the barriers at the crossings. Taking advantage of the shadow cast over the tracks by an oak, and after a brief reconnaissance, we crossed quickly. The nearer houses of the village were now quite close, a matter of a hundred paces away. A fast sprint, and we were in the shade of the first house. We had crossed the railroad just in time – at 4.45 a.m. Promptly at 5 o'clock, the Germans were on it.

We made our way cautiously from house to house, for the Boches were already patrolling the main street, and succeeded in making the wood behind our house. We entered the yard by a back door, and the sight of the château surrounded by its wall gave us a feeling of security. We entered, exhausted. I let myself drop on the sofa, my trousers and shoes heavily encrusted with mud and grime. I fell asleep immediately. But Sorin on arrival had said, "Good! It's 5 o'clock. I'll change and in half-an-hour I'll go out as I usually do, quite innocently, and reconnoitre."

He returned soon afterwards, told me to go to bed, that German patrols were everywhere about, but that he would awaken me if they approached the house so that I could make my getaway. During my sleep which was short but deep, Sorin and his wife gave further proof of their loyalty by dismantling my installation and hiding it in the yard. Now the Boches could come if they liked.[10]

Sirois kept on the move, constantly changing his place of wireless transmission to avoid detection and joining in the organization of sabotage and ambushes, especially following Corbin's arrival on 10 August. By then, the Germans were increasingly hard-pressed by the Allied advance and by the growing harassment of the underground. The long-awaited moment had finally come. On 31 August Corbin, Sirois, and the local resistance joined in a successful night attack on the now-depleted German garrison in Angoulême. With the liberation of the city, the war for Sirois was over. He arranged for his radio equipment to be smuggled to Landes in the still German-occupied port of Bordeaux. He then belatedly celebrated his twenty-first birthday, before departing for Paris and London at the end of September 1944.

8

The Triumph of the Aged
and Redundant

By early 1943, it had become evident to National Defence Headquarters in Ottawa that, with a substantial portion of Canadian army volunteers qualifying for commissions and with an army largely confined to Britain–and hence suffering few casualties–there was a growing surplus of infantry officers. Some were made available to British units through the "Canloan" scheme, but the problem remained of what to do with a number of older officers. With a reduction in the requirements for officers in Canada as the Third Division and two armoured divisions and brigades joined their predecessors in Britain, the Chief of the General Staff was eager to respond positively to an inquiry from the War Office as to whether twenty-five French-speaking officers could be made available for "special duties." On 22 September 1943, he recommended to the Minister of National Defence that such volunteers be sought, "particularly as at this time we are anxious to find useful employment for the large number of officers becoming, at least temporarily, surplus under the present programme."[1]

The scheme was both a success and a failure. It was a success in that it produced three of the best Canadian agents whom S.O.E. sent into France–and later into Asia. But it was a failure in that only these three officers of a total of forty-nine candidates were found suitable or willing to go when the moment arrived for their assignment. The basic problem was inherent in the C.G.S.'s memorandum. In its haste to identify some useful activity for surplus officers, the army nominated many men who were simply unsuitable, either physically or mentally, for special duty.

An initial twenty-four "over-age" volunteers, having first been interviewed by the Canadian Intelligence Corps, were ordered to report on 28 September 1943 to the Toronto headquarters of Military District 2 on the grounds of the Canadian National Exhibition. From there, they were passed on to a small S.O.E. camp, Special Training School 103, near Whitby, Ontario. On 25 October, the C.G.S. obtained permission from his minister for an additional twenty-five volunteers, bringing the total to forty-nine who were sent to S.T.S. 103 for a fortnight of closer examination of their suitability and for brief introductory training.* All were ordered to respond to inquiries from friends that they were beginning training for "interpreter work with commando units."

Soon after S.O.E. was established, those responsible for central Europe realized that refugees in Britain, North Africa, and the Middle East would be unable to supply an adequate number of potential agents to meet S.O.E.'s burgeoning needs in central Europe, at the time thought to be the most promising field for clandestine warfare. Prewar emigrants to Canada might, S.O.E. reasoned, afford a supplementary source. Obviously, a first screening of such volunteers could best be done in Canada before incurring the trouble of sending them across the Atlantic for final evaluation and training. But where?

---

*Special Training Schools in Britain had two digit designations; those overseas a three-digit designation. For example, as we shall see, Special Training School 101 was in Singapore (prior to its surrender in February 1942); S.T. S. 102 was in Haifa, Palestine (it opened in December 1940); other S.T. S.'s were in North Africa, India, Australia, and Ceylon. Cavelcoressi and Wynt in *Total War* (p. 275) state that S.O.E. "eventually established sixty training schools for operations in Europe besides others in Asia. These schools sent 7,500 agents ... to western Europe and 4,000 ... to Italy and southeastern Europe."

Early in 1940, almost two years before the United States entered the war, M.I.6 had contacted the F.B.I. about ways in which the two agencies might co-operate to counter espionage in the United States. In May 1940, William Stephenson, a Canadian who had flown with the Royal Flying Corps during the First World War and who had been active in European industry between the wars, was appointed to head a small M.I.6 office in Rockefeller Center in New York. (At first the office operated under the time-honoured M.I.6 guise of "British Passport Control Office"; before long, when S.O.E. and other covert agencies also sent representatives to New York for liaison work in North America, the office was more appropriately renamed "British Security Co-ordination.")* Later in 1940, with the United States still neutral, M.I.6 had obtained the agreement of the Canadian government to establish a radio station, Hydra, near Whitby, to help maintain contact with its staff in British diplomatic and consular posts in neutral Latin America and to carry some of the growing transatlantic wireless traffic between London and New York and Washington. Charles Vining, a Montreal businessman and friend of Stephenson, arranged with the Canadian government for the wireless station, the recruitment of Canadian ham operators to help man it, the employment of Canadian civilian staff for the B.S.C. office in New York, and the co-operation of the R.C.M.P. in anti-subversion and other British security activities in the western hemisphere (B.S.C.'s sole area of responsibility). On assuming other wartime responsibilities, Vining recruited Tommy Drew-Brook, another first World War flier and a Toronto stockbroker, to act, from his office on King Street, as a sort of *locum tenens* in further contacts between B.S.C. in New York and various departments of the Canadian Government.

By mid-1941, S.O.E. had become convinced that Canada could be a promising field for recruitment of central and eastern

*During the spring of 1945, a limited number of copies of a history of British Security Co-ordination were typed at S.T.S. 103. The copies were apparently distributed to the heads of government of Canada, the United States, and Britain and their respective Chiefs of Staff, but I have been unable to find one in any archives.

European and Italian agents. Its representatives in New York approached the Canadian government through the Canadian embassy in Washington and, more informally, through Drew-Brook. They obtained Ottawa's agreement to establish a small screening centre and elementary clandestine warfare school around M.I.6's already heavily-guarded Hydra wireless station in isolated farmland on Lake Ontario. Special Training School 103 – or "the Farm" as it became to be known – was the result. With the approval of the Department of National Defence and the assistance of staff at the headquarters of Military District 2 in Toronto, more than two hundred acres of additional farmland along the lakeshore were purchased by the British Government for $12,000 and, at an initial cost of $28,000, a barn and farmhouse were converted and huts built to form the holding camp. A few instructors were supplied from S.O.E. schools in Britain to evaluate the volunteers and to train the classes, which were initially limited to a maximum of sixteen. The Canadian staff at S.T.S. 103 were the adjutant (a First World War veteran), two "sapper" sergeants, and a clerical and a maintenance group of twenty-six Canadians (including C.W.A.C.s), all of a "low medical category unfit for general service."[2] In other words, administration was Canadian while operations were British. Occasionally friction arose, but on the whole the small camp was a harmonious place under its British commanding officer.

S.T.S. 103 operated for a little more than two years, beginning in December 1941. During that time it served as a holding camp for the preliminary evaluation of central and eastern European volunteers for S.O.E. For those considered suitable it provided a brief introduction to clandestine warfare before they were trained in Britain, North Africa, or the Middle East. Introductory instruction was given in both Allied and enemy weapons, explosives, surveillance, and security to a motley group of students. The fledgling Office of Strategic Services, the United States' counterpart of S.O.E., sent several of its staff for short courses before it opened its own schools in Virginia and Maryland in mid-1942. Some M.I.6 staff, appointed to British missions in Latin America, and even British embassy staff in Washington, undertook brief courses as a diversion from their more humdrum duties. Men from the F.B.I. and R.C.M.P. were instructed in what enemy agents in North America – if there were any – might be expected to do. British executives and trusted employees from plants in Latin America were taught anti-sabotage measures.*

Also passing briefly through S.T.S. 103 were the older Canadian infantry officers for whom, as we have seen, no role was readily available in 1942 in either combat or even training units. In evaluating the suitability of the forty-nine volunteers for clandestine service, S.T.S. 103 identified thirty as unfit for the mental and physical strains involved. A few were channelled into the British Political Warfare Executive or later trained as civil administrators in anticipation of the eventual Allied occupation of Germany. In the view of S.O.E. in Britain, however, their staff at S.T.S. 103 had been too lenient in allowing even nineteen of the forty-nine to proceed to Britain after their initial assessment. As Felix Walter woefully noted of the first contingent of twelve who had sailed from Halifax in late October 1943, "only two were found to measure up to [S.O.E.] standards." Eight were promptly returned to Canada and two assigned to other duties in Britain. Shortly before D-day, another six, between their final briefings and jump, chose the always-available option of withdrawing. "This was not held against them, but as they were in possession of much vital information they had to be held incommunicado in a particularly remote fastness in the Scottish Highlands before being sent back to Canada for discharge."[3]

The only S.T.S. 103 candidates in the first contingent who did successfully complete training in Britain were Jean-Paul Archambault, a Montreal post office investigator, and "Ben" Benoit, an employee of the Montreal Tramway Company. Archambault, who was to serve with distinction for seven months in occupied France, had carried his experience in civilian life into the Army Postal Corps in which he served in Canada from 1939 to 1942. An

---

*Although the trainees were varied in background, their numbers were never large. If one postwar estimate of five hundred "graduates" is correct, an average of less than five students a week must have been present at S.T.S. 103 during the little more than two years of its operation. Most were not destined for actual clandestine warfare, but for overt or covert jobs in the western hemisphere, including wireless operators in Latin America.

easy-going, likeable man of thirty-six—he is remembered by several brother officers as "fatherly"—Archambault completed his S.O.E. training in southern England during the spring of 1944. After being intensively briefed on his target area, he parachuted near Lyon on 6 April 1944 to join in the D-day preparations of "Ditcher", the same circuit to which Beauregard had been dropped two months earlier. When Beauregard had been unable to set up a new sub-circuit, he had joined "Ditcher" itself as a radio operator, so for three months three Canadian officers—Beauregard, Archambault, and d'Artois (whom we shall meet shortly)—were all serving with "Ditcher."

In the hills of Ain, the systematic and steady Archambault accomplished what he was sent to do—and more. With George Hicks, an escaped British prisoner of war, he formed and trained three groups of saboteurs. The first and largest (about 250 men) was based on Bourg to disrupt the rail lines from the great industrial centre of Lyon eastward to Bourg and Amberieu, but it soon tangled with German patrols and the hated French *milice*, who collaborated with the enemy. Against veteran troops, ably led, the *maquis* were never well advised to attempt a stand. After losing a number of men to the Germans, who were intent upon preventing disruption of their rail lines, the remnants of Archambault's first group joined his second centred on Pont d'Ain where it operated along that turbulent little river, sabotaging the Bourg-Ambérieu rail line. Archambault's team cut that line forty times, put a major bridge temporarily out of use twice and derailed two troop trains, causing many casualties among the increasingly harassed Germans. Telephone lines through the narrow valleys were disrupted so frequently that they became virtually useless. The third band of saboteurs instigated by Archambault was equally successful, until it too encountered a strong German patrol which badly cut it up. Before that, however, the group, based on the village of St. Rambert, blew up the rail line in the Rambert valley thirty times, destroyed the switches at the St. Rambert and Tenay railyards, and constantly disrupted telephone and telegraph lines.

The Germans were losing their grip on occupied France and were becoming beleaguered in much of France south of Paris.

The work of Archambault and similar agents helped to ensure that those Germans being moved to reinforce the Normandy front had first to fight to get there – or at least to suffer the delays and survive the dangers of derailment and disrupted communications. They arrived late at the front, not as fresh troops ready for battle, but already jumpy and combat-weary.

The clandestine career of Archambault, the amiable postal inspector from Montreal, ended – in Europe – on October 1944, when his circuit was overrun by the Allied units advancing through eastern France. His was an impressive record of achievement, matched by few of the Canadians in S.O.E.

One of the few whose record could stand comparison with Archambault's was that of the second S.T.S. 103 "old boy." Joseph Henri Adelard Benoit parachuted into the Saone valley on the night of 23 May 1944, a fortnight before the Normandy invasion. Dropping with Benoit were two experienced resistance workers: Henri Borosh, who had earlier served as a wireless operator in S.O.E.'s principal escape line from France, and Marianne Lavigne, whose specialty was to steal for the use of the underground identity documents from the Lyon town hall where she had been employed.

Benoit, at thirty-eight, was the second oldest Canadian sent by S.O.E. into France (Bieler was two years older). Unlike the younger Canadians, he was not only married, but also had four children at home in Montreal. Benoit had, however, special qualifications in addition to his maturity, courage, fluent French, and lively, amusing disposition. Before the war, after a year of part-time study at McGill University, he had become a switchboard inspector and power-plant technician with the Montreal Tramways Company. He knew the vulnerable points in an electric power system. He also had the advantage of looking like the then-popular film actor, George Raft; he was a dark, decisive man with a poker face and remarkable skill at all card games.

As the pre-invasion expansion of S.O.E. accelerated during the autumn of 1943, Benoit completed a short course at S.T.S. 103 with Archambault. Together they embarked in late October at Halifax for England, where they did their parachute and other training courses together.

Benoit's tour of duty in France was to end in triumph, but it began in difficulty. Agents generally jumped as low as minimum safety permitted to reduce the possibility of their parachutes being seen and to avoid their being dispersed across a wide area. Benoit, Borosh, and Lavigne, however, had no choice but to jump even though the green "go" light flashed at a higher altitude than the aircraft should have been for their drop. The result was that they were so scattered in the darkness that they were unable to find either their awaiting reception committee or even each other.

Borosh's assignment was to create a new circuit in the Champagne, many kilometres northward from where they had been parachuted. He soon learned from another circuit (whose leader he had known during his earlier service) that his two companions had dropped safely: Borosh met Lavigne in Lyon and together they went to Paris, where, during the first week of June, Benoit joined them with his wireless set intact. Paris in early June 1944, however, was no place to attempt transmissions to London. The Normandy invasion had intensified German determination to eradicate the resistance, although it had also weakened its capability to do so. Lavigne finally found two safe houses, ten kilometres apart in the Champagne near Epernay. From them Benoit finally "came up on the air," several weeks after their arrival.

Operating from Reims, Benoit organized and led sabotage teams to the targets which he had so carefully studied in London. Their speciality was blowing up ammunition and gasoline dumps and hindering enemy reinforcements and supplies from reaching the Normandy front. Benoit's knowledge of electricity transmission was also called upon: using sulphuric acid he twice cut the important Reims-Berlin telephone cable, disrupting German communications.

While the Allies were gaining a foothold in Normandy, Germany introduced one of its secret weapons, the V-1 rockets, which were launched indiscriminately at London. Not so sophisticated as the later V-2's, they nevertheless caused extensive casualties and were for many Londoners an unwelcome reversion to the harrowing days of the 1940 Blitz. Benoit, having been ordered to do whatever he could to help destroy V-1's, had been carefully briefed about their probable secret launching bases. In this task Benoit was eminently successful. As a result of his reconnaissance throughout Champagne, he helped pinpoint twelve kilometres of tunnel near Rilly-de-Montagne, full of V-1's and components. Benoit later commented laconically that he "got a great satisfaction out of seeing the R.A.F. come over soon and drop bombs on the spot,"[4] destroying the tunnel and its lethal contents.

Benoit collected some of his information in an unorthodox way. "I damned the Allies one day while drinking with a German colonel. The Nazi said, 'It's good to meet a sensible Frenchman for a change. Please have dinner with me.' He paid the checks at the bar and [we] went to his house. Before dinner was over, he got high and let slip some information that proved very useful to us. I must have looked more French than a Frenchman, for German soldiers often stopped to talk to me on the streets."[5] Drinking in bars, however, was not an entirely salutary practice. Benoit's driver, a member of a *maquis*, drank heavily. One night he talked too much, was overheard and picked up by the Gestapo, forcing Benoit to flee southward to Chaumont.

Undaunted, Benoit helped to organize a *maquis* of 250 in the woods around Chaumont, arming them in part with captured enemy weapons (ammunition for the British Sten gun and the German *Schmeisser* was interchangeable). With the arrival of Allied infantry, they and other *maquis* in contact with Benoit later served briefly with the U.S. Third Army, helping to mop up pockets of Germans, before Benoit returned to London in December 1944. Awaiting him there was a bill for $21 from his landlady in Brockville, Ontario, where he had completed his officers' training course in 1942. Army paymasters, having had great difficulty tracing him through "Special Duty" channels, were much relieved when they finally reached him upon his return from his clandestine service in occupied France.

The third Canadian from S.T.S. 103 was Lionel Guy d'Artois, a handsome, lively young infantry officer whose earlier training qualified him as a likely recruit for S.O.E. While he was given some preliminary evaluation at S.T.S. 103, he was not, unlike Archambault and Benoit, one of the over-age or redundant officers sent there. He simply happened to be back in Canada when the opportunity for service with S.O.E. arose. S.T.S. 103 was readily at hand for a quick preliminary evaluation of his suitability, pending his embarkation for Britain.

D'Artois, born in Richmond, Quebec, was one of the most thoroughly trained Canadians whom S.O.E. sent into the field. Following study at the University of Montreal, he had served with the Royal 22nd Regiment in southern England from January 1940 until he returned to Canada during the spring of 1942 as an early volunteer for paratroop training. He was assigned to the unique Canadian-American Special Service Force which trained in Montana for commando raids in Norway. The Aleutian Islands, which the Japanese had meanwhile invaded, were, however, substituted as their first destination. Following brief and uneventful service in Alaska and additional training in Vermont, d'Artois was on leave in Montreal in September 1943 when he was interviewed by an R.A.F. officer to whose guarded offer of service in a secret organization d'Artois readily responded. A brief course in clandestine warfare at S.T.S. 103 during the autumn of 1943 was followed by intensive training in Scotland. Between January and April 1944, d'Artois completed a demolition course, and he was finally assigned to the "madhouse" at 32, Weymouth Street, London, where agents both going to, and coming from, occupied Europe were frequently billeted.

D'Artois had begun his S.O.E. training in England as a bachelor; he completed it married. Upon his arrival back in London from Canada in December 1943, he had chanced to meet

Sonia "Tony" Butt, an English girl educated in France and Italy when her father was working with Caltex in North Africa. Now in the W.A.A.F., Tony was a blonde, slender nineteen, the youngest female agent "F" Section sent to France. During their training together in Scotland, d'Artois and she decided to marry, hoping to be sent together on a mission. London headquarters would have none of it. If they were captured together, the Gestapo would have no compunction about torturing each in front of the other, as they had done with other captured resistance workers. D'Artois and Butt married anyway on 15 April 1944. "F" Section was not pleased, but with D-day rapidly approaching, trained agents were urgently needed, married or not–and both Butt and d'Artois had shown great promise. "Even before proceeding to the field ... d'Artois impressed his training officers as being the perfect example of a soldier of fortune. 'The armies of General Wallenstein probably contained many men like him,'" commented one of the more historically conscious training staff.

With Archambault and Sirois, d'Artois was assigned to the "Ditcher" circuit, led by an imaginative, if not very well-organized Anglo-Spanish R.A.F. officer, Albert Browne-Bartroli. In France, d'Artois was one of the few agents sent into France who was allowed to use his own surname; his false papers only changed his first name, describing him as a former French army officer. Nevertheless, like many agents, d'Artois was to change his *nom de guerre* several times in the field, obtaining new false documents each time. With d'Artois went a young U.S. naval radio operator, "Tintin" L'Italien, whose grandparents had joined in the migration from Quebec to New England during the first decades of the twentieth century. After a false start in a U.S.A.A.F. aircraft in late April, d'Artois and L'Italien jumped from an R.A.F. Halifax bomber on the night of 1 May 1944, landing amidst the vineyards and fields of the rich, rolling Burgundy countryside.*

*D'Artois and his bride were not to meet for the next six months. About three weeks after her husband (and nine days before D-day), Butt parachuted near Le Mans to a circuit ordered to create as much havoc as possible following the Normandy invasion. Neither Butt nor D'Artois knew where the other was; they were, in fact, several hundred kilometres apart.

In the moonless night, Browne-Bartroli and his reception committee found d'Artois and L'Italien only with the greatest difficulty. During the next few days a general briefing followed, and then the two agents were on their own, operating initially from a small hotel in the village of Charolles, run by a woman whose husband and son were both in the resistance. D'Artois first undertook the unenviable task of encouraging the reconciliation of the right and left wings of the local resistance and their co-operation in a more disciplined, cohesive fighting force. He also organized a small security unit which, specializing in combing out the hated *milice* and German agents in the area, arrested 115 collaborators. Thirty members of d'Artois' group were women, "who appear to have been devoted to the dashing commander whom they knew as 'Michel le Canadien',"[6] Felix Walter later noted drily. In a Toronto *Star* interview in December 1944, d'Artois described how "the Germans considered our maquis as an outlaw army and killed our wounded prisoners, so we retaliated once by lining up 52 of their men and shooting them one by one. They killed a total of 59 of my men....Their favorite method was to club them to death with their rifle butts."

Most agents were well supplied with money, either from drops or borrowed from prosperous French supporters who were promised repayment by disguised guarantees broadcast by the B.B.C. But at the urging of his security group, d'Artois held a wealthy collaborator to ransom and thereby helped to finance the needs of his battalion. On another occasion, two million francs were dropped to enable Browne-Bartroli to pay ransom to a Gestapo agent in Cluny for seven *maquis* held in a Lyon jail. Five large arms drops immediately before and following D-day enabled d'Artois to help equip two underground battalions, one of which, numbering seven hundred men, he commanded himself with the assistance of two French army captains. In an effort to hinder German reinforcements from reaching Normandy they cut rail lines which German forced-labour units immediately repaired and which they re-cut equally persistently.

From the eve of D-day, with the repeated broadcast by the B.B.C. of brief "action" messages indicating that the long-anticipated invasion was about to begin, d'Artois and the local sabotage teams blocked sixteen troop trains in the region of Paray-le-Monial. Simultaneously, other teams blew up locks on the small canal between the village of Montceau-les-Mines and Paray-le-Monial, rendering it impassable. From D-day on, no German troops or supply convoys entered the area for which d'Artois was responsible without being attacked. His work amidst the green fields and red-roofed villages of Burgundy, Buckmaster of "F" Section reported,

> was in the path of German reinforcements straggling up through the ambushes of the Resistance to the Normandy battlefront. Here his task was to delay and harass troop concentrations; sever rail, road and telephone communications; inflict short, sharp guerilla attacks, then fade unseen into the landscape. He was outstandingly successful and was awarded the D.S.O.[7]

The success of d'Artois and the *maquis* was partly the result of having their own telephone system. Using six hundred kilometres of telephone line (some stolen from German stores) and with the co-operation of local telephone staff, they hid switchboards in barns and manned them continously, a system that permitted advance warning of local German movements and the co-ordination of ambush and sabotage. For example, girls on bicycles would appear to respond to the waves and whistles of troops in truck convoys moving along the narrow, tree-lined roads, while in fact they were estimating their numbers and arms. A nearby hidden telephone would enable a quick report to the nearest *maquis*. If the odds looked promising, an ambush would be immediately mounted. S.O.E.'s recommendation for a D.S.O. for d'Artois added that "at great personal risk d'Artois investigated cases where the functioning of the line was imperfect and personally led many attacks on enemy troops with conspicuous gallantry." The impunity with which d'Artois and his team of resistance workers were able to operate their own secure telephone system was indicative of the degree to which the German hold on large areas of France was slipping.

By the autumn of 1944, d'Artois' work was completed. With the arrival of the U.S. Seventh Army and de Lattre de Tassigny's Free French Forces (which most of his *maquis* joined), he made his way southward to Avignon and Marseille. D'Artois eventually reported to "F" Section's advanced headquarters in Paris where some days later he and Tony were reunited.

The final S.T.S. 103 candidate to complete his training and to go into France was the short, aggressive Leonard Jacques Taschereau, the second of two Saskatchewan-born volunteers with S.O.E. During the week of the Normandy invasion, he parachuted with another Canadian, the more diffident Paul-Emile Thibeault of Montreal. At thirty-four, Jimmy Taschereau was the third and last of the older officers to pass successfully through training in England. His wife, a nurse, was in Montreal with their two small children.

Taschereau had been born in Humboldt, Saskatchewan, where his father, a surveyor, had worked on the Grand Trunk Railway. When Jacques was two, the Taschereau family moved to Montreal. In 1927, having long wanted to fly, Taschereau joined the R.C.A.F. as an apprentice mechanic. The Depression, however, meant a greatly reduced air force and Taschereau was among the many released. During the 1930's he, along with most young Canadians, was grateful to have any work, taking up whatever was offered. Like his father, he became a surveyor (working briefly in Jamaica) and he joined a militia unit which was subsequently amalgamated with the Régiment de la Chaudière. Eventually Taschereau realized his long-time ambition by becoming, briefly, a bush pilot for Fecteau Airlines in Quebec and Labrador. When war became imminent, Taschereau was again in Montreal, married and employed as a bookkeeper in a hospital. Along with his three brothers, he was mobilized on 2 September 1939. Unlike them, however, he did not go overseas with the Chaudières; having been employed in aircraft production, one of Montreal's newest and most rapidly expanding industries and now a reserved occupation, the army released him back to the industry.

The army had not, however, forgotten Taschereau. During the autumn of 1943, although over age and surplus for combat requirements, he was identified as a possible candidate for review at S.T.S. 103. Like d'Artois, he excelled in his introductory course and accordingly embarked on the *Louis Pasteur* in Halifax on Boxing Day 1943 for training in England and Scotland.

Taschereau's comrade-in-arms, Paul-Emile Thibeault had, by contrast, arrived in England in 1940, a private in the Fusiliers Mont-Royal (after a brief period in the Royal Canadian Naval Volunteer Reserve and five months with the army in Iceland). With a Scots-Canadian mother and more limited formal education, Thibeault's French was not as fluent as Taschereau's but it was adequate for the unorthodox world of underground warfare.

As we have noted, Canadians served both in S.O.E. and in M.I.9. One of the Canadians in M.I.9, Lucien Dumais (of whom more later), had been Thibeault's sergeant-major in the Fusiliers Mont-Royal. During the early autumn of 1943, Dumais was being trained in London for his assignment in Brittany. He had been asked to recommend any French-speaking Canadians whom he believed might make good agents. As a result, Thibeault joined Dumais in London for training as a wireless operator for M.I.9. It soon became evident, however, that he had no aptitude for that demanding profession. Eager to continue in clandestine warfare once he had learned something of it and reluctant to return to the humdrum soldiering of southern England, Thibeault readily accepted an offer to transfer to S.O.E.

Upon completing with Thibeault a brief parachute course at Ringway, their final evaluation at Beaulieu, and a brief sojourn at 32, Weymouth Street in London (where both Archambault and Benoit were also staying), Taschereau was assigned as deputy leader and Thibeault as arms instructor to the "Diplomat" circuit led by Maurice Dupont, a young ex-officer in the French army. (Dupont had earlier been in the underground with Duchalard in Gers.) Having reached England via Spain, he had been been trained by S.O.E. and parachuted back to Troyes during the autumn of 1943. Nine months later it was to a reception committee from Dupont's well-organized circuit of four hundred *maquis,* based on the historic city and major rail junction of Troyes (a frequent target for Allied bombers) that Taschereau and Thibeault were dropped. They landed a few kilometres from where Benoit had parachuted three weeks before.

On the night of June 12th, 1944, a four-engine Liberator bomber throttled back to near-stalling speed in the dark, moonless sky over the farmland....

Inside the plane, the red light blinked on. Four men, bulky in flying suits and parachute harness, hooked up to the static line. The red light winked out and a green one glowed in its place.

"Go!" Four bodies hurtled into space and black parachutes blossomed....The leader of the team was Captain Jacques Taschereau of Humboldt, Saskatchewan, a former Quebec bush pilot. Now, if questioned, he was Jacques Taschereau, farm labourer, son of Louis who had worked in the vineyards and now lay buried beside his wife in Grenoble.

The second man was Paul-Emile Thibeault. For those who asked, he hailed from the town of Castillon and he was a salesman of farm equipment. His demobilization papers from the French army and other equally false documents attested to that. Paul-Emile Thibeault, once known in Montreal as "Kid" Thibeault, a Golden Gloves boxer, had come overseas as a sergeant with Les Fusiliers Mont-Royal. He had joined S.O.E. in 1943.

The third man answered to the name of Richard Leriche, a Paris student. His real name was James Larosée, a United States naval lieutenant from Waltham, Massachusetts, whose grandparents had been French Canadians. He was the radio man for the team.

Three North Americans posing as Frenchmen. The eccentric demands of S.O.E. reversed the process for the fourth man in the team. Gustav Duclos, a thin, wiry man and the second in command, was French. His cover story made him a Canadian, René Landrau by name, from Rivière-du-Loup, educated in France.

Landrau had been briefed exhaustively on his Canadian "home town." If the enemy learned that he was actually Gustave Duclos, who had deserted the Vichy army, crossed into Spain, and finally made his way to Britain to enlist in the fight against the Germans, it would go hard for his parents in Fabas....[8]

Having been drilled at length about the characteristics of both the area and the *maquis* to which they were going, Taschereau and

Thibeault were in action almost upon landing. Three days after their arrival, Dupont's *maquis* was attacked by the Germans, bent on eradicating all those who were making yet more difficult the already-disrupted communications to the broadening Normandy front. Despite the fact that in a battle near the village of Morvillars the *maquis* killed twenty-six Germans for a loss of five, the encounter had demonstrated once again that set pieces were to be avoided by the resistance: hit-and-run was almost invariably to the advantage of the guerrillas and pitched battles to the advantage of regular forces (especially in an area so flat and densely populated as the Champagne, features not conducive to easy underground movement). Dupont accordingly split off 125 of his men, placing them under the direct command of Taschereau in the forest of Soulaines, between the villages of Révigny and Arsonval. From a small tent camp hidden in the woods, Taschereau's detachment mounted their sabotage and raids and surreptitiously drew upon surrounding farms for food. The Germans, however, soon took the offensive. They were now hurting badly, but in the summer of 1944 their extraordinary military skill and courage were still far from finished.

In moving around under the noses of the Germans, Taschereau adopted a variety of disguises, including that of a funeral director and a carpenter. One night, disguised in the dark blue uniform of an engine driver of the French National Railway and accompanied by a picked group of saboteurs, Taschereau managed to enter a roundhouse and place bombs in twenty-two locomotives. Others of his sabotage units were engaged in blowing up rail lines, soon at a rate of almost one a day (having, wherever possible, forewarned the drivers to jump off their trains at a certain point). But all did not go well for the underground. One day in Revigny, Taschereau was picked up in a sudden, random round-up of civilians who were held hostage in the town square while the Germans sought "terrorists." Taschereau had to watch helplessly as two captured *maquis* were executed. The two young men were bound and placed on the tailgate of a truck parked against a telephone pole. Each had one end of a rope around his neck; the other end was around the crosspiece of the pole. Since they continued to refuse any information, an officer gave a signal and the truck moved forward, leaving the two dangling.

The forest of Soulaines was not only a hiding place for Taschereau, Thibeault, and the *maquis*; British, American, New Zealand, Australian, and Canadian airmen shot down during raids on the Révigny viaduct (a frequent target for Allied bombers) were concentrated there before being passed along escape lines to Switzerland or Spain or across the English Channel. They lived in crude log shelters or tents (some made from black S.O.E. parachutes), fed by the produce of nearby farms purchased with funds dropped by the R.A.F. and clothed in whatever the depleted shops of the local towns or friendly farmers could provide.

With the help of the mayor of the quiet village of Juvigny, Taschereau contacted various resistance leaders in the region, especially "Commandant Montcalm," the local *maquis* chief who claimed a following of eight thousand. Taschereau got along with them all, even the suspicious communists, consistently showing tact in dealing with them. He had, of course, a certain means of persuasion: he could deliver arms and ammunition. Although he himself lived mainly in Juvigny,* his American radio operator, James Larossé, who was the sole contact with London, was hidden in the camp in the woods (Larossé's French was even less fluent than Thibeault's). The Allied airmen awaiting guides to Switzerland or Spain joined the reception committees for air drops in the rolling farmland, helping to collect the equipment, enough for fifteen hundred men. Thibeault, like Larossé, lived in the woods, supervising and training the *maquis* in the use of small arms. During the first week of August, the *milice* were reported to be closing in on the camp. It was hurriedly moved, Thibeault and an R.A.F. sergeant being the last to leave after having placed booby traps. However, the new camp in the forest of L'Arlette, near Juvigny, proved to be no more secure. On 12 August it, too,

---

*Taschereau paid an occasional visit to Paris and to Lyon, as did d'Artois. By chance, they met in a Lyon restaurant and covertly agreed that d'Artois would spend three days visiting Taschereau's unit.

was raided by *milice*. Several Canadian airmen were among the captured, but Thibeault, firing his Sten gun as he disappeared into the thick woods, succeeded in escaping. The *maquis* had their revenge when soon after the Germans attacked on a large scale. The resistance fought well, and, with the support of Allied fighter aicraft summoned by Larossé's radio, killed about three hundred Germans for a loss of fifty-one. Nevertheless, German pressure was such that some of the *maquis* had to disperse, the remainder moving on with Thibeault, Taschereau, Duclos, and Larossé deep into another wood, this time at Vernonvillers, about seven kilometres from L'Arlette.

When advance units of the U.S. Third Army reached Troyes in early September 1944, Taschereau was operating an efficient intelligence service, sending agents on bicycles to keep the U.S. vanguard informed about the disposition of the enemy and removing explosives which the Germans had placed on bridges to delay the American advance. A final ambush of the retreating Germans was planned, but it was abandoned at the urging of the mayor of Juvigny, who feared needless, last-minute reprisals on innocent civilians. Their area having been overrun by the Americans, Taschereau, Thibeault, Larossé, and Duclos, back in their uniforms which they had carried with them when they parachuted into France three months before, travelled by car to Paris to report to the advance S.O.E. headquarters there.

9

D-Day

During the weeks immediately preceding and following D-day, "F" Section poured into France every agent who had completed at least a minimum of training. Some who were sent in 1944 would not have been sent in 1942 or 1943. Standards were relaxed, especially when it could be assumed that the volunteer would likely have little contact with the local populace, his needs being looked after largely by his circuit chief and his presence masked by the more numerous *maquis*. By 1944, the story of S.O.E. had become one of both rapid expansion and increasing efficiency. Its amateur and fumbling beginnings had gradually been replaced by growing professionalism. With D-day, the moment had arrived for S.O.E. to emerge from the shadows to make its greatest effort in Europe to kill, sabotage, terrorize, and confuse the enemy. Included in this wave of agents were the last two Canadians who parachuted into France from Britain, seven who went from Algeria, and one who apparently was sent by the Political Warfare Executive.

There was no question of the ability of Pierre Charles Meunier of Montreal to pass himself off as a Frenchman. One French friend later characterized his French as "un français sans défaut, recherché même." Meunier was in a sense going home; he had been born in Paris during the First World War, where his Canadian father, a correspondent for the Montreal *Le Devoir*, had married a French girl. They sailed for Montreal when Meunier was three years old. By 1938, Meunier was completing his schooling, and, convinced that another world war was imminent, he believed that his knowledge of French might be useful to the British secret service. He volunteered in a letter to the War Office who in reply sensibly urged him to continue his education. Meunier, however, is convinced that his letter, retained on file, eventually led to his work with S.O.E. In any event, in 1939 he volunteered for an English-speaking Montreal regiment, the Canadian Grenadier Guards, partly to improve his English. Following training and staff appointments at the Brockville Officers' Training School and at Defence Headquarters in Ottawa, Meunier was sent overseas in August 1942 as a reinforcement officer for the Fusiliers Mont-Royal. Whether or not Meunier's prewar letter was the cause, guarded inquiries via C.M.H.Q. led to an interview with Buckmaster and recruitment by "F" Section. In its haste to place as many agents as possible in the field prior to D-day, S.O.E. gave Meunier accelerated training and on 11 April 1944 parachuted him as "Pierre Mornet," a Vichy police inspector, into the southwest corner of France near Lanton.

His circuit, "Actor," was led by Roger Landes, the singularly brave and resourceful agent with whom Sirois had parachuted on 2 March. Landes, an architectural student in London of Franco-Jewish origin who had joined the Royal Corps of Signals, had been a radio operator as early as 1942 in a network operating in and around Bordeaux. He had survived the betrayal of his circuit by one Maurice Grandclement, a right-wing French colonel. After himself working with Landes' circuit, Grandclement had, under duress, revealed much about it to the Gestapo during the autumn of 1943 in the conviction that by doing so, he was really helping to stem the spread of communism which he loathed. Landes had escaped this treachery by a hair's breadth, arriving back in England via Spain in January 1944. Two months later, a month before Meunier, Landes nevertheless returned to the same area where Grandclement was still collaborating with the Gestapo.* In doing so, Landes was running a great risk of detection – and so was Meunier in serving with him – but Landes was one of the most capable of "F" Section's agents.

London's faith in his ability to re-create a secure circuit based on Bordeaux was, in the event, fully repaid. Landes resurrected a few of his old circuit: "Working his own wireless set from several different places, approaching people through cutouts whenever he could, checking and counter-checking every move, [he] managed to get over two thousand armed men organized and set their tasks by D-day. When de Gaulle's [representative] reached Bordeaux in May, he found that Landes had already got the area so well in hand that there was hardly anyone outside [his] zone of influence...to recruit."[1] The fact that the Bordeaux docks which the Germans had intended to demolish were still intact was also in part the result of Landes' work.

At first, Meunier played a useful role in furthering Landes' successful efforts to recruit, organize, train, and lead a significant underground force. At Arcachon, sixty kilometres to the west of Bordeaux on the heavily guarded Biscay coast, Meunier, in the disguise of Police Inspector Mornet, instructed over three hundred *maquis*, and subsequently forty more at Mormont, in the use of the small arms and explosives dropped to them. However, as D-day approached, it became known that Meunier, a tall, handsome, and likeable young man who had already established in London something of a reputation as a Casanova, had a mistress who was passing on whatever she could glean to a friend of the traitor Grandclement. A similar incident of carelessness by Meunier soon endangered another underground unit. Landes decided that Meunier must go. "He sent a signal to...Buckmaster requesting...immediate recall....It had become necessary because several of the Resistance leaders had complained to [Landes] that the young S.O.E. officer was endangering the organization." Although no great distance from the

---

*Grandclement, his wife, and his principal assistant were secretly tried and executed by Landes' circuit at the end of July 1944.

Spanish frontier, "it took more than two weeks before Baker Street arranged for 'Edouard's' journey...and he was taken there by one of [Landes'] men."[2]

On 14 July, Meunier was safely guided across the Pyrenees and conducted to Gibraltar. He arrived back in Britain on 11 August, four months after having parachuted to his assignment in Bordeaux and a fortnight before Landes and the resistance liberated the port.

S.O.E. was not, however, finished with Meunier. He volunteered to go back to France three weeks after his return to London, presumably having had the need for greater security and prudence driven home. S.O.E., for its part, was reluctant to lose a trained agent when such heavy demands were being placed on its limited resources. On 1 September 1944, Meunier parachuted a second time, on this occasion in uniform into the Auvergne in central France. He joined John Farmer's "Freelance" circuit which had been established four months earlier to help seek out and evaluate the Auvergne resistance, put it in touch with London, instruct it in small arms and sabotage, and prepare it for D-day action.

John Farmer was an energetic, even wild, circuit chief. With him were two equally colourful agents: Nancy Wake, a young, flamboyant, and determined Australian nurse who was *chef du parachutage*, and Dennis Rake, an ex-actor radio operator. Wake had already earned a remarkable reputation during more than two years of work with an escape line in Vichy France. With the Gestapo closing in on her following the German entry into Vichy, she escaped across the Pyrenees and made her way to Britain. After gruelling S.O.E. training, Farmer and Wake had parachuted to the large, if somewhat chaotic, underground of the Auvergne. Through the force of their personalities, they soon made themselves dominant among the local resistance units. By late August 1944, London knew that it was sending Meunier to one of its more successful circuits. So did Meunier, who was told,

"You'll drop here"...and given a map of reference. [Meunier] looked it up on his Michelin map and then uttered a howl of disbelief. "But

that bearing is clearly marked as a chateau." A brief nod was the
answer. "Well, who fixed that crazy field?" demanded the irate
Canadian. They told him. "Oh," he said, "Nancy! Well that explains
everything!" [Meunier] had trained with Nancy and nothing she
would do would any longer surprise him. On the other hand,
knowing her, he accepted her judgment and prepared himself
cheerfully for his flight and the drop into France.[3]

Within the loose framework of the "Freelance" circuit, Meunier
acted as a liaison officer to de Gaulle's representative a little
farther north in the prosperous farmland of the Allier. There he
had found Free French agents and underground forces attempting unsuccessfully to enter the usually quiet market town of
Moulins. Although it was now well into September and German
units elsewhere were being pushed back relentlessly toward their
own borders, the garrison in Moulins showed no sign of departing.

On orders from London, Meunier first surveyed the local
situation in Moulins before travelling the sixty kilometres
southward along the Allier River to Vichy. There Meunier
undertook a dual task. First, he encouraged the few heads of
diplomatic missions still accredited to the now virtually defunct
puppet government of Vichy to withdraw to Paris. To the Turkish
and Spanish ministers, Meunier provided *laissez-passer*. The
Swiss minister, however, was essential for Meunier's second task.
In the hope of avoiding more killing, Meunier succeeded in
persuading the tall, distinguished Walter Stuki to accompany
him back to Moulins to attempt the negotiation of the garrison's
surrender.

Upon their cautious entry into Moulins, however, they found
that the Germans had already withdrawn, leaving the ancient
cathedral town untouched. Their humanitarian mission rendered unnecessary, Meunier returned to Vichy with Stuki, who
organized a reception to mark the arrival of John Farmer, Nancy
Wake, and their boisterous *maquis* comrades. Meunier borrowed
a jeep from arriving U.S. forces to make his way through the
disintegrating German front to Paris to report to "F" Section's
advance headquarters.

Marcel Veilleux of St. Perpetué, Quebec, the last of the Canadians sent to France by S.O.E. from Britain, was a slight, quiet young man, the oldest of eight children of a foreman at a chemical plant in Shawinigan Falls. He had left school at fifteen to help his hard-pressed father provide for their large family. At first, he had worked as a delivery boy on coal and ice trucks, but by the time he joined the Royal Canadian Ordnance Corps in Montreal in December 1942 at the age of twenty, he had become an apprentice machinist. His recruiting officer noted that Veilleux had a co-operative, friendly manner and balanced judgment. He also soon showed an aptitude for wireless work. When he disembarked in England at the end of 1943, he was a sergeant in the Signal Corps. Within seven months, he was with a circuit in the Jura Mountains near the Swiss border, one of the regions where *maquis* were especially active and persistent.

Veilleux had the good fortune to go to one of "F" Section's best and most experienced circuit chiefs, Richard Heslop,* a stocky Englishman in his thirties who before the war had spent several years in France and in Thailand. He had been deposited on a Riviera beach by a felucca one night in August 1942. During the next two years he had become one of S.O.E.'s most peripatetic and versatile agents: he had been in and out of a Vichy prison; had returned to England in June 1943; gone back to France in September to reconnoitre the Jura and the Savoy; returned to London in mid-October for two nights to report on the potential of the burgeoning resistance in the rustic, mountainous area along the Swiss frontier; and finally gone back to France to help organize and train *maquis* there.

Heslop was an extraordinary man. Foot, the historian of S.O.E.

*For a detailed description of Heslop's remarkable adventures, see George Millar, *Horned Pigeon* (London: Heinemann, 1946) and Heslop's own *Xavier* (London: Rupert Hart Davis, 1970) with a foreword by Colin Gubbins.

in France, pauses in his narrative to praise him in a way he does few other agents:

> Heslop had *mana*, or whatever else you call that mesmeric quality that makes men follow another man through flood, through fire; he soon assembled a formidable underground army, fit to play its part in the battles to come. Unluckily for the historian, he was a proverbial strong, silent man, who disliked putting pen to paper. When "F" section insisted ... on a final report from him, it was hardly longer than Caesar's account of his victory over Pharnaces. Most of the details of what Heslop did are now beyond recall; but [his] will be a name of power for centuries in the Alpine hamlets that knew him.[4]

An escaped British army officer, an ex-journalist, met Heslop while en route to the Spanish frontier and left a brief sketch of him:

> He was a man who called himself Xavier, and who became quite famous in all that part of France. A short, square man with a powerful though nondescript face. There were tired lines around his eyes.... His hands were big for his size, big and rounded with muscle. He wore poorish clothes.... A British officer doing a hard job, and doing it without bogus theatricals and paradings.[5]

In the summer of 1944, the *maquis* of the Jura and the Savoy, distant though they were from the fighting in Normandy, could harass the now-depleted enemy forces with some hope of sustained success. German garrisons throughout France had been reduced to reinforce the Normandy front, and frequently old men, boys, and Russian mercenaries took the place of regular units. A large *maquis*, especially in a lightly garrisoned and thinly populated area of woods and mountains, was tempted to take the offensive, but this often called forth a devastating riposte. The bloody experience of the underground in the Jura was no exception. Daylight arms drops were added to the more surreptitious night drops to the point where, between January and May 1944, Heslop's "Marksman" circuit and an adjoining circuit shared between them almost one thousand containers of arms. Some were delivered by U.S.A.A.F. Flying Fortresses on pioneering daylight drops which proved neither accurate nor satisfactory from a security point of view: they attracted widespread local and German interest, putting in peril those in the pastures and valley flatlands receiving the drops. Heslop was assigned the welcome addition of a Royal Army Medical Corps surgeon with an abbreviated field hospital before the Germans attempted to put an end to the continued strengthening of "Marksman" and its increasingly bold harassment. Early in February 1944, almost six months before the arrival of Veilleux, the Germans had attacked in force, partly using the *milice*. During the next month, almost forty-five hundred *milice* and others in the employ of the Germans had been sent against the *maquis* in the Jura. Several pitched battles – which the guerrillas would have been well advised to avoid – led to a thousand arrests and many summary executions in various towns and villages of the valleys.

The German offensive was repeated beginning in July – the day after a Hudson landed Veilleux in a small valley near the hamlet of Izernore to assist an American radio operator in dealing with "Marksman's" increasingly heavy wireless traffic with London. Veilleux was taken at once to the nearby Château Voluvres, the headquarters of Henri Romans-Petit, a First World War veteran and the resistance leader of the Ain region.

As a reinforcement, Veilleux's timing was impeccable. At dawn the next day, nine thousand German troops attacked with light artillery and air support in a three-pronged effort to eradicate the troublesome *maquis* of the Ain. The American radio operator remained with Romans-Petit, while the newly arrived Veilleux moved southward with another local resistance leader. Veilleux joined in maintaining radio contact between the two main units which ranged through the hills during the ensuing battle. The Germans encircled many of the *maquis*, who urgently needed supplies. Despite constant enemy attacks and although the security of selected dropping points changed constantly, Veilleux nevertheless succeeded in keeping London informed of where drops might be safely made to *maquis* now scattered through the valleys and mountains. A difficult night drop by nine R.A.F. aircraft and a hazardous daylight drop by thirty-six U.S. aircraft provided desperately needed arms, explosives, and medicines (the latter in part for the civilian population upon whom, in their frustration, the Germans took many reprisals). Veilleux moved on to Lyon to act as a clearing house for information about the whole battle.

After Lyon was liberated, Veilleux returned to London at the end of September, having served with distinction for two months with "Marksman." Heslop, with some understatement, later reported that Veilleux had arrived when things were "pretty sticky," but by working his set up to eighteen hours a day, he had accomplished "an especially fine feat."[6]

The last Canadian sent into occupied France from England before D-day seems also to have been the only Canadian employed by the Political Warfare Executive. The qualifications of John Hippolyte Wickey for secret service were certainly varied. Born in France but educated in Switzerland, Wickey spoke such fluent French that he was never in any danger of it betraying him. His knowledge of argot was assured by four years' in a Moroccan division of the French army and in the Foreign Legion in whose service he won the Medaille Militaire and both the French and the Belgian Croix de Guerre. Upon discharge from the Foreign Legion in 1921 as a twenty-one-year-old sergeant-major, he sailed for New Zealand where he worked for three years before emigrating to Canada where he became a school teacher in Manitoba. There, before the war, he joined the Fort Garry Horse (with which he subsequently went overseas) and qualified in 1938 as a first-class French interpreter. He also spoke passable German.

Wickey was returned to Canada from England in January 1944 to become a senior instructor at the tank gunnery school at Camp Borden. Three months later he sailed back to England, ostensibly in preparation for the Normandy invasion. Within a few days of his arrival, however, Wickey was summoned to C.M.H.Q. for interviews both there and at the War Office. Having agreed to volunteer for clandestine work in France, yet more interviews followed. After initial evaluation at Hinchfield, Wickey spent five weeks in Scotland, training with a group of Free French commandos. His hurried parachute training consisted of three practice jumps at Ringway before he was dropped in May near the village of Sées in Normandy. D-day was only weeks away.

Wickey's Swiss-French accent and his knowledge of German suggested an Alsatian background. His primary disguise was accordingly that of "Joseph Garnier," born in a small village near Strasbourg who had lived part of his life in Algeria. Now he was an insurance and real estate agent, based in Le Mans. If he found himself in a corner, Wickey had been instructed to destroy his Garnier identity papers and present his authentic Swiss documents. Claiming Swiss nationality, it was hoped, might save him from the worst that the Gestapo could do.

As Joseph Garnier, Wickey's mandate was varied. By spreading rumours about an impending Allied invasion in the Pas de Calais area, he was part of a massive and successful effort to direct German resources away from the selected beaches in Normandy. Along with the other P.W.E. officers who parachuted into France immediately before D-day, Wickey was also ordered to drop hints about possible use of poison gas by the Allies, to report to London on German troop train movements and, most important, to help pinpoint launching ramps for V-1 missiles. In carrying out his rumour-spreading role, Wickey was reinforcing a variety of other successful stratagems that the Allies were employing to deceive the Germans into believing that the invasion would come across the Channel at its narrowest point, distant from the actual landing beaches in Normandy. And in attempting to identify V-1 launching sites, Wickey was fulfilling an urgent assignment similar to that of many other agents parachuted shortly before D-day.

From Sées, near Le Mans, Wickey made his way to Argentan, shortly to be severely damaged in the invasion. During the confusion following D-day, Wickey sent information about troop movements to London which resulted in the bombing of two trains. More important, Wickey, like Benoit, pinpointed V-1 launching sites for destruction by the R.A.F. His missions for the

Political Warfare Executive now completed, Wickey made his way, disguised as a French refugee, to Allied lines. By chance, he crossed over to fellow Canadians of the Régiment de la Chaudière near Cairon on 10 June, four days after D-day and four weeks after parachuting into France.*

*As a major trained in military government, Wickey became governor of Wuppertal after the German capitulation. He remained in the Canadian army until his retirement in 1959. He lives in Lethbridge, Alberta.

10

Assignments from Algiers

The final group of seven Canadians who volunteered to serve with S.O.E. in France arrived from the south – from Algeria – rather than from Britain. Operations from Algeria offered the advantages of good airfields, better weather, and shorter flying time into southern France.

S.O.E. was not new to Algiers. Soon after the Anglo-American occupation of Algeria in November 1942, Massingham, a largely autonomous S.O.E./O.S.S. training camp, was established at Guyotville a few kilometres west of Algiers. In the commodious villas of a prewar resort, the "Club des Pins," near the beaches and the main coastal road, accelerated courses were provided, with exercises in deception in Algiers itself.*

Another Canadian, Ray Wooler, had already been at Massingham by the time the seven volunteers arrived on transfer from their units in Italy. Following almost eighteen months of pioneer work at Ringway, Wooler had become responsible for all supply and other preparations for drops from Tempsford in

---

*Unfortunately, many of Massingham's records were destroyed after the war, as were many of those of S.O.E. in Asia.

Surrey. In May 1943, Wooler was transferred to Algeria as an instructor at the joint S.O.E./O.S.S. parachute school, training British, Free French, Americans, Thais (on their way to Asia), and his fellow Canadians. From there he soon moved on to the Protville airfield near Tunis to supervise the preparation of supply drops into the Balkans and northern Italy.

During the spring of 1944, there passed through Algeria three Canadian officers and four Signals sergeants who had volunteered to serve in occupied France with inter-Allied missions being sent to help the resistance and later to assist in the establishment of civil authority in liberated areas. The four sergeants (three after having been commissioned) were parachuted to *maquis* to provide communication with London and Algiers, to encourage the resistance by their presence, and to offer advanced weapons and sabotage instruction. None had to live, as had Bieler and Chartrand, the lonely, terrifying existence of disguised agents in the rain and cold of northern France. Theirs was para-military service in the bright summer sunlight of the south.*

The first Canadian to train in Algeria was the only regular army officer among the total of twenty-eight Canadians who waged clandestine warfare in France: the twenty-two-year-old Pierre Edouard Chassé of the Royal 22nd Regiment, the "Van Doos." Chassé's father had commanded the regiment in the First World War. At seventeen, Pierre had joined the reserve army, transferring to the regular force in 1941. He was a company commander in the difficult fighting up the boot of Italy ("ce n'était pas un cadeau") when he and a fellow subaltern, Paul-Emile Labelle of Montreal, were asked by their commanding officer whether they would like to be considered for service as "liaison officers with Free French units in Italy." The offer proved, however, to be only a security cover. Robert Searle, a British

---

*These operational units which remained together and were generally composed of British, Americans, and Free French became known as "Jedburghs." They parachuted into France in uniform, especially in the south, with increasing frequency as D-day approached.

major in the S.O.E. and second in command of "F" Section at Massingham, came to Naples to interview candidates. He asked them – in perfect French – whether they wanted to volunteer for highly dangerous but unspecified work behind enemy lines. The challenge of adventure was irresistible to the two young officers, as was the opportunity to escape the mud, squalor, and death of the Italian campaign of the winter of 1943 – 44.

At Guyotville, Chassé was transformed into a Frenchman – or as close to one as his own ingenuity and that of the training staff could make him. Free French instructors drilled him constantly in French argot and mannerisms and in ways of dressing and eating. Gradually the young Pierre Chassé of Quebec became Pierre Duval of Versailles. The only remaining trace of the Canadian officer was his given name. His clothing, including a beret, carried French labels, tobacco dust in the folds of his clothing was French, and he was equipped even with a French paint set, for Chassé, who was an amateur painter in real life, went disguised as an artist. Impossible though it would have been for security reasons in Britain, the welfare of the seven Canadian S.O.E. volunteers in Algeria was followed with interest by Georges Vanier, the then Canadian minister to de Gaulle's Free French government in Algiers, who had been second-in-command to Chassé's father during the First World War. Both Vanier and Mme. Vanier visited the Canadians during their training at Guyotville, and received Chassé at their residence the night before his departure. They were even at the airfield to wish Labelle godspeed on his hazardous mission.

Chassé and Labelle's training at Guyotville was brief: they had already survived months of grinding combat in Italy, and in any case time was short before the Normandy invasion. Both were taken on brief exercises in civilian clothes in Algiers, and Chassé was instructed on three practice parachute jumps by a U.S. sergeant before being dropped from a Halifax bomber into the Ardèche one night in February 1944. With him parachuted a Free French colonel and two radio operators. With invasion preparations well advanced, de Gaulle was determined to ensure that no time was lost in establishing his writ throughout France. He anticipated liberation in many areas – in the case of the Ardèche by four months – by sending officers to assert by their presence the representation of the only legitimate French government. The Free French colonel with whom Chassé parachuted carried a letter from de Gaulle accrediting him as his representative and as a sort of military governor of the Ardèche. Chassé went as the liaison officer between Allied headquarters in Algiers and the mission. The French colonel had been ordered to report back to Algiers on German troop movements and on what help was necessary to ensure the greater effectiveness of the underground in the Ardèche and Haute Loire. This meant determining whether the tough communist Francs-Tireurs et Partisans were willing to co-operate with the pro-Allied Armée Secrète.

Beginning in the village of Le Cheylard in the centre of the Ardèche, the mission saw plenty of evidence of the animosity within the resistance, as well as internecine cruelty and brutality. A near civil war was being waged, parallel with the fight against the common enemy. The Free French colonel and Chassé had only limited success in inducing the communists and their opponents to co-operate, but their mission was more productive against the Germans. Upon the Allied landings in the south of France in August 1944, S.O.E. headquarters in Algeria ordered Chassé and his colleagues to concentrate their forces along the Rhône, to harass German troop movements. Their ambushes and sabotage became so effective that much of the German traffic on the west side of the valley was virtually halted, with five thousand casualties inflicted. An excerpt from the daily combat diary of the Forces Françaises de l'Intérieur reflects their success:

> 7 *Août* – 2 camions allemands attaqués sur la route BOULIEU-DAVEZIEUX; l'un d'eux détruit, 2 allemands tués et 1 fait prisonnier.
>
> 10 *Août* – 2 sentinelles allemandes abattues sur le front d'AN-DANCE.
>
> 11 *Août* – 2 motocyclistes allemands remontant vers Lyon sont tués à la hauteur d'ANDANCE.
>
> – Un camion arrêté près de BOGY et 6 Allemands tués au cours d'un combat qui dure depuis 20 H.45 jusqu'à la nuit.

13 Août – Une section de la Ire compagnie A.S. rencontre à, ST
ETIENNE-de-Valoux, un groupe d'Allemands dotés
d'armes automatiques; elle en tue 4.

14 Août – Combat près de PEYRAUD et à la gare de Peyraud, avec
une dizaine d'allemands tués au moins.

15 Août – Dans le même secteur, rencontre d'une patrouille en-
nemie dotée de canons de 37; une dizaine d'Allemands
mis hors de combat.

– Gros accrochage avec les Allemands qui ont passé le
Rhône à la Voulte, sur les bacs et y attaquent avec appui
d'aviation et d'artillerie.[1]

Chassé attempted to restrain the guerrillas in their enthusiasm
to begin open warfare. He had the satisfaction, before such folly
could occur, of negotiating with a German general the surrender
of more than seven thousand of his men in the town of Privas on
the night of 25 August 1944. The general had sought out Chassé
to avoid surrendering to the *maquis*, who had a widespread and
sometimes well-deserved reputation for mistreating or even
executing captured Germans. The general, in his fifties, was not
much pleased at the thought of surrendering to a twenty-one-
year-old acting lieutenant-colonel, but the alternative was even
less attractive. For a month, Chassé ensured that the German
prisoners of war were protected and fed before passing them on
to the regular Free French forces advancing up the Rhône.

In their work, Chassé and the *maquis* were assisted in the later
stages by the members of two U.S. "Operations Groups" who,
though trained in sabotage, in Chassé's opinion spoke deplorable
French. They were also joined by three R.A.F. sergeants and nine
U.S. airmen who had evaded capture upon baling out of their
damaged aircraft and had fought with the *maquis* for several
months. Chassé was able to arrange their evacuation to Algeria,
along with several British, U.S., and Polish civilians who had
been interned in the Ardèche since 1942. He completed his
service in Lyon, which he had visited several times from the
Ardèche, maintaining some contact with the local resistance
through a safe house, a bar run by an enormous Frenchwoman
who was always a mine of information about what was happening.

A fortnight after D-day, Lucien Joseph Durocher parachuted into France from Algeria. He had trained with the other three Signals sergeants and, after the squalor and dangers of Italy, had, like them, sampled the many diversions of night life in wartime Algiers. Born in Casselman, Ontario, a village a few score kilometres from Ottawa where he received his schooling, Durocher had left his electrical course at the Ottawa Technical High School at the age of nineteen to join the Royal Canadian Corps of Signals on 3 September 1939, the day Britain declared war on Germany. He was with the advance units of the First Division which arrived in Britain in early December 1939. Durocher was also with the Canadian brigade sent to Spitzbergen in August 1941, and from June 1943 to early 1944 he was a wireless operator at battalion and divisional headquarters in Sicily and Italy. From there, he was recruited by S.O.E. and, like Chassé, sent to Algeria for accelerated training.

In two respects Durocher was unique among the Canadian volunteers with S.O.E. in Europe: he was not commissioned (he parachuted into southern France as a sergeant); and he went with an O.S.S. mission. By mid-1944, many mixed teams were being sent into France: Americans, Canadians, Free French, and British. Some were commando units, others sabotage teams, and yet others military administrators. Durocher, a tall, lanky young man who spoke fluent French and who was a skilful and experienced wireless operator, was dropped with an O.S.S. mission on 24 June 1944. Details of where Durocher served are now unavailable, but the American major who headed the small team was full of praise for his "perfect radio contact with Algiers from behind enemy lines. He was required to make long trips in civilian clothes carrying his radio set with him,"[2] before his area was liberated by Free French forces.

Paul-Emile Labelle, first of the Régiment de Maisonneuve and later of the Van Doos, had volunteered with Chassé in Italy. A slight, dark young man, Labelle went into France in uniform, but he carried with him the disguise of a lavender salesman from Lyon, supposedly employed by a Marseille perfume firm (which had been contacted covertly to include "Paul Bourget" on its payroll). The disguise was apt; Labelle was to parachute near the cliff-hanging village of Sault, the centre of the lavender trade. (In fact, Labelle knew little about scent; before the war he had been a salesman in Quebec for a subsidiary of the Imperial Tobacco Company).

From the hatch of a Halifax bomber, Labelle parachuted on the starry night of 18 July 1944 with three French officers all destined for various *maquis* in the Vaucluse, that sunny, hilly, arid area of Provence. Labelle carried with him the usual credentials signed by the Supreme Allied Commander in the Mediterranean, appointing him a link between Allied headquarters in Algiers and the resistance in the Vaucluse. His inter-Allied mission was somewhat more successful than Chassé's in encouraging the various rival elements to co-operate, but the frustrations were nevertheless manifold in attempting to create a united resistance.

Labelle became an adviser to the First World War veteran Colonel Beyne, a leader of the Vaucluse underground and former postmaster of Montelimar. From Labelle's arrival near Sault (about eighty kilometres due north of Marseille) until the liberation of the Vaucluse three months later, he was constantly in action with the *maquis*, keeping them in wireless contact with Algiers. Within three weeks of his landing, the *maquis* to which Labelle was attached had carried out a highly successful ambush of a thousand-strong column in the rocky, picturesque hills around the massif of the Ventoux, killing 250 of the enemy and forcing the survivors to withdraw. Seldom did the *maquis* enter a German-held town; continually on the move at night, they fought the classic warfare of the guerrilla. There was little need for Labelle to employ his false documents or disguise as a perfume salesman; generally he wore his Canadian army uniform. Nevertheless, on one occasion when in disguise, a traitor in the *maquis* attempted to betray Labelle by providing the Gestapo with a charcoal sketch of him. "Luckily, I had a man working right in the German commandant's office and he warned me. I shaved off my mustache and parted my hair down the centre instead of the side and moved out of that sector as fast as possible."[3] On a later occasion, Labelle had an even narrower escape.

> One of the most important parts of my training was to learn an alibi in case I was caught.... It's a lucky thing I learned it so well. I was picked up in a routine round-up. At Gestapo headquarters after three hours of questioning, a big officer came in and slapped my face until the blood came. I never suffered anything more humiliating in my life, but I had to take it.... I took plenty of time in answering his questions. The sweat was rolling down my back, but outwardly I remained calm. I was finally released.[4]

Beyne's Radical Socialist *maquis* with whom Labelle fought under the hot Mediterranean sun, and for whom he provided almost daily wireless contact with Algiers, was disciplined, honest, and intensely patriotic (the local communist units, he later recalled, seemed more interested in caching captured or parachuted arms for undefined purposes). Moving westward, Labelle helped to direct the almost daily sabotage of Rhône rail lines – which the Germans with almost equal speed restored. "One of our best jobs was sabotaging rails on the line from Marseilles to Lyons and turning a normal five-hour trip into a three-day journey for German trains. Three days was our standard. It was hard to keep to this standard later on because the Germans had excellent equipment for repairing and started placing guards along the right-of-way every 200 yards."[5]

It was on the right bank of the Rhône near Sault that Labelle was "overrun" by U.S. infantry, following the Allied landings on the Mediterranean coast on 15 August 1944. He then borrowed six jeeps in which he and his *maquis*, with a U.S. armoured car, probed the rate and extent of the German retreat northward. Before returning to England on 10 October, Labelle spent several weeks in the Vaucluse, assisting the Free French authorities now governing the Department, before turning northward to Paris and London.

The fourth Canadian to go from Algeria into southern France was, like the others, a veteran of the fighting in Italy. John Harold McDougal Dehler of Ottawa, a prewar clerk and militia signalman, had volunteered for active service in the Royal Canadian Corps of Signals a few days before Canada declared war on Germany. Three months later, he and Durocher, who had known each other in Ottawa before the war, disembarked in Scotland with the First Division, with which Dehler served briefly in Brittany in June 1940. Dehler and Durocher both went as radio operators with the Spitzbergen expedition of July 1941 and, as sergeants, were in the Sicily landings two years later. Unlike Durocher, however, Dehler's French was not fluent. The fact that S.O.E. was ready to send him as a wireless operator into occupied France was indicative both of the shortage of operators and of the degree to which, by August 1944, the conflict in southern France had evolved from clandestine to more open warfare. Little of the special instruction in evasion, disguise, silent killing, or the other cloak-and-dagger techniques taught in various S.O.E. schools in Britain were provided Dehler during his two months at Guyotville: his brief training centred on sabotage, small arms, and clandestine wireless transmission.

On 7 August, the day after he was commissioned, Dehler was dropped near the town of Mirepoix, between the fortress city of Carcassone and the frontier with Spain. More than four years after his brief excursion into Brittany, Dehler was back in France, this time with a five-member inter-Allied mission to help co-ordinate the various resistance forces in the Departement of Ariège. Within forty-eight hours of their night landing, Dehler's messages began to be received in Algiers, opening the way for drops of arms and ammunition in such quantities that the local resistance was able to take the offensive against German garrisons, killing or capturing two thousand.*

The next two Canadians to drop from Algeria into occupied France were Bentley Cameron Hunter and Joseph Ernest Fournier. The contrast between the two could hardly have been greater: Ben Hunter was an urbane McGill graduate from Montreal, and "Rocky" Fournier, a hard-rock miner from the village of Petit Rocher in New Brunswick.

Fournier had, from the age of seventeen, lived a hard life in New Brunswick and in northern Ontario as a truck driver and a miner at the remote Pickle Crow gold mine north of Lake Superior. Despite his short, slight stature, Fournier was a tough, resilient man, accustomed to improvising and living in the rough – good qualifications for a guerrilla. Upon enlisting in the Royal Canadian Corps of Signals in Toronto in April 1942, the recruiting officer had noted that Fournier was a "very willing, agreeable chap. Anxious to do whatever will be most useful in the army. Very sociable and an easy mixer." It was an initial impression which proved valid throughout Fournier's varied and taxing military career in both Europe and Asia. He also made a good impression upon a young English girl in the W.A.A.F.; they married between his arrival in Britain on New Year's Eve 1942 and his landing, as a wireless operator, with the first Canadian units ashore in Sicily in June 1943.

*Dehler, along with many who were commissioned for service behind enemy lines, had agreed in advance to give up his commission upon being requested to do so (generally upon completion of the assignment). Dehler was so requested following his return from France in late 1944. Rather than revert to N.C.O. status, he took his discharge from the army in early 1945. He worked for the Department of Veteran Affairs in Ottawa until his retirement in 1976.

From the First Division in Italy in early 1944, Fournier was recruited for S.O.E. training in Algeria. There he met for the first time his fellow Canadian who was to be second in command of his team. Hunter, then twenty-eight years old, had been commissioned in July 1942 in the Royal Artillery (like Duchalard and Macalister, he was in the British army), following a prewar career as a surveyor after his graduation from McGill. Where the tall, dark Hunter was trained, or where he served during the two years between July 1942 and his arrival at Massingham in May 1944, is now unclear, but on the warm summer night of 12 August 1944 he parachuted with Fournier and the seven other members of the team into the foothills of the Alps.

With a total of nine members, it was one of the larger teams sent to link the resistance with the Allied forces which landed in southern France three days later. Green, its leader, after serving a prewar prison sentence, had taught lock-forcing and safe-cracking to S.O.E. trainees in southern England. By 1944, he, like many instructors, was so eager to see action before the fighting ended that he finally persuaded headquarters to let him go on a mission. He was not disappointed in his assignment. In Hunter he had an able deputy and in Fournier a radio operator who was as adaptable and skilful as he was himself. The ultimate destination of Green's team was the Haute-Savoie, a wooded, mountainous area south of Geneva bordering on Switzerland and Italy. There the resistance, operating from the mountains, had long been involved in continuing skirmishes with the enemy. With an active and mobile German garrison, the Haute-Savoie offered little hope of a secure reception, so the mission was dropped close to the village of Seyne, nearer the Mediterranean in the Basses Alpes, "an area so free of the enemy that they could all travel together in a charabanc, carrying all their equipment with them" ("neuf paras dans un chara").[6] Their orders were to make their way somehow through the French Alps – admittedly it was summer, but there was little available road transport – and then to spread out through the Haute-Savoie to act as a link between the local, very active underground and Allied headquarters in Algiers.

Guyotville had earned itself a certain notoriety among S.O.E. volunteers; the cannisters which came from there were more frequently damaged upon landing than those from Britain. The problem arose partly from the shortage of either the traditional silk or the more recent nylon for parachutes; only heavy cotton parachutes made in Egypt were available for supply drops. They frequently tangled, did not open, or otherwise failed to deliver intact their precious loads. One result was that initial radio contact with Algiers was sometimes delayed as a consequence of damage to wireless batteries. So it was with Green's team. Transmission was difficult enough from mountain valleys far from receiving stations, but it became doubly so with a faulty set. Nevertheless, Fournier succeeded in finding new acid for his set's batteries, recharged them, and within four days of landing began transmission, thus enabling the mission to receive air drops and co-ordinate attacks on retreating German columns. On 4 September Hunter hastened the German garrison at St. Michel-en-Maurienne on its way by leading an attack on the "telegraph fort" covering the approaches to the town. "Carrying out the preliminary reconnaisance in person, Captain Hunter killed four Germans, and sited the company's mortar to such effect that enemy mortar fire was silenced with only seven rounds, and of the garrison of sixty men in strong positions, twenty-two were killed and the Germans forced to withdraw."[7]

Of the seventh and final Canadian to parachute into southern France from Algeria, little is recorded. S.O.E. archives are inconclusive about whether he even went to southern France; Canadian records confirm that he did, but do not state where. All that is clear is that Ferdinand Joseph La Pointe was, like Fournier, a New Brunswicker, born in Restigouche County. Originally an infantryman in the Carleton and York Regiment, he had served as a sergeant with the Royal Canadian Corps of Signals in Italy. Upon completion of his S.O.E. training in Algeria, he was commissioned with Dehler and Fournier on 6 August 1944. La

Pointe was dropped into southern France ten days later, presumably to serve as a radio operator with an inter-Allied mission. The last Canadian into occupied France, he was with the underground for six weeks until 28 September.*

An estimated eighteen hundred S.O.E. agents were deposited in occupied France between 1941 and September 1944. Of this total, twenty-five were Canadians. Not a large proportion – less than 2 per cent – but the ratio of Canadians to other volunteers cannot be a measurement of the individual courage required to jump in the night into an alien land held by an enemy aided by informers. Of the twenty-five Canadians, seven were captured and executed, a higher proportion than for S.O.E. in France as a whole. But this statistic too is of little real moment; ultimately what matters is the resolve of those Canadians who, coming from remarkably varied backgrounds, risked their lives in the land of their ancestors or in a land which they regarded as sharing the same transcendental values of their own homeland – the antithesis of Nazi ideology. To defeat Hitler's brutish regime and to help restore Europe to the mainstream of its traditions was to them worth all the many risks of clandestine warfare.

*La Pointe died in California in 1965.

11

Yugoslavia

During 1942, S.O.E. also began to take an interest in Canadians of European or Mediterranean background. The initial influx of refugees from central Europe had largely dried up; now Canada might prove a fertile recruiting ground.

Well before the war, Germany had dominated eastern Europe economically. With the outbreak of war, the domination became yet more direct. Yugoslavia was invaded by the Germans in April 1941, the beginning of a bitter four-year conflict. In Hungary, the kingdom was in the grip of an anti-Soviet regent who, in co-operation with Hitler, declared war on the U.S.S.R. in July 1941 and on Britain six months later. German troops passed through Hungary on their way to the Balkans, finally occupying the whole country in March 1944 and establishing a fascist government. Romania was even more under the direct control of Hitler, who gave pieces of it to Bulgaria and Hungary and, when Russia was still an ally, condoned Russian annexation of two other areas. The remnants of the helpless Romania, reduced by almost half its territory and more than half its population, Hitler occupied and ruled through a puppet government. Italy was an Axis power. It was only following Italy's capitulation to the Allies

129

in September 1943 that Italian partisans – many communist – reached such numbers that they became an annoyance to the German occupation forces. To all these enemy-held countries – Yugoslavia, Hungary, Romania, and Italy – many score of Canadians who had been born there or whose parents had been born there volunteered to return with S.O.E.

The predecessor agencies of S.O.E. had been active in all four countries before the war. In Romania, British planning had long been concentrated on the destruction of the oil fields – the largest in Europe – which were seen as a vital supply source for Germany. In the event, the various plans came to nothing. Nevertheless, the fantasies of clandestine warfare denying essential raw materials to the Germans, current when S.O.E. was formed in 1940, were reinforced by the simple fact that it was primarily in the Balkans that such opportunities were thought to exist. Later the manifold opportunities for diversion and subversion offered by organizing a Balkan front against the Germans persisted in Churchill's thinking, despite Roosevelt's insistence on an invasion of France and Stalin's determination to exclude British influence from the Balkans. S.O.E. in Cairo and Istanbul did what it could to contact possible resistance elements throughout the Balkans. The way ahead was, however, anything but clear. The question of whether to assist communists, never easy of resolution in London, gradually became acute. As Elizabeth Barker has observed, from mid-1943, as the eventual defeat of Hitler became more certain, an uneasy Foreign Office

> began to urge on military planners, and on S.O.E., the importance of taking into account Britain's post-war interests; and ... what they saw as the Soviet threat to South-East Europe. What might have been expected in such circumstances would have been a clash between the Foreign Office and the military; ... such clashes did in fact happen, but ... when the two sides felt bitterness or anger, they turned them against a third party, S.O.E., which sometimes found itself violently attacked by both simultaneously – mainly, though not solely, because, in its operations in the field, it had failed to solve the quite insoluble contradictions between foreign office policy and military policy .... Yet another source of inter-departmental friction was the mistrust felt by the permanent Secret Intelligence Service

[M.I.6] about S.O.E.'s discretion, security and judgement. This meant the S.O.E. was at times starved of information.... Personal antagonisms at the top and inter-departmental ill-feelings lower down made it still more difficult to reconcile the conflicting requirements of obtaining the more efficient possible resistance effort in South-East Europe – which meant backing communist-led resistance organizations – and securing British post-war interests – which, it was thought, meant backing exiled kings and anti-communist resistance groups.[1]

Throughout the war, but especially when Soviet intentions became more obvious, the Balkans remained for S.O.E. an uncertain and frequently treacherous theatre. British policy was ambiguous, alliances shaky, agreements fragile, and directions occasionally contradictory. It was into this maelstrom of duplicity, brutality and foreboding that the first Canadian volunteers of Balkan origin parachuted.

With the possible exception of Greece, S.O.E. was more involved in the internal politics of Yugoslavia than of any other occupied country in Europe. As early as 1938, one of the predecessor organizations of S.O.E. had begun to explore various means of blocking the Danube River as one way of disrupting the flow of Romanian oil and other Balkan raw materials to German industry. In the end, opposition within the Yugoslav government, misgivings by the British Foreign Office, and the swift German advance in Yugoslavia in April 1941, combined to ensure that the planned attempts achieved little. However, a foundation for S.O.E. operations in Yugoslavia had been laid, even if most of the contacts established were to prove valueless during the subsequent conflict between left and right in the Yugoslav resistance. During 1942 and 1943, as the true nature of Yugoslav resistance became clearer, the flow of Allied support was diverted from royalists to communists. In supplying confirmation on the spot of what the Allies had come to suspect through the decoding of intercepted enemy wireless messages, several Canadians contributed to the evolution in Allied–essentially British–thinking about the true nature of the Yugoslav resistance.

Following the German invasion of April 1941, a royalist army officer, Draza Mihailović, had been extolled widely in the west as a leading example of the national resistance leaders who, it was hoped, would soon emerge throughout occupied Europe. For a while, Mihailović's units in Montenegro and his Chetniks in Serbia were the only Yugoslav underground about whom anything was heard. Gradually, however, the existence of a determined, much more effective communist resistance was recognized, even if details remained few. The realization began to spread in British headquarters in Cairo and in London that the hitherto much vaunted Chetniks were compromising and collaborating with the enemy against their fellow Yugoslavs, Tito's communist Partisans. When intercepted German and Italian messages were deciphered, it became irrefutable that only Tito's Partisans were wholly committed to fighting the Germans and that many Chetniks had become little more than collaborators.

To complicate an already confused and bitter situation, traditional animosities flared among Serbs, Croats, Slovenes, and other Yugoslav nationalities, intensified by the disappearance of any central authority other than German. It began to be recognized in Cairo and London that a civil war was being fought within the resistance: Tito's Partisans against Mihailović's Chetniks. It was all very confusing, brutal and savage; the war in Yugoslavia was as fierce as anywhere. What gradually became clear was that Tito's National Liberation Army was tying down dozens of enemy divisions needed elsewhere: by the end of 1943, it was estimated that three hundred thousand Partisans were keeping occupied over five hundred thousand German, Bulgarian, and Hungarian soldiers and almost four hundred thousand pro-Nazi Yugoslavs.

A British officer had been with Mihailović since late September 1941. He had also contacted Tito and had been able to get an occasional wireless message through to Cairo, but a clear picture remained wanting. In February 1942, a second British officer was landed by submarine on the Dalmatian coast. He too made intermittent contact with Tito and with Mihailović, but by late April 1942, Cairo had lost radio contact with both officers (one, in fact, had disappeared, probably murdered for the funds he was carrying).

By mid-1942, the situation was substantially this: little was known about either the Chetniks or the Partisans or the fate of the two British officers sent to attempt to determine more precisely what the degree of Yugoslav resistance was and what co-operation, if any, existed between the royalist and the communist guerrillas. Something had to be done urgently to clarify the confusing situation if the maximum help possible was to be sent to those guerrillas most likely to tie down the largest number of Germans who would otherwise be available for other fronts.

Few British officers spoke Serbo-Croatian fluently or knew the country well; why risk any in testing the best way to make further contact with the Partisans? Better to hold them in reserve. Why not send volunteers of Yugoslav background who knew the country intimately, were communists and hence sympathetic to the Partisans' ideology, and yet were recruited and controlled, at least initially, by S.O.E.? They could in turn signal how more qualified agents could be sent. But where could volunteers combining these characteristics be found?

Prospective recruits were available among Yugoslav emigrants to Canada, many of whom had left their homeland during the difficult years of consolidation following the creation of Yugoslavia in the wake of the collapse of the Austro-Hungarian Empire. Others had arrived during the first years of the Depression, seeking work. By the time of their recruitment, most were older men in their thirties or forties, largely unschooled, a few barely literate. They were, on the whole, simple men who had lived simple, hard lives as miners in Ontario and Quebec, as longshoremen and lumberjacks in British Columbia, and as factory and construction workers in Winnipeg and Toronto (where one had earned local renown as a heavyweight wrestler). Most were members of the Communist Party of Canada or of left-wing unions and several had police records for what was simply described as "labour agitation." Two were already privates in the Canadian army. Others had served in either a Slav regiment or the Mackenzie-Papineau brigade in the Spanish Civil War. Their combat experience there augmented military training which many had already received in the fledgling Yugoslav army in the 1920s. They were, for S.O.E.'s purposes, a unique resource within the British Commonwealth.

When S.O.E. decided early in 1942 that Yugoslav emigrants to Canada might be a promising source of recruits for an initial contact mission to Tito's Partisans, the S.O.E. staff at the office of British Security Co-ordination in Rockefeller Center in New York City was asked to facilitate a recruiting mission to Canada. The aim was to recruit as many as one hundred volunteers, and the man chosen to do so was Colonel William Bailey, a prewar metallurgist in a British-owned mining company at Trepca in southern Serbia who spoke such fluent Serbo-Croatian that he could almost pass as a Yugoslav. He had undertaken intelligence work in Belgrade during the summer of 1940 (where he had known Mihailović) and had soon become a leading S.O.E. expert on Yugoslavia. On his trip to Canada, Bailey was accompanied by Captain William Yull Stuart, who knew both Yugoslavia and Yugoslav immigrants to Canada intimately, and was fluent in Serbo-Croat, Hungarian, and German. Born in Bosnia of a Scottish father and a Hungarian mother, Stuart had been educated in Hungary and Yugoslavia. In 1927, he had emigrated to Canada to work on farms and in the mining and forestry industries of Manitoba. He became a Canadian citizen in 1932. Given his intimate knowledge of central and eastern Europe and its languages, Stuart was a well-qualified recruit to the immigration department of the Canadian Pacific Railway in the early 1930s. His work took him to Europe frequently, culminating in appointments in Prague and Zagreb. In 1939, with the outbreak of war, he and his wife returned to London where he was asked by the Foreign Office to return to Zagreb as a vice consul.

In 1941, he joined with the few remaining British consulate staff in destroying its records upon the approach of the Italian army. As instructed by London, they then made their way to the Dalmatian coast for pick-up by Sunderland flying boats. On the coast, however, many Yugoslavs who had congregated there were so seriously compromised by their anti-German activities that all available places on the aircraft were ceded to them by the British ambassador and the staff of the embassy and consulates. As a result, the British were overrun by an Italian division advancing down the coast and spent the next six months as civilian internees in Italy. A Red Cross exchange of such internees between Italy and Britain led to Stuart's arrival in Gibraltar and his eventual assignment to British Security Co-ordination in New York City.

Bailey and Stuart arranged through contacts in the R.C.M.P. and in the departments of National Defence and External Affairs in Ottawa, and through Tommy Drew-Brook, B.S.C.'s man in Toronto, to interview a large number of Yugoslav-Canadians. Until the German invasion of the Soviet Union, the Communist Party of Canada—along with communist parties everywhere—had been opposed to the Allied war effort. Now, through R.C.M.P. contacts, it helped enthusiastically in identifying likely volunteers, drawing in part upon the knowledge of a representative of the Yugoslav communist party resident in Canada. Drew-Brook later recalled that some of the communists were not in his view really volunteers: "They were simply ordered to go by the Party."[2] Since the recruits were to be parachuted to Tito's communist Partisans in Croatia, neither the Royal Yugoslav government-in-exile in London nor its consul general in Montreal were informed of S.O.E.'s activities (although the consul general appears to have learned later of their recruitment).

All that the volunteers were told by Bailey, who travelled by train across Canada to interview them, was that their part in the anti-fascist struggle would be to return to their homeland (by unspecified means) to join in the fight against the invaders. "For the assignment, although difficult and hazardous," one of the volunteers, Stevan Serdar, later recalled, "so many of our comrades volunteered that it would have been possible, without exaggeration, to recruit an entire brigade."[3]

On a warm summer evening in August 1942, the volunteers from British Columbia congregated at the communist workers' club in Vancouver for a farewell party before boarding a train for the four-day journey to Toronto. About forty Yugoslav-Canadians from across Canada were brought together at the barracks of

Military District No. 2, where they were further screened before being driven to S.T.S. 103 near Whitby. There, for a few weeks during August and September 1942, they were evaluated while being given some elementary training in demolition, small arms, hand-to-hand combat, and other commando practices (one volunteer was so grievously injured that he had to be rejected for any further service).

Preliminary training completed, a farewell party in Toronto by the volunteers selected marked their departure to embark in St. John for Cairo. A British radio instructor working at Hydra present:

> When I had the privilege of being invited to a banquet by a big group of our Yugoslav volunteers, it proved to be an emotional affair. They were of all trades: Pacific coast fishermen, Ontario miners, woodsmen, trappers and craftsmen. Despite my language limitation in their various Slav ethnic divisions, their courtesy made me feel myself a member in good standing. Their ages ranged up to the middle forties. When the evening ended, the departing ones embraced the friends who had planned the evening. The Anglo-Saxon goodbye parties I had attended lacked the dignity of that Yugoslav send-off.[4]

The Yugoslav-Canadians, now called "civilian technicians," divided into two groups, eight sailing on the Greek freighter *Andreas* and the remainder following in the more appropriately named *Star of Alexandria*. Their route was a long one: south through the Caribbean to Brazil, across the southern Atlantic, around the Cape of Good Hope, up the east coast of Africa to Suez and from there overland to Cairo. From Trinidad the two freighters sailed unescorted since their Atlantic crossings would be well to the south of the busy northern trade lanes favoured by U-boats. Nevertheless the *Andreas* was torpedoed off Recife, Brazil, on 4 November 1942. Two of the volunteers were killed in the machine-gun fire with which the surfaced submarine raked the sinking ship. Two others were seriously wounded. They and the remaining four volunteers spent two days and three nights in lifeboats before being picked up by another freighter which deposited them in Recife. After several weeks there and in

Trinidad they re-embarked on 15 December in the *El Nil*, finally arriving in Egypt during the first week of February. A week later, the second group also arrived, having crossed the south Atlantic without incident, to bring the total of Canadians training at the S.O.E. camp at Khataiga to sixteen (with five from the United States).

Additional instruction followed: with Stuart they received parachute training at Ramat David near Haifa, Palestine, where Special Training School 102 had been established in 1940 to help train agents for the Balkans and Middle East (one Yugoslav-Canadian was so seriously injured that he could not be sent on a mission). Upon their return to Egypt, a few were given wireless instruction before they were all restricted to a large, heavily guarded villa near Cairo, pending their departure. Of the few recreation opportunities available to them, the club run by the wife of William Stuart was the most popular. She had followed her husband to Cairo upon the completion of his New York assignment. Unknown to her, he had volunteered to return to Yugoslavia. For her part, Didi Stuart helped establish a "Canada House" for the use of the growing number of Canadian airmen and other servicemen on leave in Cairo from their war in North Africa.

Meanwhile Bailey, having returned from his recruiting mission to Canada, had been parachuted to Mihailović's headquarters on Christmas Eve 1942. His assignment was to determine Mihailović's real intentions in light of growing evidence that the Chetniks were becoming increasingly less active against the Germans and Italians, and to see whether co-operation between Chetniks and Partisans might still be fostered. Following Bailey's mission, there were, beginning in April 1943, a total of nine small British missions sent to various Chetnik factions and units. The British, as postwar documents indicated, believed that it might somehow yet be possible to reconcile royalist and communist.

The policy of the British government was still the reconciliation – if possible with Russian diplomatic aid – of the two rival guerrilla parties .... Any departure from this hopeful formula must inevitably affect and disturb the political balance of power within post-war Yugoslavia. On the other hand, the military needs of the Allies were pressing, and on their fulfilment depended the issue of the war. These were increasingly at variance with the official policy of exclusive support to Mihailović. Bailey's proposal of "spheres of influence," of supporting both sides in separate defined areas, and attempting to get agreement, at this stage not on joint action but on at least a demarcation of areas of operation, was doomed to failure from the start. Any suggestion also that local non-aggression agreement could be made between Tito and Mihailović was equally fated. After two years of isolation and uncertainty as to ultimate Allied intentions, Mihailović was opposed to any compromise, and progressively – if reluctantly – driven into varying limited stages of collaboration with the Axis.[5]

With the completion of their additional training near Cairo, the Yugoslav-Canadian volunteers were ready to attempt the risky task of opening up a reliable, direct link between Tito and Cairo. As late as the spring of 1943, Cairo and London were still unclear about the strength of the Partisans, their longer-term intentions, and their willingness to co-operate in what might be a "united front" of the communist Tito and the royalist Mihailović. As a further step in attempting such an evaluation, the Yugoslav-Canadians would be dropped where it was believed that Partisans were operating in Croatia.

The first mission consisted of two Croatian-Canadian veterans of the Spanish Civil War: Peter Erdeljac, a stone mason, and Paul Pavlic, a worker in the wartime shipyards that had sprung up in Vancouver. They were accompanied by Alexandre Simic, an Anglo-Serb.* On the night of 20 April 1943, the three volunteers departed from an R.A.F. field near Derna, Libya, to be dropped blind into western Croatia thirteen kilometres north of Brinje. Unlike all but the earliest S.O.E. drops in France, no reception committee awaited them, but Erdeljac and Pavlic knew the area intimately from their childhood. The next day peasants led them to a nearby village where the Partisan headquarters for Croatia

*The variations in the spelling of the names of the Yugoslav-Canadians are many. I have followed the most anglicized, used by the Canadian army.

was temporarily housed. After checking with Tito in Montenegro by wireless, the three S.O.E. agents were allowed, from the
last days of April, to operate one of their two wireless sets to
Cairo. Thereafter, Tito and Cairo were never for long without
contact. This was a major achievement, a first step in concentrat-
ing Allied support on Tito.

Within an hour of Erdeljac, Pavlic, and Simic parachuting into
Croatia, a second group of Yugoslav-Canadians also parachuted
blind, this time to Sekovic in eastern Bosnia, from a R.A.F.
Halifax with a Canadian crew. Evidence had been accumulating
in Cairo that the Partisans were also active there, as in parts of
Croatia. If one mission failed, the other could attempt to contact
Tito. The third, fourth, and fifth Yugoslav-Canadians to parachute were Stevan Serdar, George Diclic, and Milan Druzic, all
three miners in Quebec before the war. They were followed
almost immediately by an agent whose qualifications were
primarily courage and perseverance – and no knowledge of
Yugoslavia.

S.O.E. sent many unlikely agents into occupied Europe and
Asia – and some of the most incongruous proved to be the most
successful. But few were more unlikely than Major William
Jones, a one-eyed veteran of the First World War and an incorri-
gible romantic. One British officer who met Jones in Yugoslavia
later recorded his impression of him: "A grizzled Canadian,
brave as a lion and guileless as a child. But what could that
affable middle-aged gentleman, with his well-thumbed [New]
testament, his passion for bee-keeping, and his touching enthusiasm for the Partisans, do?"[6]

There is no ready explanation of why Jones was selected to go
on a highly risky mission to Croatia. He had undoubted courage,
rare enthusiasm, and determination; but he had never before
been in Yugoslavia; he spoke no Serbo-Croatian, and he appears
to have received little detailed instruction about his assignment
or even about the country to which he was being sent. The nature

of his military duties in North Africa appears to have been such that he could be readily spared. The impression remains that Jones, as well as the Yugoslav-Canadians, was regarded as expendable. If they could help to establish contact between Tito and Cairo, they would make a valuable contribution. If, on the other hand, they were lost in the attempt, no significant reduction would have occurred in S.O.E.'s limited Yugoslav resources.

Jones was a curious figure. Born in rural Nova Scotia in 1893, he volunteered as an infantry private as soon as the First World War began. By the end of the war, he was a lieutenant, having served in all the intermediate ranks and having demonstrated such battlefield courage that he was awarded the D.C.M. and – what was most unusual – a bar. Jones was badly wounded twice.

The interwar years were not easy for Jones. He attempted successively, and always vainly, to qualify for the medical schools of the universities of Dalhousie, McGill, and Toronto so that he could become a medical missionary. The beginning of the Second World War found him in the real estate business in Toronto. Given his age and war wounds, the Canadian army rejected him on each of his repeated efforts in both Toronto and Ottawa to rejoin the army. Nothing daunted, Jones worked his way across the Atlantic as a deckhand on a Liverpool-bound munitions ship – a job not sought by many. Once in England, he renewed his efforts to enlist, this time in the British army. Upon failing again, he spent several months helping to clear rubble during the London Blitz. Finally, Alfred Critchley, a Calgarian who had been a brigadier-general in the R.A.F. at the end of the First World War and who had become an R.A.F. air commodore in the Second, arranged for Jones to be commissioned in the R.A.F.

Jones had achieved his first goal, but he was still some distance from his second: to see action against the enemy. According to a biographic note on the dust-jacket of his postwar book of reminiscences about Yugoslavia, he had hoped to become an R.A.F. fighter pilot – at forty-nine years of age, with one eye – but when his application was rejected he did manage to get himself posted first to Cyprus and later to North Africa where he helped to organize ground defences of advance airfields. This was still not enough. Shortly before his fiftieth birthday, Jones accepted an inexplicable army offer of parachute training in Palestine, where he met some of the Yugoslav-Canadians. Upon completion of the course in February 1943, he was given some commando training, including demolition instruction. Now finally informed that he was being trained for a special mission in the Balkans, he "applied for permission to wear the uniform of his old regiment—the Canadian 'Black Watch'—13th Canadian Battalion, Royal Highlanders of Canada. The authorities went one better, and affiliated him with the parent Scottish regiment, the Imperial Black Watch. So it was that on the moonlit night of 18 May 1943, the Canadian floated out of the sky with a Black Watch tam o'shanter jammed on his head."[7]

Parachuting with Jones from the Liberator on that late spring night were Anthony Hunter, a British army captain, and Ronald Jephson, an R.A.F. radio operator. They were flown from the heat of Derna on the coast of Libya to the cool and remote woodlands and pastures of Croatia. Simic and Erdeljac, who were on hand to greet Jones and his small team, immediately came under his orders as the senior Allied officer in the region (as did Pavlic who had made all the arrangements for their reception and who became Jones' principal interpreter).

In a sense, Jones' mission had become unnecessary even before it had begun: upon landing, Jones and Hunter learned from Pavlic that, two days before, he had radioed to Cairo confirmation of Tito's agreement to receive a British military mission at his headquarters near Mount Durmitor in Montenegro.

As a result, Jones never became the essential link between Tito and the British headquarters in Cairo which he might otherwise have briefly been. On 28 May, ten days after Jones' arrival, William Deakin, a perceptive young Oxford don, and William Stuart were parachuted together to Montenegro "as the official representative of the British General Headquarters in the Middle East accredited to the central command of Yugoslav Partisans."[8] They had arrived at a dangerous moment. A German offensive had encircled the Partisans, who, fighting for their lives, attemped to break out. Soon after Deakin's team reached Tito's headquarters, it was bombed by the Germans; Stuart was killed

CENTRAL EUROPE

instantly, and Deakin and Tito were wounded by the same bomb.

By June 1943, a total of twenty British personnel had been dropped to the Chetniks and thirteen to the Partisans, including eight Yugoslav-Canadians; Jones, Hunter, Jephson, Deakin and Stuart; their wireless staff and their interpreter, and a ninth Yugoslav-Canadian, Ivan Starcevic (who had been selected from those still housed near Cairo). With the arrival of Deakin's mission at Tito's headquarters on 28 May, ten days after Jones' arrival in Croatia, there was established for the first time a direct link between Tito on the one hand and Cairo and London on the other. However, five days before Deakin's arrival,

> Major Jones sent the first of a series of messages reporting on the existence of a strong Partisan organization in Croatia. One of these signals, dated 26 May, asked when British G.H.Q. Cairo would reorganize the Partisans as a Second Front. "What could be done to equip four Partisan divisions?"...
>
> These ... telegrams were disturbing in their wild and irresponsible enthusiasm, and indirectly had unfortunate consequences.
>
> The development of these "Croat" operations had gathered such speed that London was only aware of the barest details, and not even that the first ... operation had been successful.... But the British General Headquarters in Cairo were acting, through S.O.E., on the general instructions of the previous March instructing them "to infiltrate British officers to other resistance groups."
>
> But a reception of Partisan delegates in Cairo, proposed by Jones within three days of landing, and requests for material aid for four divisions, coupled with Tito's request for explosives ... went beyond any instructions or authority upon which British military command in the Middle East could act.
>
> Even appreciating the gallant eccentricity of Jones, the S.O.E. Staff in Cairo realized that the sending of explosives would be an admission of future support, which they were ordered not to send until the British mission, [Deakin and Stuart] now on the point of departure to the Partisan command in Montenegro had arrived and been able to report reliable evidence.[9]

Thereafter, Jones' messages were regarded by Cairo as secondary and only marginally useful in terms of what was happening in his part of the country rather than in Yugoslavia as a whole. Long, rambling messages about the wonderful socialist democracy being built on the ruins of the rotten Yugoslav monarchy were so repetitive and devoid of military or indeed of any significance that the hard-pressed cryptographers in Egypt simply put them aside (whether some were ever decoded remains uncertain). Allegedly, certain of his messages were addressed "For Churchill's and Roosevelt's Eyes Only." In turn, Jones passed to the Partisans messages addressed to him, despite Cairo's specific injunction that they were "for his eyes only." When S.O.E. finally learned of this unauthorized practice, its messages to Jones became decidedly fewer and terser.

What exactly Jones did in Yugoslavia is unrecorded, since he died in 1969 still under the erroneous impression that he was obliged to remain silent until 1973 about actions in which he had been involved. In any event, S.O.E. does not appear to have made any determined effort to bring him out of Yugoslavia; nor, for that matter, does it seem that he wanted out. At the end of the war, Jones wrote a short book about his impressions of the Partisans. More an uncritical polemic on their behalf than an objective narrative, it leaves no doubt about Jones' enthusiasm.

> The people with whom we were living, and all whom we had the opportunity of meeting from time to time, were the most friendly, frank, unpretentious, matter-of-fact, simple-in-taste, modest folk imaginable. Not only were they incapable of pretence, but their fine qualities of honesty and understanding made them scorn all semblance of such. Whether we met them in council, at headquarters, in detached units, in towns, villages and rural areas, in groups or individually, in office, workshop, in the fields, or in the army, we found these qualities to be characteristic of all. Their earnest application to the task in hand; their firm conviction of the righteousness of the cause for which they were fighting; their confidence and trust in their leaders; their mutual interest and concern in one another's welfare; their unity in effort and purpose; their readiness to endure hardship; their lack of self-pity in the face of hideous, brutal torture and death of loved ones; their songs that never failed to emanate from a crude, lean-to shelter, all that was left from the ruins of a former home; in all these expressions the same true, honest qualities of a virtuous people were observed.[10]

Rather unkindly although accurately enough, another S.O.E. officer later described Jones as "The uncritical admirer of the Yugoslav Partisans...who seems to have found the movement barely distinguishable, in several respects, from a religious revivalist meeting."

With no further responsibility for communication between Tito's headquarters and Cairo following the arrival of Deakin and later of Fitzroy Maclean as head of all Allied liaison with the Partisans, Jones became, in effect, a Partisan himself. Maclean noted of him, "a picturesque figure, whose personal courage was equalled only by the violence of his enthusiasms...had... somehow contrived to have himself dropped into Yugoslavia, where his powers of endurance and his spirited, though at times somewhat unorthodox behavior, astonished all who met him."[11] For a year Jones was with the Partisans, sharing their dangers and omnipresent hardships in the forests and mountains of Croatia and Slovenia. "Language was no barrier," Jones later told *Maclean's* magazine. "It was amazing how many of those fighters had worked in Pittsburg or Detroit. And there were hundreds of university students and professional men who spoke English. You could find two or three interpreters in any village or mountain station."[12] And in his memoirs he added:

> Wherever we went...we found many English-speaking peasants living there. Our interest was even more aroused when we learned that there were one or two gentlemen living in that area who had spent several years in Toronto....
>
> We had not been in Croatia very long before, as a result of moving about and meeting people, we discovered to our pleasant surprise that very many of them could speak English fluently. Thousands of citizens of that country and from all parts of Jugoslavia had lived for as long as twenty-five and thirty years in the United States and Canada. They left home when they were quite young, often leaving their wives and families behind them. They worked, usually in the mines, factories, in the woods, then returned to their homeland, hopeful of living comfortably for the rest of their lives on their small farms, aided by their hard-earned savings.[13]

Early in July, about six weeks after his arrival, Jones decided to move northward into Slovenia, that most affluent of Yugoslav republics, bordering on Italy, Austria, and Hungary. Leaving Hunter, Jephson, Erdeljac, and Pavlic* at Croatian headquarters, Jones and Simic (who accompanied him as radio operator) rode on horseback for ten days across the mountains into the rolling farmland and woods of Slovenia. They were led by ten Partisans, who between them had six horses and a mixture of Yugoslav, German, and Italian uniforms and weapons.

Three Italian divisions had garrisoned Slovenia, part of which had been incorporated by Mussolini into Italy. Jones, who arrived in Slovenia at the moment when Italy surrendered, helped to disarm the Italian divisions following discussions with their general. By early September 1943, the Partisans had gained a great arsenal of Italian weapons, vehicles, and clothing, freeing themselves from dependancy on either British or Russian supplies and support. But they now also had to face a much more formidable foe in the Germans. With the withdrawal of the Italians, Slovenia came under direct German occupation, local collaborators alone being ineffectual against the growing strength of the Partisans. Additional German divisions, which would have been more useful against the Allies who were now pushing northward from the toe of Italy, had to be diverted to Yugoslavia. The Partisans, however, were too wily to be drawn into direct confrontation with them. Ambush, hit-and-run attacks, and rail sabotage remained the rigid Partisan principle, leaving the Germans few targets during their savage two-month offensive in Slovenia during the autumn of 1943. What Jones did during the offensive is unclear, although he speaks of "having been hidden in caves and most secret hide-outs."[14] Once Jones "spent a week with a troop of Partisans trapped in a cave while German tanks rumbled back and forth...scouting for the guerrillas who'd recently attacked them. The Germans eventually gave up the hunt."[15] Jones made himself a nuisance to the Germans in Slovenia in another way. *Maclean's* magazine in December 1944, some months after Jones left Yugoslavia, described him as "particularly proud of the psychological cam-

*Pavlic was killed later in a German ambush and Hunter in the Normandy landings.

paign in which he played a prominent part. Through leaflets, posters, and even released prisoners the enemy is constantly made conscious of his position as an invader."[16] Jones was, however, also on the receiving end of poster warfare. He was apparently sufficiently troublesome that the Germans put up notices offering a substantial reward for him, dead or alive.

After almost a year with the Partisans, the R.A.F. carried Jones across the Adriatic to Bari, Italy, presumably in the early spring of 1944 since he speaks in his book of attending Partisan political rallies in January. At one such rally, Jones apparently became carried away with his never-failing enthusiasm for the Partisans and contributed S.O.E. funds for the support of a women's anti-fascist league in the name of a non-existent "Canadian Anti-Fascist Women Fighters for Freedom."

He made a considerable impression wherever he went. A New Zealand surgeon, who arrived in Slovenia some months after Jones' departure, found that

> the notorious Major Jones ... a rough Canadian type, had incurred displeasure and was at the moment writing a book in Bari at the Imperiale Hotel; probably a rather outspoken book on the political manoeuvrings of the British in Yugoslavia. I heard a year afterward that he was still trying to get his book published and still trying to get home to Canada, but unfortunately a passage at that time "could not be given." He must have been a grand chap in his own way ... and echoes of his exploits will be heard for years down the valley of the Kupa.[17]

After reporting in detail his knowledge of local operations, Jones was returned to England, where he continued his fervent advocacy of the Partisan cause. He gave a long, if cautious interview to *Maclean's*; eventually published his own glowing account of the communist resistance, *Twelve Months with Tito's Partisans*, campaigned on behalf of a Labour candidate in Edinburgh in Britain's 1945 general election, and offered unsolicited pro-Yugoslav advice to Vincent Massey, the Canadian High Commissioner in London, about the postwar disposition of Trieste. A senior officer of the mission recorded for Ottawa his impressions of Jones' visit to Canada House:

Major Jones has called on me in order to explain his views on Yugoslavia at some length, and I am passing this information on to you because I think it possible that when Major Jones returns to Canada, as he expects to shortly, he may be communicating with the Department, or at least making efforts to spread his views in Canada. I have no reason to believe that his views are not sincerely held, although he is perhaps somewhat ingenuous, and his close association in the field with the Yugoslav Partisans has made him an unquestioning devotee of Marshal Tito. I should doubt if Major Jones is a Communist. Politically he is not very widely informed, and undoubtedly accepts the Partisan view of events categorically. Nevertheless, his picture of a devoted body of men enduring great hardships for an ideal in which they believe is one to which due consideration must be given. One interesting aspect of his viewpoint is his firm belief that the Western Allies deliberately failed the Partisans at almost every point. In this view he undoubtedly reflects, and helps to explain, the suspicion of the West which is so large an element in the policy of the present authorities in Belgrade.

If Major Jones should appear in Ottawa for an interview with a member of the Department, I should suggest that he be allotted a specific period of time, as he is inclined to take the floor and deliver a sermon which it is impossible to interrupt, and which might well continue for hours.[18]

On the margin of the despatch, Norman Robertson, the Under Secretary of State for External Affairs in Ottawa, noted "Dedijer [whom Jones had known in the woods of Croatia] of the Yugoslav delegation [to the United Nations Conference] in San Francisco, spoke with real affection and respect for Jones, who he seemed to feel had been demoted by the military for his unorthodox support of the Partisans' effort." In 1954 Dedijer, by then a leading member of the Yugoslav Communist Party, wrote, "Jones made an excellent impression from the very beginning, because of his sincerity and courage. The Partisans liked him because he was very brave, never wanting to bend down or to take cover in battle. He always stood erect, wearing his beret defiantly. Major Jones was remembered among the Partisans to the end of the war as the most popular Allied officer in Yugoslavia." Certainly Tito's postwar government highly valued Jones' willingness to share the wartime dangers and hardships and appreciated his postwar support. In London in September 1945 and on several occasions during the following decades, both in Ottawa and Belgrade, Jones was repeatedly decorated or otherwise honoured before his death at "Belgrade," his farm in Wellandport, Ontario, in 1969.

While Jones' odyssey amongst the Slovenes ran its uncertain course, Yugoslav-Canadians fought with Partisans in all principal regions. Serdar, Diclic, and Druzic had parachuted together on 21 April 1943 to the Partisan headquarters in eastern Bosnia. Serdar, a prewar miner in Quebec, was a much-wounded and decorated veteran of the Spanish Civil War, as was Diclic. A British officer met them in eastern Bosnia late in 1943.

> Two Serbs, born in the Lika and emigrated to Canada early in their lives ... had dropped in "blind" in a gallant effort to find touch with the partisans the April before. They had saved their wireless set in spite of hideous difficulties and had been lucky enough to find their way out of the forest tangle they were dropped into, after some anxious days of uncertainty, to the headquarters of one the Voivodina brigades ... and since then they had been moving round in Eastern Bosnia.
>
> Now they were a little thinner, tougher, more decided; their battle-dress hung in rags about them, only their eyes shone. They were bubbling with things to say:
>
> "Gee, what a time we've had. Why, you should have seen us ..." they said, laughing. Their great delight was to pull each other's legs. They were quite different from each other in everything except physical strength; both, having been miners, were hard and bent and muscle-bound and immensely strong. They thought slowly; and such was their good humour that whenever they could manage to produce a thought it came up like a bubble that sailed into the air and burst in their laughter. Both were radical; both had fought in Spain and were enormously proud of it; both were well aware of what they had come to do. For them there were no degrees between black and white, and accordingly they were accustomed to voice strong and immediate views on what was good and what was bad. But while George was an individualist who, in spite of all his years of trying, could never see anything but from the angle of what George Diklitch ought to do about it — and he was supremely

confident of being able to cope with any situation – Steve was more cautious, and liked to be strictly level with the party line, and for this reason he was better in co-operation with others. They made a good combination.

"George, he says he's afraid to lie down night-time for fear the lice'll walk away with him," said Steve, laughing so loud that nothing more he said could be understood.

"Well," George asked, "I'm going to get a bath and then I'm going to get some new clothes. Steve here, he's got a way with the girls, you know, they wash his clothes..." and George, too trailed off in billows of laughter....

George told a long story that had no beginning and no end about a bridge he had blown up on the Krivaja River during the spring; and Steve helped out with details of their travels since then.[19]

Yugoslav-Canadians continued to join the Partisans following the arrival of the initial groups.* For example, a communist from Vancouver, Nikola Kombol, a tough, squat, forty-three-year-old lumberjack had, before leaving Yugoslavia in 1926 to emigrate to Canada, served briefly as a sergeant in Albania. Kombol, who parachuted on 3 July 1943, was welcomed as an interpreter for several British liaison missions in Bosnia and Serbia. The extreme hardship of life with the Partisans so undermined Kombol's health that in May 1944 he had to be evacuated to a military hospital in Cairo, via Bari. Kombol was a convinced communist so committed to the Partisan cause that he returned twice to Yugoslavia. Upon his recovery in September 1944 from his first mission, he parachuted a second time, on this occasion into Macedonia where he remained until January 1945. After another brief sojourn in Bari, Kombol crossed the Adriatic by R.N. motor gunboat for a third surreptitious entry into Yugoslavia where he remained until the war in Europe ended.

---

*I am unable to state precisely how many Yugoslav-Canadians fought in Yugoslavia. From British and Canadian records, it is certain that twenty went into Yugoslavia with S.O.E. and two with M.I.9. A British Cabinet document of 14 October 1943 states that serving with eight British missions with the Partisans were "twenty-eight Yugoslav O.R.'s [other ranks] recruited from Canada and the U.S.A." There is, unfortunately, no indication of exactly how many of these were from the United States (P.R.O. CAB/122/762, appendix A).

Kombol's bravery was not unique. All the Yugoslav-Canadians showed abundant courage and determination. They shared
the terrible hardships and deprivations of life with the Partisans,
one becoming so severely ill with tuberculosis that he had to be
evacuated in January 1945, and another being so badly injured in
a parachuting of supplies that he too had to be evacuated to Italy.
At least five disappeared in action: Joe Sharic, Janez Smrke,
Marko Pavicich, Mica Pavicich, and Paul Stichman. Most, however, survived, a few to resume their prewar occupations in
Canada but more to remain in Yugoslavia where the communist
government offered them employment (at least two became
minor local government officials) and an opportunity to help
create a new order in their ancestral homeland.*

The final Canadian volunteer to parachute to the Partisans was
not of Yugoslav background. Colin Scott Dafoe was a surgeon,
born in Madoc, Ontario, and a graduate of Queen's University
medical school. Following prewar study in Sweden, he and his
physician wife did postgraduate work in Britain. There, in 1940,
Dafoe joined the Royal Army Medical Corps, serving in casualty
clearing stations of the Eighth Army across North Africa. By 1943,
with the British advance into Tunisia, Dafoe knew that his days of
desert warfare were ending. An adventurous, restless man, he
had heard of irregular missions being sent into Greece, but his
offer to go there was altered by S.O.E. to Yugoslavia.

There the shortage of medical help and of supplies was
desperate. Most battle wounds were in the limbs, generally
necessitating amputation, since no alternative treatment was
available. Partisan "hospitals," at best no more than log huts,
were primitive and the patients subjected to sudden and agonizing moves if their place of hiding was approached by a German
patrol. Such patrols were brutal in their treatment of even

*Stevan Serdar, Nikola Kombol, and George Diclic were among those who
elected to remain in Yugoslavia. Serdar lives in Belgrade; Kombol and Diclic
are dead.

wounded "Slav brigands. " The Germans shot all the patients and medical staff or even burned them alive in their huts.

To this underground world of brutal retaliation, extreme deprivation, and great courage, Dafoe parachuted into Serbia from a Bari-based U.S.A.A.F. Dakota on 12 May 1944, after two false starts because of bad weather. With Dafoe into the mountains of eastern Bosnia went two British sergeant orderlies. S.O.E. Bari acted as their control and channel of supply, whenever air drops or landings on rough fields could be managed, to bring desperately needed medicines, bandages, and other chronically short supplies. Two days after their arrival, Dafoe realized fully the magnitude of the task that awaited them in the hospital huts at the Partisans' headquarters. In his diary, he noted,

> I examined the patients and was shocked to see their condition and the type of treatment.... Dirty dressings over serious wounds full of pus.... Some of the patients were very pale ... 70-100 of them ... I was amazed to find the patients in one house singing; what they had to sing about, I could not see.... I was stunned by what I saw.... The filth and the uncleanliness of the patients, the rooms and even the surrounding ground.... The smell of latrines or the lack of them.... My first impression was of a callousness towards suffering and the wounded, as if life didn't mean so much there.[20]

More than a year later, Dafoe had still not forgotten his initial shock. During a talk on the C.B.C. on 13 August 1945, Dafoe added,

> Here we saw the results of total war in gruesome detail – a sight which I still find hard to believe. In about twenty, one-room peasant houses were crowded together 350 seriously wounded Partisans. They lay on bare wooden floors, with closed windows. They were crowded together for warmth with but one blanket for every two patients. The odour of decaying flesh was almost overpowering. Many of them were sickly green in colour, having recently spent seven to ten days underground in camouflaged bunkers – in damp, continuous darkness, with little food or water.
>
> All had severe war injuries which received very little treatment due to the lack of supplies, doctors and nurses. Some of them

literally were just bags of pus. Most pitiful of all was the fact that about one-third of the patients were women and young boys; for by the beginning of 1944 nearly 25% of the Partisan army consisted of women.... The death rate at the Hospital was about six per day.[21]

After two months in the village, Dafoe established his own hospital in the woods. During the warm summer, tents made from captured Italian groundsheets provided all the shelter required. Wooden bedframes were built with springs of parachute strapping and mattresses of parachute silk stuffed with straw. A Flying Fortress crashed nearby. Soon rubber pipes, aluminum, and electrical apparatus stripped from it provided more of the needs of the sylvan hospital. Parachuted Red Cross supplies, including vitamin tablets and dried milk as well as sulpha drugs and penicillin, helped to raise the small hospital to a level of efficiency and equipment unknown in the underground. A crude airfield was cleared nearby. At night U.S.A.A.F. Dakotas evacuated the wounded to hospitals in Bari, removing almost all of Dafoe's more than seven hundred patients.

Fortunately the airlift was almost complete before a major German offensive began which discovered the remaining fifty patients, despite their being hidden underground in the woods. "Those unable to walk had their throats slit. The rest were taken prisoner and subsequently tortured. The nurses were raped and taken prisoner. Our supplies were found and looted, except for a small amount we had been able to take with us, strapped to the back of five horses."[22]

From August to November 1944, Dafoe and the Partisans were constantly on the run, travelling light, ready to move at a moment's notice, and equipped to survive indefinitely if cut off from the main force. With a rare mixture of stoicism and cheerfulness that never failed to impress Dafoe, the Partisans endured the winter of 1944, surviving several enemy offensives before taking the offensive themselves in the early spring. As large parts of Bosnia were liberated, Dafoe was on hand, tirelessly working to save the limbs of the wounded and to reduce their torment and pain. Only when the German defeat was virtually assured did Dafoe agree to be himself evacuated by air to Bari, ill and exhausted but forever impressed with the courage, perseverance, and sacrifice that he had seen during his six months with the Partisans.*

*Dr. Dafoe practised as a thoracic surgeon in Edmonton until his death in 1969. During a visit to Waterton National Park that year, he disappeared. His body was found three years later. The Alberta coroner concluded that it was impossible to determine whether the fatal accident had occurred as a result of a heart attack or whether Dr. Dafoe had tripped in the rough terrain and had fallen to his death.

12

The Balkans and Italy

The Yugoslavs who embarked during the autumn of 1942 on the initial stage of their long journey to contact Tito's Partisans were followed into Europe by a heterogeneous collection of volunteers of Hungarian, Romanian, and Bulgarian ancestry. Several more were of Italian parentage and one or two of Dutch or Danish.*

Housed briefly in the austere huts of S.T.S. 103, following the departure of the Yugoslavs, was a smaller group of Hungarian-Canadians. Although residents of Canada, several had not become Canadian citizens. Consequently, upon Britain and Hungary declaring war in December 1941, as enemy aliens they were required to report regularly to the R.C.M.P. In any event, some were communists already known to the police. They too were encouraged by the Communist Party of Canada to volunteer,

---

*The anonymous Dutchman, upon being vetted at S.T.S. 103, was sent to Britain in May 1943. The Dane was Jens Peter Carlsen, a waiter on C.P.R. trains from 1927 to 1941. He volunteered for service with the Bedfordshire Regiment (of which the King of Denmark was colonel-in-chief). From that regiment, he transferred to S.O.E. and spent several months in Denmark – where all S.O.E. agents were of Danish origin – as a sabotage instructor before being smuggled out through Sweden.

once the Soviet Union and Germany were at war. The first two Hungarian-Canadian volunteers, however, never saw S.T.S. 103; they were already in Britain by the time that S.O.E. took up their offers of service.

Steve Markos was born in 1903 in that part of Transylvania which, following the wholesale reshuffling of the borders of eastern Europe upon the collapse of the Austro-Hungarian Empire, had become part of Romania. In part to avoid compulsory service in the Romanian army, Markos emigrated to Canada in 1927. A window-washer in Winnipeg for many years, he later became employed concurrently by both the left-wing *Canadian Hungarian Worker* and by the Independent Mutual Benefit Association in Toronto.

Markos, by then a communist, joined the Royal Hamilton Light Infantry soon after Germany and the Soviet Union broke their pact of friendship and went to war. While on leave in Toronto in April 1942, a friend in the Communist Party told him that the Department of National Defence was seeking "five Hungarians to be used in the Hungarian question." Markos asked his friend to submit his name, but in a fortnight, before he had heard anything more, he had embarked for Britain. Within a month of his arrival in Britain, however, S.O.E. had interviewed him. By July 1942, he was being trained as one of the first Canadians in S.O.E. (Bieler had begun his training a few weeks before). Following a winter of instruction in clandestine warfare in Scotland and England, Markos, having been commissioned in the British army – an unusual experience for a communist "of peasant stock" from Transylvania – was briefed for one of the earliest missions into Hungary, which at that time was not occupied by the Germans. S.O.E.'s plan was to attempt to infiltrate him into Hungary via Poland. The well-organized and courageous Polish underground had indicated a willingness to assist in passing Markos across the frontier so that he could try to establish contact with whatever Hungarian anti-Nazi movement there was and to open the way for additional agents to be dropped directly into Hungary. At the last moment, however, Markos' pioneering assignment never materialized. The Poles in London had concluded that the risks for all who would be involved were unacceptably high.

S.O.E.'s Hungarian section nevertheless remained determined to place Markos in Hungary in some way. After numerous delays, in August 1943 he was flown to Cairo via Gibraltar and Algiers. There arrangements were made to parachute Markos into Yugoslavia in the expectation that Tito's Partisans could smuggle him back into the land of his birth. After a month in Cairo and two in Tunisia, Markos became "Istvan Damo," the first of the Hungarian-Canadians to embark upon his mission. His assignment remained unchanged: to help establish secure routes for additional missions to enter Hungary.

From this point, Markos' activities are largely unrecorded. That he was parachuted into Yugoslavia a few months after the first Croatian-Canadians and that he joined Basil Davidson's "Savannah" mission there is clear enough. He must have subsequently been passed successfully into Hungary since he is reported to have sent back to Davidson in Yugoslavia (presumably for onward transmission to Cairo) "valuable reports about German and Hungarian armies' movements and about factories making war materials." When Markos is next heard of in October 1944, a year after crossing into Hungary, he is in the midst of a battle between the advancing Russian army and the Germans who were supported by fascist Hungarians near the town of Szenttamáspuszta. Markos' mission being completed and apparently not wishing to be overrun by his fellow communists of the Red Army, he attempted to return to Yugoslavia to rejoin Davidson. Before he could do so, however, he was arrested by the Russians.

Given the paucity of information, it is impossible to estimate how long Markos was in Hungary or how much he accomplished. Clearly he was one of the few S.O.E. agents in Hungary who remained at large for any length of time. We shall return later to the imprisoned Markos, once we have surveyed the efforts of other less successful Hungarian-Canadian volunteers.

The second Hungarian-Canadian who joined S.O.E. in England never even reached Hungary. As in the case of Markos, the Hungarian-born Steve Mate from Thunder Bay was initially approached in Canada when he was at the Canadian Armoured Corps School at Camp Borden; but it was only on his arrival in England in October 1943 that his offer was taken up by S.O.E. Upon completion of his training, Mate was to be flown from Cornwall to Italy, via Gibraltar and Tunisia. A Warwick (which had a Canadian pilot and wireless operator) was to carry him to Brindisi where he was to join an S.O.E. team led by Peter Boughey, a senior S.O.E. staff officer. The team was to attempt to establish secure ties with the Hungarian resistance. The other passengers aboard the plane were a motley group destined for various clandestine assignments: two Polish officers on their way to join the underground Home Army; a Free French major and an O.S.S. officer initially assigned to Algeria; an S.O.E. Greek expert; a staff officer destined for Cairo; and Air Commodore the Viscount Carlow who, presumably on behalf of M.I.6, was on his way to join Tito. An unexplained explosion occurred soon after the Warwick took off, plunging the aircraft into the English Channel near Newquay, Cornwall, and killing all those aboard.

Of the remaining six Hungarian-Canadians who completed their training for service in their ancestral homeland, most came from Ontario towns or from Toronto, where they were first interviewed by Eric Curwain, a British radio instructor at Hydra who also helped Major R.F. Lethbridge of S.O.E. in New York in his recruiting activities in Canada. During mid-1942, in interviews in small cafés, shabby hotel rooms along Queen and King streets, and in a small, bare office on Bay Street, Curwain sounded out a number of potential volunteers in a preliminary, tentative way about their willingness to volunteer for a "special duty assignment directed toward Hungary." Twenty-two volunteered; some of whom were urged on by the Canadian Communist Party. But for some months after, as the spring of 1943 came to Toronto, nothing more was heard by them about their possible assignment. At least five were by then in the Canadian army. As is so often the case with military forces, months of boredom were suddenly ended by frantic activity. One day in mid-June, seven volunteers, most of whom knew each other from prewar life, were hurriedly assembled at the barracks of Military District 2. There, in accordance with a decision taken by Ottawa six months earlier, the two not already in the Canadian army were immediately enlisted. The group was told little more about their terms of service than that all pay and allowances were to be met by the British army upon arrival in Britain.

From the Canadian National Exhibition grounds, they were driven to S.T.S. 103 to begin a few weeks of evaluation and preliminary training. Physical exercise was constant and rudimentary instruction in parachuting was given with the aid of a crude ninety-foot tower. One volunteer was so severely injured that he was withdrawn and discharged from the army. Their day and night exercises included visits to Toronto railyards where they learned at first hand something of the most vulnerable points in a marshalling yard (although rail equipment in Europe was markedly different). They also ranged through the woods and farmlands as far north as Rice Lake on feigned sabotage assignments. From S.T.S. 103, with their lethal lessons fresh in their minds, the Hungarian-Canadians sailed from Halifax to Greenock in September 1943 on the *Queen Elizabeth*. In Britain, however, the instructors at various S.O.E. schools soon required them to forget some of the things that they had been taught in Canada on the grounds that such instruction was out of touch with actual conditions in occupied Europe.

Two of the volunteers, André Durovecz and Adam Magyar,

were flown via Gibraltar to Cairo where more training followed between January and the early summer of 1944. At British barracks in Cairo they were drilled in such diverse subjects as recognition of German unit insignia and likely rail sabotage targets. Newspapers from Budapest (which reached Cairo via Istanbul) helped to ensure that they were as informed as possible about the conditions which they could expect to encounter on their missions. In fact, it later became evident that British intelligence about the state of Hungary was inaccurate in several important respects.

By April 1944, all the Hungarian-Canadian volunteers had congregated in Bari from where, following the Allied capture of southern Italy in 1943, missions to central Europe, the Balkans, and northern Italy were mounted. Airfields and ports were now available for more active S.O.E. involvement in encouraging resistance throughout the Balkans. Until then, forays from North Africa had been difficult, stretching aircraft to the limits of their range. Bari, the Adriatic port of Brindisi, and the town of San Vito dei Normanni between the two, became the principal centres for both S.O.E. and O.S.S. operations into Yugoslavia. The aircraft mainly employed were Halifaxes, Liberators, C-47's, and Dakotas. In addition, R.N. motor gunboats (several officered by Canadians) ferried supplies to, and wounded from, Partisan-held islands of the Dalmatian.

Eric Curwain was fascinated by the size and scope of S.O.E.'s base activities at Bari when he arrived there in 1944.

Bari...had a facade of "modern" buildings as nondescript as the grubby town they hid. The cobbled streets were a sounding board for the country carts that crashed through the streets every weekday at sunrise.... The Germans had left the city with little apparent damage....There were so many Allied troops that one hardly noticed the civilians, and the opera house was always filled with troops–the operatic genius of Italy had already risen from the chaos of war.

Our Special Signals Unit in Bari was administered from a building next to a church and had everything a field office of that type should have: photography unit for faking documents, engraving and printing equipment, coding and decoding staff.

Attached was a radio interception and transmitting station to maintain contact with agents in Yugoslavia, northern Italy, Austria and Hungary, and with our Ops. room at headquarters in England. There was also a school for training agents in morse and in the use of mobile field transmitters....There was a store of foreign-type clothing for agents dropping into countries of which they were usually native or linguistically suited to pass as such. It contained a strange collection of gadgets and stores for the use of the parachute types, ranging from currency to whisky, cigarettes to fly buttons containing tiny compasses and beautiful maps printed on silk.[1]

The "parachute types," including the Hungarian-Canadians, benefited from the presence of the inventive Ray Wooler who had come from Algeria to take charge of parachute drops. During their weeks of waiting in San Vito dei Normanni, the Canadian volunteers helped to instruct Italian partisans who were going behind German lines in northern Italy. They also trained wolfhounds for parachuting behind enemy lines from where they would carry messages from partisan units to the slowly advancing Allies. Bari was, however, as close as two of the Hungarian-Canadian volunteers, Adam Herter and Adam Magyar, came to seeing action. Their mission to eastern Hungary was cancelled as the Russian army moved west across the frontier westward.*

Indeed, the prospects for success had never been hopeful for S.O.E. agents in their efforts to stimulate an active resistance to the German suzerainty over Hungary. Intermittent contact with anti-Nazi elements had been maintained since Britain and Hungary had gone to war, but more active involvement was limited by a later British agreement with the U.S.S.R. which had the effect of restricting S.O.E. activities in Hungary. However, despite the increased peril resulting from the German occupation in March 1944 and the known Soviet opposition to a British presence, three S.O.E. missions were sent into Hungary between April and June. Tito had agreed that Yugoslavia could be used as

---

*Adam Herter, a forty-three-year-old volunteer from Windsor, Ontario, had served for two years in the Canadian army before transferring to S.O.E. but, like Magyar, he was unable to employ his particular skills against the enemy. No co-operation was to be expected from the Russians; they remained deeply suspicious and hostile toward S.O.E. and all its works.

a base for such excursions, but they proved wholly unsuccessful. Two missions were captured soon after crossing the frontier and the other had to return hurriedly to Yugoslavia. However, S.O.E. was nothing daunted. The planning of additional missions proceeded, with Hungarian-Canadians included in almost all.

The first of the remaining Hungarian-Canadian volunteers to return to his country of birth was Gustav Bodo, a forty-two-year-old farmer who had lived in Canada for twenty years. On 3 June 1944, he was dropped to an S.O.E. mission attached to a Partisan unit in Croatia which had agreed to assist him across the River Drava, the wooded and flat border area with Hungary. In the nearby Hungarian city of Pécs, Bodo would contact an underground group believed to be willing to work with a larger team which would also enter Hungary with the help of Tito's Partisans. This larger team, for which Bodo was to prepare the way, was led by a British officer, John Coates. It included two other Hungarian-Canadians, Michael Turk and Joseph Gelleny. Turk, born in the Tokai wine region of Hungary, was more than twenty years older than Gelleny who, although also born in Hungary, had arrived in Canada in 1931 when he was only eight years old. The two men were dissimilar in other respects: Turk had a butcher shop in Kingsville, Ontario, while Gelleny had been a laboratory technician in Toronto, his entry into S.O.E. was unusual among the Hungarian-Canadian volunteers. He was already a private in the Canadian Army when recruited by army officials, and became a second lieutenant in the British Army after entering the S.O.E. Unlike some of the others he was a strong anti communist.

Whether Bodo, in entering Pécs, walked into a trap—Hungarian police having watched him since his night crossing of their border—or whether he was betrayed when once there is uncertain; what is clear is that one or more of those in Pécs whom he had taken for resistance workers were in fact in the pay of the German or Hungarian police. Apparently Bodo realized his jeopardy, since he managed to send several wireless messages to Bari which were innocuous in themselves but from which he omitted the agreed security checks. Bari duly noted the omissions, rightly inferring that Bodo had either been captured, had become an unwilling accomplice of a *Funkspiel,* or at the least was uncertain about those whom he had contacted. His messages in any case soon stopped. Bodo had been arrested by Hungarian police who, after interrogating him at length, handed him over to the Gestapo.

By then, however, Coates, Turk, and Gelleny had already parachuted into Croatia where they were awaiting a signal to follow Bodo's route across the Drava into Hungary. Instead, a message arrived ordering the team to return across the Adriatic to Bari where Coates, despite the misgivings about the fate of Bodo, eventually convinced the Hungarian section staff that resistance contacts could be established through industrial workers in Pécs. The team duly parachuted near Pécs in early September, a full three months after Bodo had disappeared.

Coates' team was no more successful than Bodo; it was arrested almost upon landing and taken to the Pécs prison. Gelleny was fortunate to have been in uniform when he parachuted; he was less harshly treated than Turk who, for some reason, was in civilian clothes and was accordingly treated as a spy. Turk was so badly beaten that his jaw and many teeth were broken; he was subsequently held under guard in a Budapest hospital while the more fortunate Coates and Gelleny were sent to the Zugliget prison camp in Budapest.

Soon after Bodo had been smuggled across the Drava and before the arrival of Turk and Gelleny, yet another Hungarian-Canadian parachuted into Hungary. The slight, dark-haired twenty-one-year-old Alexander Vass of St. Catharines, Ontario, had volunteered in early 1943 for service as an orderly with the Royal Canadian Army Medical Corps. But within a few months S.O.E. efforts to locate suitable volunteers for Hungary meant that Vass, fluent in both English and Hungarian, found himself with the other volunteers on the *Queen Elizabeth,* outward bound for Scotland. Vass was highly strung, but he was also alert and responsive. He had been twelve years old when his parents had taken him to Canada. Six years as a linotype operator in Toronto had taught him to be methodical and systematic. The youngest of the volunteers, he distinguished himself during his training in

England; his instructors repeatedly characterized him as one of their best students. He even excelled in his parachute instruction at Ringway.

To replace Steve Mate who had been killed in the aircrash off Cornwall, Vass was assigned as an interpreter to the "Deerhurst" mission headed by Lieutenant-Colonel Peter Boughey, the fourth S.O.E. team to be sent into Hungary since the German occupation. Boughey had served with S.O.E. almost from its inception; he would have been a prize catch for the Gestapo. His disguise for "Deerhurst" was as a sergeant in the Black Watch charged with the reception of supplies; the nominal leader of the mission was a regular army major, "Dickie" Wright. The mission was a disaster. On 3 July 1944, after one abortive attempt, an R.A.F. Halifax dropped the team near the small porcelain centre of Herend, several kilometres away from the designated point in a forest north of Lake Balaton where a reception committee awaited it in vain. Instead, Boughey, Wright, Vass (whose code name was "Vincent") and their wireless operator were arrested upon landing and their aircraft shot down with the loss of its crew. Boughey later recorded how his small team had been dropped in the wrong area in the middle of a forest, with the added disadvantage that it was divided two and two on either slope of a steep hill.

> Our parachutes were draped over the tree-tops and I for one was left hanging about 30 feet up a tree....
>
> There was no hope of concealing our whereabouts. At dawn the [Hungarian] Army assisted by the Home Guard, were soon out in force. Despite this, both Vincent and I (Vincent found himself with me on our side of the hill) managed to conceal ourselves for about 24 hours, escaping detection by only feet from the lines of troops who were combing the area. On a subsequent drag, a soldier came right upon our hideout. We were lucky that he did not shoot us in his fright! We were captured and taken down the hill to join our other companions at the Staff HQ set up in the woods.
>
> After a thorough search when we were stripped naked and a brief interrogation, we were taken by truck to Vesperem where we were told that we were going to be shot the next day! Instead, we were taken by train to secret police HQ in Budapest for a detailed

interrogation which lasted some days. We were next told that the recently installed Arrow Cross Government had agreed to hand us over to the German authorities for further interrogation by the Gestapo at the HQ in Buda. Consequently, we were soon moved to the Gestapo wing in the notorious Fu Utca prison along the river in Buda.

During August and most of September we were spasmodically interrogated by the Gestapo . . . . In October, with the approach of the Russians into the Balkans, we were suddenly transferred by train with a number of Jews to Vienna where we found ourselves in the notorious Elizabetstrasse Prison. Here we were all separated and it seemed that this time with many other nationalities and types we were really to be liquidated – a daily ritual in the prison. However, after some days, we found ourselves once more together and on our way by train we knew not where, but going West. Our destination turned out to be the Luftwaffe interrogation centre at Ober Ursel near Frankfurt-am-Main. Here our interrogation was not severe and after a few days we were on our way to the Luftwaffe distribution centre at Wetzlar . . . the Gestapo made strong representations for us to be returned to them, but the Luftwaffe opposed that as they considered us POWs and so sent us on to their distribution centre. At Wetzlar, as we were in Army uniform we were again forwarded to the Wehrmacht distribution centre near Limburg. Here, during a [R.A.F.] raid on the railway sidings, unfortunately the officers' quarters of the POW centre was hit and both Major Wright and Lt. Vincent were killed.[2]

Today Vass who, like the Canadians captured upon landing in France, never had a chance to put his skills and training to work, lies buried in Germany.

Bodo, Turk, Gelleny, and Vass had been arrested as soon as they entered Hungary. Other S.O.E. missions had been equally unsuccessful. Nevertheless, another effort was decided upon. Poland was so hazardous as to be excluded as a possible route in, and teams crossing from Yugoslavia had been apprehended. Now an effort would be made to infiltrate from Czechoslovakia.

Like the Poles, the Slovaks had risen against the Germans as the Russian armies approached Czechoslovakia's eastern frontier in September. Unfortunately, the Red Army did not cross into Slovakia until late November. By then, the uprising, which had begun in early September, had largely been crushed by the Germans. For a few brief weeks, however, Slovakia seemed to offer a more secure reception for S.O.E. agents destined for Hungary than Hungary itself. The team selected for the drop was led by an Anglo-Irish major, John Seymour; the other members were a Romanian in the British army who spoke fluent Hungarian, a British N.C.O. wireless operator, and André Durovecz, a dark, sturdy thirty-one-year-old journalist from a small left-wing Hungarian newspaper in Toronto. After two false starts from Bari, they finally parachuted on 2 September 1944 near Banska Bystrica in Slovakia, from an R.A.F. Halifax with a Canadian pilot and navigator. Durovecz recalled that

> we could each have a flask of rum...in our jump suits....I managed...a few swallows...just before I jumped. Halfway down I was stone sober. By the time I landed, I was cold as death....After several minutes more, I had found my jump-mates, one of whom, an expert map reader, informed us that we were lost. Although later evidence was to prove him correct, this intelligence was not at all well received at that moment. [3]

While Seymour and the other two team members remained hidden with Slovak insurgents in Banska Bystrica, Durovecz was to cross the frontier into Hungary and, with the assistance of Slovaks, contact the Hungarian underground for the reception of the whole team. Disguised as a peasant, but with "more money than I knew what to do with" and with poison for unduly inquisitive dogs, Durovecz was safely passed across the border. He reached Budapest by train and registered at a small hotel as a clerk in a textile factory. But at that point his luck ran out. Unable either to make satisfactory contact with the small and not very secure resistance – the initial contact whom S.O.E. had given him had, in fact, been dead nine months – or even to obtain genuine identity papers (his forged documents were inadequate), Durovecz was in a perilous position. Contrary to what he had been assured in Bari, there was no radio contact between the Budapest underground and the headquarters of the Slovak partisans. Not knowing that Seymour and the other two members had by then been betrayed to the Germans and were already dead, Durovecz decided that the only way to inform his team of the increasingly chaotic situation in Hungary was to recross the border into Czechoslovakia. On 15 October, as the Slovak uprising was being brutally put down, and on the same day that a fanatical pro-Nazi became head of the Hungarian government, Durovecz was arrested during the late afternoon while attempting to slip back across the frontier, a little less than a month after he had first entered Hungary. Some evidence suggests that he was betrayed by an underground contact in Budapest.

Persistent interrogation by Germans and by pro-Nazi Hungarians in the prison of Miskolc did not break Durovecz's determination to reveal nothing. Such severe interrogation followed in Hadik prison in Budapest, before he was transferred to the Zugliget prison camp, that Durovecz was badly concussed and his hearing temporarily affected.

Almost every day one or more prisoners in Zugliget were executed. Durovecz arrived in the camp on a Friday to find John Coates and Josef Gelleny already there. On Monday a Russian prisoner was shot. Durovecz learned that he was to be executed the following day. Willing in such circumstances to take any risk, he and Gelleny managed to escape with the help of Poles who had been in the camp since 1940. Both successfully hid in Budapest during the bitter house-to-house fighting that raged through the shattered city from the entry of advance units of the Red Army into the suburbs at Christmas 1944 until the capture of the whole city in early February 1945. Durovecz lived in the cold, dark basement of a church and cellars of resistance houses for almost two months. During that time he worked with the underground in helping the Red Army, existing partly on the tough, rank flesh of horses killed in the street fighting.

In mid-March, with their capture of Budapest, the victorious Red Army moved Durovecz, Coates, Turk, and Gelleny from the now half-demolished city to Debrecen, a market town on the Great Plain of Hungary near the Romanian and Soviet borders.

There a communist-dominated provisional government had been established in December 1944, and from there the U.S.A.A.F. flew them back to Bari, en route to Britain where they arrived by ship a few days after VE-Day.

Steve Markos, the first of the volunteers to be infiltrated into Hungary, had preceded their return to England by about six weeks – but only after severe treatment from suspicious and hostile Russians. As we have seen, he was caught in the fighting between them and the Germans in October 1944. Having been arrested by the Red Army, for three months he was brutally interrogated before being transferred to a week of solitary confinement in Romania. On 7 February 1945 he was finally handed over by the Russians to the British military mission in Bucharest, which put him on an R.A.F. transport for Bari. Throughout eastern Europe, several S.O.E. agents who, like Markos, had the misfortune to fall into Soviet hands were grossly mistreated. What the communist Markos thought of this is not recorded. At least the physical impact was evident. He had to be hospitalized in Scotland as a result of the Russian maltreatment.

Bodo recovered sufficiently from his broken jaw and other injuries to be moved from hospital to a Budapest prison. When the Russian army besieged the capital, he was transferred to Komaron, a town a few kilometres west of Budapest. There he was forced to join a Hungarian army unit deployed alongside the Germans against the advancing Russians. However, in the confusion of the fighting, as the Germans were pressed back on the Austrian border in the spring of 1945, he managed to make his way back to the ruins of Budapest where a family sheltered him until the arrival of a British military mission in late April. It despatched him to Bari, which he reached on 21 May 1945, the last of the Hungarian-Canadians to return.*

*Durovecz and Gelleny live in southern Ontario. Turk lives in Hungary where both Markos and Bodo (the chairman of a collective farm) died in 1955.

S.O.E. had less success in recruiting suitable Romanian-Canadians. Missions to Romania were not, in any case, notably fruitful. The British had hoped that they might succeed in inducing a leading pro-Allied politician to head an uprising against the pro-German government. To this end, an S.O.E. officer was smuggled into Romania via Yugoslavia in mid-1943. He was soon murdered. The likelihood of any real anti-Axis movement in the country was limited by the British inability to guarantee that Romania would not fall under Russian domination once the Germans were expelled. Nevertheless, S.O.E. sought additional agents to disrupt German communications and to organize, if possible, a pro-Allied *coup d'état*.

Alfred Gardyne de Chastelain, an affable and outgoing former sales manager in the British-owned Unirea de Petrol Company in Romania who was also active in various covert activities there before the war, came to Canada in June 1943 from New York to identify potential S.O.E. agents. On 12 August 1943 he reported to London that he had not been very successful. The majority of those he had interviewed in Toronto, at Camp Petawawa, and at the large summer camp at Niagara-on-the-Lake were unsuitable. Mainly the sons of immigrants from Transylvania who did not speak fluent Romanian or who were over-age, he considered only four to be possible recruits. Of these, the records of only two are now available.

One, George Eugene Stephane Georgescu, was, like de Chastelain, an employee of oil companies. Born in Brussels but educated in Romania and at Birmingham University as a chemist, Georgescu came to Canada in 1926. He worked mainly in western Canada as a petrochemist, but in 1943 he was with the Canadian Oil Company in Sarnia, Ontario. There he was interviewed by de Chastelain before being given brief introductory training at S.T.S. 103. More instruction followed in Cairo during the autumn of 1943, preparatory to parachuting into Romania. His mission, however, never materialized "due to changed circumstances." What had happened was that de Chastelain himself had parachuted into Romania on 22 December 1943, and a secret Romanian emissary had been smuggled out to Cairo in

February 1944. With the connivance of King Michael of Romania and certain pro-Allied factions, de Chastelain was able to contact S.O.E. headquarters in Cairo. The *coup d'état* to oust the pro-Nazi government, which S.O.E. had been working for, occurred six months later as the Red Army approached. More S.O.E. teams could serve no useful purpose; indeed, they might merely draw attention to de Chastelain's team, about whose presence in Romania the Russians, who regarded the country as being within their sphere, had already protested to the British. Georgescu's talents were not, however, lost to S.O.E. He joined its technical section in Cairo where he remained until he visited Bucharest on behalf of S.O.E. following the entry of the Red Army.

Victor Moldovan was also unable to undertake his mission to Romania. Although born in Canada in 1915, he had attended school in Romania before returning to work as a machinist with the Ford Motor Company in his native Windsor. Sometime in 1942 Moldovan joined the Canadian army–where he soon established a reputation as an expert poker player. By mid-1943 he had passed through S.T.S. 103 and was on his way to Cairo, via Britain. He completed his S.O.E. training in Egypt, but ill health and the same cancellation of missions into Romania that had affected Georgescu meant that Moldovan was returned to Britain in April 1944 and to Canada that October.*

Toncho Naidenoff, one of the few Bulgar-Canadians among the S.O.E. agents, was also one of the oldest volunteers recruited in Canada.† An organizer for the International Fur and Leather-workers' Union, he was already forty-nine years old when he volunteered in Toronto for the Queen's York Rangers. He completed sabotage training near Cairo, but illness prevented him from going on his assigned duties. Naidenoff was returned to Canada in December 1944, fortunate that he had not been sent

---

*De Chastelain also returned to Canada: in 1954 he settled in Calgary where he died in 1973.
†Durovecz recalls that two Bulgar-Canadian and possibly one Romanian-Canadian volunteer were drowned in a torpedoing in the Mediterranean, but I have been unable to find any evidence to support this recollection.

since the mortality rate was high among those few agents whom S.O.E. did manage to infiltrate into Bulgaria.

Following the capitulation of Italy in 1943, S.O.E. (in the guise of "No. 1 Special Force") took an increasing interest in the possibilities which Italian partisans offered for anti-German sabotage and harassment. But here again the problem of extending assistance to largely left-wing resistance units had somehow to be resolved. In Yugoslavia and Asia, the assistance was generally as extensive as supply and transport obstacles would permit; in Italy it was tempered with growing misgivings that communists might come to control the postwar government.

As early as February 1943, S.O.E. headquarters had contended that increased attention should be paid to Italy where, "unless the liberal elements are strengthened by moral aid, communism becomes the only alternative to fascism." Care had to be taken that the partisan units did not proclaim socialist or communist "republics" behind enemy lines, challenging the authority of the Italian government in Rome. However, as David Stafford has added,

> the partisans existed, they could make a useful military
> contribution, and there was no question of ignoring
> them .... Sixty-two S.O.E. personnel and nineteen W/T sets were
> infiltrated into northern Italy in August [1944] alone, a higher figure
> than for any other Mediterranean country with the exception of
> Yugoslavia, and in October fifty new parties were ready to go either
> to reinforce or supplement the existing fifteen S.O.E.
> missions .... Even in this period, however, political precautions
> remained to the fore .... So far as supplies to the partisans went,
> while there appears to have been no overall discrimination against
> communist groups, care was taken not to provide large-scale
> deliveries of rifles, small arms and ammunition, but to concentrate
> instead on clothing, sabotage equipment and sten guns.[4]

About the Italo-Canadians who volunteered to return to their homeland to fight with the largely left-wing partisans against the Germans, frustratingly little appears to remain on either S.O.E. or Canadian army files.

In October 1946, the Department of External Affairs compiled a list of fifty-six Canadian S.O.E. volunteers of central and southern European background. The list makes no claim to be definitive – and demonstrably it is not. Included are seven Italo-Canadians: Ralph Vetere and Peter Lizza of Toronto; John de Lucia and Frank Fusco of Niagara Falls; Angelo di Vantro and Peter Manzo of Montreal; and Joseph Stefano of Ottawa. An eighth Italo-Canadian, Vincent Nardi of Montreal, also served with S.O.E. in northern Italy.* A little is known about the service of Ralph Vetere and Peter Lizza, rather more about that of John de Lucia. Of the remaining five, almost nothing is recorded.†

As long as Italy was an Axis power, Vetere and Lizza like all Italo-Canadians volunteering for active service had first been vetted by the R.C.M.P., who in turn passed their names through the Department of External Affairs to S.O.E. in New York, along with those of several other young Italo-Canadians already serving in the Canadian forces. Vetere, born in Montreal, was a nineteen-year-old clerk in Toronto when he volunteered for the Queen's Own Rifles in November 1942. Lizza, born in Ottawa,

---

*A tenth and eleventh Italo-Canadian would have been included, but one was eventually rejected as a "troublemaker" and the other deserted before embarkation for Britain.

†Manzo, a machinist in a Canada Dry bottling plant in Montreal, was trained with the other Italo-Canadians in Britain, Algeria, and southern Italy. Where or for how long he fought with a partisan unit in northern Italy is unrecorded. Joseph Gabriel Stefano, a printer in prewar Ottawa, was assigned as an interpreter to an S.O.E. mission in Italy (where he had never been). Only the same limited information is available about Angelo di Vantro, a food company employee in Montreal before he joined the Canadian army in 1942. Frank Fusco, a factory worker in his native Niagara Falls, served as an interpreter in the Cuneo region, assisting in the protection of "vital installations" from destruction by the retreating Germans. Frank Misercordia, born in Cattona, Italy, was trained in Britain and Algeria as a wireless operator, but after five vain efforts to land him along the Gulf of Genoa, he was found, perhaps not surprisingly, to have a severe heart problem. He was returned to Toronto in November 1944.

was a cobbler who had worked briefly in Rome before the war. Both Vetere and Lizza were at Camp Borden in May 1943 when they were suddenly asked whether they would volunteer for "special duty" overseas. Along with five other Italo-Canadian volunteers, they passed briefly through S.T.S. 103, before sailing from Halifax for Britain in mid-June 1943. Upon completion of their training there, they were sent to Algiers for yet more instruction at Massingham. They were subsequently transferred to Bari where, Vetere later noted, "we waited a long time for any action, but meanwhile we did other duties such as training, interpreting and instructing."[5] The date and place of Vetere's drop to the partisans in the Imperia area of northwestern Italy as a sergeant interpreter is unrecorded; Lizza parachuted near Milan in October 1944. In a brief postwar note, Vetere stated, "we fought hard against the rigorous weather, fatigue and all our enemies." Certainly the fighting in Italy was hard. The highly professional soldiers of the German army roughly handled the partisans in the valleys and mountains of northern Italy. Dissension and rivalry among the communist and non-communist partisans did not increase their effectiveness. Treachery was not unknown. All that is clear is that Vetere and Lizza survived the war, presumably after having been overrun by Allied forces painfully fighting their way northward against well-entrenched German units.

More is known about John (Giovanni) di Lucia who was born in Ortona, Italy, in 1913. At the age of thirteen, he had been moved to Niagara Falls with his parents, and later he attended the University of Rochester. Di Lucia, a highly competent linguist, graduated in romance languages, but in 1942 was an accountant with the Borden Dairies in Niagara Falls. While on an R.C.A.F. officer training course at the University of Western Ontario in December 1942, he was invited to volunteer for "special duty." Following training with other Italo-Canadians in Britain, Algeria, and southern Italy, di Lucia parachuted to the partisans north of Verona in early 1944, as part of a "Rankin" mission, the designation of Allied missions sent to assist partisan units in protecting bridges, hydro-electric installations, and other important works from destruction by the retreating Germans. Di Lucia joined in the harassment of German units until early May 1944 when he was captured. On 12 May he was executed. It was not until a year later that his father in Niagara Falls received a short note which the Germans had permitted di Lucia to write immediately before they shot him. "I am giving my life for a good cause," he wrote. "This was expected and I am ready to face it. I die happily. May God bless and protect both of you."[6]

Much more is known about George Robert Paterson, not an Italo-Canadian, but an officer whose extraordinary wartime career was spent almost entirely in Italy.*

Born in Kelowna, British Columbia, in 1919, Paterson was not yet eighteen when he left his family orchards to become an undergraduate at Edinburgh University. Two years later, with the outbreak of the war, Paterson immediately volunteered to join the British army. During the spring of 1940, he served as intelligence officer to a Royal Engineer Chemical Warfare Group before joining D-Troop, No. 2 Commando. Paterson was one of the first Canadians to undertake parachute training at Ringway (in July 1940) and the special combat training in Scotland at which commandos excelled: unarmed combat, small arms, stalking, boat handling, surreptitious landings, and sabotage.

Paterson's mission with the commandos was the first British airborne operation of the war. He was among thirty-eight commandos who volunteered to parachute into Calabria in southern Italy on 19 February 1941 with orders to blow up the Tredgino aqueduct near Monte Voltore. Their daring went unrewarded. The damage which they were able to do was only temporary and the whole group was soon captured. The fact that the attack did

---

*A romanticized account of Paterson's adventures, complete with reconstructed dialogue, is in John Windsor, The Mouth of the Wolf (Toronto: Totem, 1978). A description of the paratroop raid in which Paterson participated is in Anthony Deane-Drummond, Return Ticket (London: Collins, 1953). (A second Canadian in the British army on that pioneering drop was Geoffrey Jowett of Montreal).

not succeed was, however, not the result of any failure of courage – the commandos acted throughout with great gallantry.

Following their capture, Paterson and the other commandos were held at an Italian air force base before spending the next two and a half years in a series of dreary camps for Commonwealth prisoners of war in the Apennines and in Tuscany. From them Paterson made repeated and vain attempts to escape. Eventually he was incarcerated in an ancient walled fortress thirty kilometres north of Genoa. There Paterson and the other Commonwealth prisoners were ordered by a secret message from British headquarters to remain in the camp, despite the sudden disappearance of their Italian guards when Italy surrendered. The assumption was that Allied troops would soon move rapidly northward through Italy, releasing and succouring all P.O.W. camps en route. In fact, the Allied armies soon became bogged down and at the camps hard-bitten German troops quickly replaced the Italian guards. Finally, Paterson managed to work his way through the boards of a crowded box car on a train carrying Allied prisoners to Germany. A rag-tag partisan unit near Brescia passed him on to Milan where arrangements could be made to assist him to cross into Switzerland.

An intrepid Italian engineer in contact with British secret services in Switzerland induced Paterson to help round up escaped British prisoners of war who were scattered over the Italian countryside and to smuggle them into Switzerland. The Germans raided the escape line's transit houses along the road to the Swiss frontier and in early January 1944, Paterson was seized on a train near Erba by an anti-communist patrol of Republicans who handed him over to the S.S. During the next six months, he was joined in the cells of the black hulk of Milan's San Vittore prison by most of the members of the escape line, including its leader. Against all odds, he and Paterson escaped together on 8 July 1944, when the Allied forces were still attempting to push northward from Rome. Paterson crossed safely ten days later into Switzerland, having made part of the trip to the frontier hidden in a small Milan fire truck.

At the British embassy in Berne, John McTavish, head of its press office was, in fact, the S.O.E. representative in neutral

Switzerland, responsible for infiltrating agents, money, and supplies into northern Italy. He asked Paterson to return across the border which the Canadian had with much danger and difficulty only recently crossed. Despite three and a half years of hardship and captivity, Paterson agreed to return to Italy to report on the reliability and needs of the various partisan bands gathering strength in the border area around Domodossola. Having been a prisoner of the Italians and Germans for so long, Paterson was given the cover of "Major George Robertson of the Royal Engineers," supposedly one of the many British prisoners of war who were on the run in northern Italy since the disintegration of Mussolini's regime.

With another escaped P.O.W., a British wireless operator who had been on the original paratroop mission with him three years before, Paterson went back into Italy in September 1944. He was with a partisan unit for almost two months, returning once briefly to Switzerland to obtain more money and supplies. "During this period," his S.O.E. record notes laconically, "he became a legendary figure of courage and leadership." On 14 October, Paterson was captured in a savage encounter with a tough German Alpine unit near Domodossola. Fortunately for him, the Germans remained ignorant of his connection with S.O.E. in Berne, reluctantly accepting his story that he was simply one of the legion of British prisoners of war hiding in northern Italy. Once again, imprisonment in the bleak, sprawling San Vittore in Milan followed for Paterson, this time from November 1944 to April 1945 when the prisoners were finally able to force their release, the partisans having seized control of the city from the few remaining German troops. Even then Paterson was not finished with Italy; for another year he voluntarily remained with the Allied forces in Milan, assisting in the assessment of partisan claims, before finally resuming his forestry studies at Edinburgh University.*

*Upon graduation from Edinburgh University, Paterson worked for several years in East Africa before returning to his native British Columbia where he is a forest management consultant.

13

Asia

The S.O.E. in Asia was known as Force 136.* Under that bland designation, the S.O.E. of Europe was recognizable in Asia by the same basic mandate: the raising, training, and arming of local underground forces; the sabotage of rail lines and industrial and military targets; the collection and transmission of information; and the deception of the enemy. There, however, the similarity between the S.O.E. of Europe and the S.O.E. of Asia largely ends. S.O.E.'s role in Asia was more comprehensive. It collected intelligence in a way that M.I.6 jealously regarded as an in-

*When S.O.E. headquarters in Cairo transferred to Bari in 1943, it was known as Force 366; earlier S.O.E. in the Middle East had been designated Force 133 and in Australia and the Pacific, Force 137, but none of these or other similar designations had the durability of Force 136. Indeed, I have had several veterans deny that they served in S.O.E. (a few had not even heard of it), but rather in an organization called Force 136.

fringement of its particular preserve; it engaged in propaganda for which, in Europe, the Political Warfare Executive was responsible; and despite an M.I.9 network throughout much of Asia, it assisted escapers and evaders who in Europe would have been wholly under the aegis of M.I.9.

Asia imposed its own unique conditions on S.O.E. operations. Skin of a different colour made it impossible for European agents to move about in Japanese-occupied countries as their fellow agents could in occupied Europe. An agent of European background could not travel unnoticed by train from, say, Singapore to Kuala Lumpur as one could – given the necessary papers – from Marseille to Paris. European agents could not hope to escape detection in, for example, the cities of the Netherlands East Indies, Malaya, or Burma; what they could hope to do was move through the jungle undetected. Accordingly, S.O.E. activities in Asia were generally more rural than in Europe. As a further consequence, the activities of Force 136 had much more of a para-military air about them; there were few opportunities for agents to attempt to pass themselves off as local civilians.

For European agents, even those who had long lived in Asia, operating from the jungle meant months in an alien and sometimes terrifying world of unknown plants, animals, diseases, and climate – wholly unlike the basic rhythms of life in, say, rural Italy. For most Europeans, adaptation to the jungle came slowly and seldom completely.[1] In Asia, many S.O.E. agents of European background had the triple challenges of concurrently fighting a fanatical enemy, adapting to an alien culture, and living surreptitiously in an unknown or hostile environment. Agents sought in vain for help from cowed, indifferent, or antagonistic native peoples, many of whom had been so terrified by Japanese brutality that they remained passive to Allied appeals to take up the fight against the invader. Others suspected the Europeans of being eager to push out the Japanese merely to regain their old colonial supremacy. Against all these and a multitude of other obstacles – such as the dearth until the final months of the war of long-range aircraft and submarines – it is astonishing that Force 136 accomplished so much.

Another obstacle S.O.E. had to overcome in Asia was partly self-inflicted. Over the vast territory of Asia there was a confusion of commands and an extraordinarily complex organization. Force 136 was responsible for clandestine operations in Burma, Malaya, and the Netherlands East Indies (the Southeast Asia command of Lord Mountbatten) but also to a degree in China, Siam, and French Indochina. A senior S.O.E. staff officer from London noted in some astonishment the tangled web of S.O.E. commands in Asia:

> Our operational headquarters for work into Burma, Siam, China and French Indo-China was in Calcutta....Work into Malaya and Dutch East Indies was controlled by a second sub-headquarters... in Colombo. Each had its own country sections and signals arrangements, which required the employment of vast numbers of F.A.N.Y's and native servants and transport.... Administrative and financial arrangements were looked after... in Delhi... stores depots were at Bombay, Poona and Jubbulpore in central India. There were para-naval bases at Madras and Trincomalee. Parachute training took place up on the North West Frontier at Rawalpindi. Jungle training was arranged at Horana near Colombo, but there were other training schools near Bangalore, and a most impressive "agents'" training establishment like that at Beaulieu in the palace of the Tagores outside Calcutta. [S.O.E.] had the use of airfields at Jessore outside Calcutta, and a forward base at Chittagong [and] later... the use of the airfields of Sigirya and Mineriya in the centre of Ceylon, and were preparing to move them forward...when the war came to an end. This farflung but loosely-knit empire was connected, if that is the word, by a telephone network on which it was almost impossible to have any coherent conversation, even if you and the man at the other end remembered the elaborate code system you were supposed to use, because of the innumerable exchanges through which the land line passed. It was in any case subject to interruption by the monsoon.... The bustling activity of all these centres was supposed to be controlled by... H.Q. in Kandy [Ceylon].[2]

This structure appears unnecessarily complicated, but it was not so much the result of hurried improvisation by S.O.E. as it was a function of the huge, alien terrain of Asia and a reflection of the complex organization of Southeast Asia Command itself.

By mid-1940, six months before the Japanese entered the war, a nucleus of Force 136 was already at work in India, considering what might be done to hinder and harass the invader if the Germans were to pass through the Caucasus (with Russian connivance) and invade India via Iran. The growing threat from Japan was not, however, neglected. After war did come to Asia, the year 1942 at S.O.E. headquarters in India was spent largely in improvisation and organization, as the embryonic Force 136 attempted to digest what the sudden extension of Japanese dominion over Hong Kong, Malaya, Burma, the Netherlands East Indies, Siam, French Indochina, and the Philippines meant in terms of plans and organization and what exactly infiltrated S.O.E. agents might hope to achieve.

In Malaya, a nucleus for resistance existed among the communists of the Chinese community which comprised about 40 per cent of the population and represented the most determined element in Malaya. Long before the Japanese attacked the British colonies in Asia in December 1941, the Malayan communists organized a bothersome wave of strikes in principal industries. Once Germany attacked the Soviet Union in June 1941, however, the party – along with all overseas communist parties – promptly threw support behind the hitherto hated imperial power.

In anticipation of a Japanese invasion and despite regular army scepticism, Special Training School 101 had already been established in Singapore by S.O.E. to train British and local volunteers for small "left-behind" parties to attempt the ambush and sabotage of the invader.* At the end of 1941, with the Japanese already beginning their unexpectedly rapid advance through the rain forests and mountains of the Malay peninsula,

---

*At least one instructor at S.T.S. 101, Frederick Spencer Chapman, came from a special forces jungle training camp at Wilson's Point, the southern tip of the State of Victoria, which later, following the extension of S.O.E. to Australia, contributed to the growth of several other training camps in the Pacific theatre.

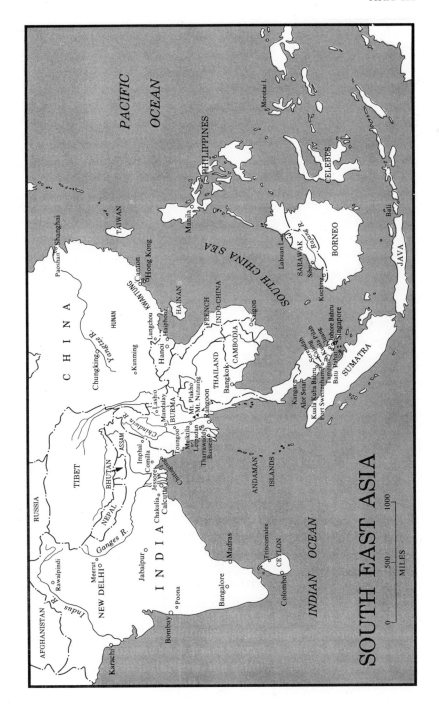

SOUTH EAST ASIA

MILES
0   500   1000

the Malayan Communist Party agreed to send the first of its members to S.T.S. 101. When Singapore fell on 15 February 1942, about two hundred had received some initial training, doing so well that their British chief instructor characterized them as "probably the best material we had ever had at the School."[3]

These trainees of S.T.S. 101 were the nucleus of the Malayan Peoples' Anti-Japanese Army (M.P.A.J.A.) which, by the end of the war, numbered more than seven thousand, supported by a much larger number of peasants and village merchants. However, the thick, humid jungle and the central mountain range of Malaya made communication among the major guerrilla groups difficult. Gradually there formed in eight states semi-autonomous "regiments," under the broad general control of the Central Committee of the Communist Party. Accordingly, it was with the executive of the party that contact was first made in 1943 when, after more than a year, S.O.E. managed to re-establish communication with the Malayan resistance. As in Yugoslavia, the difficult decision was taken to support local communists against the common enemy. Thereafter, Force 136 was increasingly active in Malaya, fighting side by side with communist guerrillas.

In Burma as well as in Malaya, indigenous resistance to the Japanese eventually replaced the initial indifference or even welcome given to their fellow Asian "liberators." The willingness of Burmese to take up arms against the Japanese was welcome to British and American strategists who sought the reconquest of at least northern Burma so that they might supply Nationalist China by a route more direct than flying "the Hump"–the dangerous airlift from India across the eastern Himalayas. If the massive though not very effective Chinese armies could be supplied to enable them to move decisively against the Japanese, enemy forces could be drawn away from the Pacific and southeast Asia. From Burma too could come some of the essential supplies for heavy bombers to operate from China against Japan itself. The reconquest of Burma was, however, no easy matter. Not only were the British and Indian forces themselves under-equipped; as General Slim, the British commander who was eventually to lead them from India to Rangoon, noted, the Indo-Burmese frontier was a "wide belt of jungle-clad, precipitous hills, railless, roadless, and for six months of the year during the monsoon rains, almost trackless."[4]

While Slim's Fourteenth Army was organizing and equipping for its eventual push southward against the Japanese, Dutch and British submarines operating from Ceylon began during 1943 to land small parties of agents – frequently prewar planters or foresters, police or government officials – on the Andaman Islands and then along the coasts of Malaya and Burma. Their assignment was to offer the local underground arms and medical supplies in exchange for support and sanctuary for Force 136 agents. At the same time, S.O.E. in Australia, under its cover name of the Services Reconnaisance Department, was increasingly active: it launched a daring and successful attack on Japanese shipping in Singapore harbour and carried out raids along the coasts of Malaya, the Netherlands East Indies, Portuguese Timor, Borneo, and New Guinea. However, throughout 1943 and into 1944, the southeast Asia theatre remained something of a sideshow for the Allies compared with Europe. "But from the moment the Japanese advance in Burma was checked [in June 1944] and the British assumed the offensive, the outlook for [S.O.E.'s] activities improved very quickly. During 1944 the Force had rapidly grown into a large but straggling para-military unit with a ration strength of all ranks and colours which was to become about 6,000."[5]

The key word here is para-military. The use of Europeans as clandestine agents had obvious limitations in Asia. They could operate in the jungles, but they could never pass as locals. For clandestine operations requiring disguise, the answer was to employ those who could pass unnoticed: overseas Chinese offered an immediate prospect.

For centuries, imperturbable and persistent, the Chinese had spread throughout southeast Asia, becoming a dominant feature of the urban landscape as hard-working merchants and traders. Here was one promising route for the infiltration into Japanese-occupied countries of agents who might, at least in a cursory way, pass as inhabitants. The challenge was to find reliable candidates within the British Commonwealth. Chinese were few in those parts of the Commonwealth not occupied by the Japanese – "white Australia" and South Africa had excluded them, but Canada was a possibility. Chinese had been brought to Canada as the essential labour for building the Canadian Pacific Railway through the Rockies, and others had found the necessary "head tax" to migrate before the people of British Columbia had deployed the full panoply of prejudice against further migration.

Before the war, traditional animosity had excluded Chinese-Canadians from professions and public office. Now, suddenly, they were valued for the special role that they could play in a global war. To recruit them there arrived in Ottawa in November 1943 a Canadian major in the British army who had long been involved in both M.I.6 and S.O.E.: Francis Woodley Kendall. Thirty-six-year-old "Mike" Kendall was a cheerful mining engineer from Vancouver who had worked before the war in south China. There he had been recruited by M.I.6 to help expand an intelligence-gathering network along the coast of the South China Sea from Taiwan to Hainan. According to the meagre records extant, Kendall must have led a highly dangerous life during the first half of 1942. Upon the surrender of Hong Kong on Christmas Eve 1941 and the internment of the survivors of the British and Canadian garrison there, Kendall escaped to the south China coast on an R.N. motor torpedo boat with seventy-five British naval, army and civilian "evaders" – and a one-legged Chinese admiral.[6] Included among them was Ronald Holmes, a young colonial civil servant whom we shall meet again. For the next six weeks, as he made his way northeastward from Hong Kong, Kendall came under the direction of Leslie Ride, an Australian who had been a professor of physiology at the University of Hong Kong. After himself performing the near-impossible feat of escaping from a Hong Kong prisoner-of-war camp, Ride had organized the "British Army Aid Group" which based itself on Kweilin and operated a combined intelligence, propaganda, and escapers' and evaders' assistance organization. Under him, Kendall worked briefly as a resistance organizer in northern Kwantung Province before leaving China in June 1942. Upon reaching India, he became an instructor at S.O.E.'s Eastern Warfare School at Poona, in the hills above Bombay. In November 1943, after more than a year at the school, Kendall was sent home to Canada to negotiate the recruitment of Chinese-Canadians for clandestine service with Force 136.

Even the easy-going Kendall found his assignment in Ottawa frustrating and time-consuming. In the hectic, overcrowded capital of a young country striving to achieve its full and unexpected potential for making war, S.O.E.'s request for Chinese-Canadian volunteers for "special duty with the War Office" raised unwelcome political as well as military problems. Many in Ottawa, including Prime Minister Mackenzie King, were sensitive to the distinct lack of enthusiasm in British Columbia for army recruitment of "Orientals." There were ample problems in wartime Ottawa without raising the longstanding issue of the rights of Canadians of Asian background to play a full and free role in Canadian life. Despite the mounting difficulties in reinforcing Canadian infantry as the war in Europe intensified and despite the ingenuity employed to attract volunteers so as to avoid the imposition of conscription, King's government had rejected repeated offers of service from both Chinese and Japanese-Canadian volunteers. It was only in March 1944, after several months of perseverance, that Kendall finally obtained both ministerial approval and army headquarters' co-operation in his search for volunteers. Even then Kendall's problems with Ottawa red tape were not quite over: the government required that the Chinese-Canadians be loaned to the British army which would then train, equip, and pay them.*

As Hudson had done before him in the case of Yugoslav-Canadians, Kendall crossed Canada by rail to interview possible volunteers. In Toronto, Kendall recruited the twenty-nine-year-

---

*The Canadian government did, however, eventually agree to make the volunteers eligible for Canadian pensions and other benefits.

old Roger Cheng, a brilliant electrical engineering graduate from McGill University who had been born in Lillooet, British Columbia. Upon completing officer training at Brockville, the Cantonese-speaking Cheng had been the first Chinese-Canadian to be commissioned in the Royal Canadian Corps of Signals. Following a wireless course at Kingston, Cheng was serving with the Directorate of Electrical and Communications Design at headquarters in Ottawa when Canadian Intelligence sounded him about volunteering for "special duty" in Asia. An interview with Kendall in a Toronto hotel room followed, before Kendall departed for western Canada.

Although Kendall did not spell out to the candidates whom he interviewed where their hazardous special duty might take them, their intended destination was in fact southern China. Before leaving London, Kendall had received S.O.E.'s approval for a risky operation that Ronald Holmes and he had conceived: an R.N. submarine would land a team composed largely of Cantonese-speaking Chinese-Canadians near Hong Kong. They would attempt to make contact with Chinese guerrillas (most of whom were communist and a few of whom Kendall had known before his escape from China). With their help, the team would then arrange for supply drops and would instruct the guerrillas in the latest small arms and demolition equipment. London, however, had an additional motive in sanctioning this operation: whenever the Japanese capitulated, it would be useful to have on hand a team to enter Hong Kong promptly to help re-establish the British writ there. It was a patently dangerous plan, but at least Holmes and Kendall, as leaders, were not asking others to face dangers that they themselves were unwilling to risk. The project was assigned the decidedly unpromising code name of "Oblivion."

When Kendall had been sent to Ottawa to seek the approval of the Canadian government for S.O.E.'s recruitment of Chinese-Canadians, he had also been instructed to obtain the government's agreement to the establishment of a temporary camp for their training somewhere in the Pacific Command of the Canadian army. There the volunteers would be instructed in wireless, sabotage, and other aspects of clandestine warfare. Boat work and weapons training would follow in Australia, before the volunteers finally crowded aboard an R.N. submarine for the long voyage to China.

Twenty-five young Chinese-Canadians were first interviewed by staff of Pacific Command or, in the case of four from Ontario, of Military District 2. From among them, Kendall selected twelve volunteers. All were bright, but to Kendall's regret, only four had had the opportunity in their childhood to learn fluent Cantonese. All except Cheng were privates in their late teens or early twenties. All were enthusiastic at the prospect of secret service against the invader of their ancestors' homeland and the enemy of their own.

There was an additional reason for their volunteering so readily. A British S.O.E. instructor at their camp later recalled, "From what they said to me . . . they were hoping that as a result of their efforts the Chinese in British Columbia would achieve equal status . . . and at the end of the war they would be accepted in complete equality."[7] During September 1944, the need for infantry reinforcements in western Europe had become so pressing that even Chinese-Canadians had begun to receive conscription orders under the National Resources Mobilization Act. By then, a number, including the twelve destined for S.O.E., had finally been successful in their repeated efforts to volunteer. Major-General George Pearkes of the Pacific Command had, however, urged that Chinese-Canadians should be restricted to separate training units to obviate "difficulties arising from racial characteristics and language." Perhaps partly because of this advocacy of separate units for Chinese-Canadians, Pearkes became an enthusiastic supporter of the establishment of an S.O.E. camp on Lake Okanagan to train an all-Chinese unit for special duty. The army, however, was more practical: it integrated other Chinese-Canadian volunteers into regular units. Nevertheless, the army remained decidedly slow in commissioning Chinese-Canadians, despite the fact that some were better qualified than their officers. The twelve volunteers for S.O.E. were no exception. Unlike most other volunteers, they were never commissioned:

they remained sergeants until their discharge in 1946.* General
Pearkes, on a brief visit to the camp,

> had the opportunity to talk at some length with the men and
> learned a great deal from them. They were anxious about their
> status upon their return to Canada and especially concerned about
> the franchise which had been denied to them for many years. They
> were bitter about the anti-Oriental feeling prevalent in British
> Columbia for decades. They felt themselves to be Canadians, they
> had volunteered to fight for Canada, and it was only right they
> should expect the privileges as well as the duties of citizenship.[8]

Pearkes later added his voice to those calling for Chinese-Canadians to have the right to vote, and Parliament eventually
enfranchised them.

Fortunately, the principal instructor whom S.O.E. selected to
join Kendall at the small Okanagan camp was free of the racial
prejudices that had so marred prewar life in British Columbia.
Hugh John Legg was an ideal choice: hardy, imaginative, experienced, and capable of endless improvisation. A wireless expert
from the British merchant marine of the First World War, an
employee of an international merchant bank between the wars,
and a wireless instructor in the R.A.F. until 1941 when S.O.E.
recruited him, Legg had already distinguished himself in operations of S.O.E.'s "Shetland bus" infiltrating agents into Norway;
in the capture of Madagascar; and in the tracking of suspected
German wireless stations and agents in South Africa. In March
1944 he was recalled from South Africa to London to go at once to
Vancouver to help Kendall train the twelve Chinese-Canadians.
At a site selected by the army in the low hills near Penticton, they
established a training camp of tents along the Okanagan lakeshore. Two sergeants from the Royal Canadian Engineers,
experts in small arms and explosives, arrived from the now
depleted S.T.S. 103 to complete the staff. The young volunteers,
despite their mainly urban backgrounds, soon adapted themselves to their rustic environment—which included morning

---

*One among them, Tom Lock, recalls some discussion during their later
training in Australia of being offered British commissions as lieutenants,
but, if they had been, at least Lock would have preferred to retain his
Canadian sergeant's pay.

plunges into the lake, physical training, and an abundance of peaches picked in nearby orchards. Early in the course, the instructors were augmented by Roger Cheng who had come from Ottawa, both to be trained himself and to provide some instruction in Cantonese. With Kendall and Holmes, Cheng would lead Operation Oblivion.

The twelve volunteers were divided into two groups for their four months' training: four were given intensive instruction in wireless, while the remainder concentrated on sabotage and small arms on the rocky secluded benchlands above the lake and in boat work on the placid lake itself. The Okanagan valley in summer is hot, dry, and salubrious; the volunteers were able to train seven days a week from mid-May until September when they were granted a few days' pre-embarkation leave in Vancouver. Finally, on 6 September 1944, the volunteers—now all sergeants—literally folded their tents and departed. Cheng and the four wireless sergeants flew from Gander to Rabat, Bahrein, and New Delhi for several weeks' specialized training in cryptology at the S.O.E. school at Meerut. In contrast, Legg and the eight remaining volunteers crossed the Pacific by ship, armed with vitamin pills to augment their expected diet in China of rice and fish. When they departed to join their ship in San Francisco, Kendall left by air for S.O.E. headquarters in India to report on the group's progress before he rejoined it in Australia.

The prewar Pacific liner *Lurline*, now converted to a grey troopship, was to carry Legg and his group to Brisbane. While at sea, however, General Douglas MacArthur, satisfied with the progress his forces were making in retaking the Philippines, ordered U.S. troopships to proceed there directly, rather than via Australia. In the face of these unexpected orders, Legg obtained the reluctant agreement of the *Lurline's* captain to deposit his team somewhere closer to Australia than the Philippines. They were rather unceremoniously landed by one of the liner's lifeboats at an almost-abandoned U.S. naval camp on the south coast of New Guinea. From a small nearby Australian radio station, they contacted Australian army headquarters in Melbourne, which diverted an Australian coastal liner to collect them and carry them from New Guinea to Townsville in

Queensland, where they finally arrived in early November 1944. From there they made their way by rail to Mount Martha, a camp near Melbourne, for final pre-operational training. This consisted of exercises under the direction of Kendall, Holmes, and Cheng, partly to test equipment being taken on the mission. The Royal Australian Navy provided the camp with a small harbour craft for boat and beach work, and training schemes were carried out in Port Phillips Bay, including mock attacks on airfields, oil installations, and gun sites. Weekends were spent in civilian clothes in Melbourne; questions about why Canadian sergeants of Chinese origin were in Australia would have been unwelcome.

By mid-December 1944, all training had at last been completed, all stores assembled and an R.N. submarine assigned to land Operation Oblivion on the south China coast. The total party consisted of Kendall, Holmes, Cheng, the twelve Canadian sergeants, and a Nationalist Chinese sergeant who had been added in Australia. Then, as an S.O.E. summary report observes laconically, "a distressingly long period of waiting followed. The team continued training, every effort being made to maintain the men's morale."[9] Parachute instruction at Leyburn in Queensland was included, but to what end was never made clear. In fact, at no time were the volunteers told that it had been intended to send them to China.

Meanwhile, unknown to the team, following the Anglo-American allocation of the Chinese theatre to the United States,* Roosevelt had appointed General Albert Wedemeyer commander of U.S. forces in the "China War Theatre" and Chief of Staff to Chiang Kai-shek, the Nationalist Chinese leader. A man of decided, if simplistic, views, Wedemeyer was flatly opposed to Oblivion. He contended that if such an operation were essential, it could be carried out more economically by U.S. forces from Chungking employing long-range aircraft than by the British sending a team by submarine from distant Australia. In any event, Wedemeyer was convinced that Chiang Kai-shek would

---

*A British military mission was nevertheless active in south China, attempting to co-operate with Nationalist forces, including those in northern Burma. A C.W.A.C. captain, Mary Dignam, was deputy to the S.O.E. officer attached to the British embassy in Chungking, following service on S.O.E. staff in Washington and Meerut, India.

never countenance an operation involving Allied contact with Mao Tse-tung's communists. Wedemeyer might also have added that Chiang was also, to say the least, unenthusiastic about any operation which would, even incidentally, help the British to re-establish themselves in their crown colony of Hong Kong. This was a point of view with which Wedemeyer was sympathetic: in his postwar memoirs he described Chiang as fighting concurrently the Japanese, Mao's communists, and the British who, "thanks to their strategy of self-interest and their attitude toward China, he had no reason to trust."[10] The net result of the combined opposition of Chiang and Wedemeyer was the cancellation of Oblivion.

In his opposition, Wedemeyer was far from alone. The Pacific and China theatres were never hospitable to S.O.E.; many senior U.S. officers regarded proposed British operations there as little more than attempts to re-establish British hegemony over its former colonial territories. During the spring of 1945, S.O.E. vainly attempted to devise an operation into south China acceptable to all, but, finally, on 25 April 1945, Oblivion was written off as impracticable, more than eighteen months after it had first been mooted.

For Holmes, Kendall, and the Nationalist Chinese sergeant, assignments elsewhere followed; for eight of the twelve Chinese-Canadian volunteers waiting in Australia, the war was now over.* On 1 June 1945 they were placed under the orders of Colonel L. M. Cosgrove, the Canadian military attaché in Canberra, who arranged for their passage from Sydney to Vancouver on the Matson Line's *Monterey*.† However, for the remaining five volunteers (including Cheng) the war was far from finished. They had the wireless skills urgently needed in Sarawak where several S.O.E. teams had parachuted a few months earlier to contact anti-Japanese tribes of the hinterland and to prepare the way for yet more teams.

*Today Legg lives in retirement in southern England; in 1976 Kendall died in Hong Kong where he had returned after the war.
†Two of the eight had married Chinese-Australian girls; when they arrived in Canada some months after their husbands, they were among the few women of Chinese background to enter Canada legally since the Orientals Exclusion Act of 1907.

14

Sarawak

Sarawak, that part of northern Borneo which for a century had been the personal realm of the Brooke family – the "White Rajahs" – had been seized by the Japanese in January 1942. Much of the coast is mangrove swamp. The jungle inland is dense and humid, with alternating heavy rainfall and hot, hazy sunshine. Occasional contact with Borneo had been maintained by S.O.E. sending by submarine an officer knowledgeable about the island to collect intelligence and to begin to arm potential resistance volunteers along the coast.

The first major operation was not, however, until 25 March 1945, in the fourth year of the Japanese occupation, when an officer and three sergeants were dropped by an R.A.A.F. Liberator to the Kilabit tribe on a high plateau in the interior. Several other missions followed, parachuted blind into the remote Borneo mountains. For a few days their lives remained in balance as the chiefs of the Kenyah and the neighbouring Kayan tribes debated the prudence of assisting these few returning representatives of the distant European government. Once they had decided to do so, however, they never wavered in their loyalty.

Hid and fed by the Kenyahs, the teams gradually contacted other mountain tribes, seeking their help against the hated Japanese. Bill Sochon, a former officer of the Sarawak Constabulary, undertook the dangerous task of contacting and then leading volunteers from the Ibans, the most aggressive and dynamic of the head-hunting tribes, against the Japanese along the Rejang River, one of the great highways of the roadless Sarawak jungle. Sochon had little difficulty in securing the Ibans' co-operation:

> With few exceptions the people of Sarawak detested them. The pagan tribes in particular were wretched under their rule. Since the principal anxiety of the Japanese was to secure for themselves all good things of the country, they commandeered the natives' crops of rice, made the chiefs hunt jungle game for them, and confiscated their shotguns for fear of insurrection. They showed no respect for pagan custom.[1]

Now reappears Ray Wooler, that most ubiquitous of all Canadians in S.O.E. Following his service in Britain, North Africa, and Italy, Wooler had sailed to Australia (via the Panama Canal) to assist S.O.E.'s Australian branch, the Services Reconnaissance Department. He became responsible for expanding its parachute training at Richmond and Leyburn, organizing drops from Liberators, and instructing volunteers in the use of S phones and Eureka beacons. R.A.A.F. Liberators were carrying increasing numbers of supplies and trained agents (frequently prewar colonial police or civil officials) to the islands of Portuguese Timor, the Netherlands East Indies, Borneo, and Sarawak. On seven of these missions, Wooler flew as despatcher with the teams whom he had trained. Having for four years watched other agents depart on secret missions, Wooler could no longer deny the urge to go himself. Three months after arriving in Australia and with Sochon's team in place on the upper Rejang River, Wooler, an ex-Sarawak civil servant, and three Australian N.C.O.s were dropped to Sochon on 7 July 1945, after being flown from Darwin in northern Australia. Parachuting into Sarawak was especially dangerous, given the low cloud that often hid mountains and obscured valleys. However, once landed along the Rejang and clear of the jungle, Wooler's team was safe enough at Sochon's small, secluded camp. The Rejang scenery, an articulate British traveller noted a year later,

> was beautiful, presenting various aspects of a river twisting through equatorial jungle. The thick vegetation was uniformly green, but the limbs of some of the lankiest trees were grey, and the shadowy woodland depths were black. Almost everywhere the forest came to the water's edge, a confusing mass of close-growing timbers and tangled undergrowth; but occasionally a space of pebbly shore or mudbank intervened between it and the river, and here or there a small clearing in the jungle contained a longhouse.
>
> In some places islands stood in the river, rocky and wooded.... No taming hand of men had touched them; only the beasts of the jungle and the fowls of the air knew them as habitations. The same was true of almost all the land which passed before our gaze in a splendid succession of savage, unkempt landscapes.
>
> Sometimes we caught glimpses of its inmates. At one spot a party of monkeys gambolled on a sandbank beside the water.... At another place a giant lizard, three feet long, basked lazily on a grassy path.... Brilliant kingfishers were plentiful. Hornbills flapped their ponderous way above our heads. Eagles, kites, crows, doves, swifts, swallows, sandpipers and bitterns were common. They eyed suspiciously our invasion of their territory.[2]

The river was also treacherous, complete with dangerous rapids, shallows, and poisonous fish and crocodiles. To add to Wooler's problems, the Australian maps which he had been given showed few elevations, providing him with only an approximate indication of where he was going, as he moved downriver toward the Japanese.

Fortunately for the Force 136 teams, the small enemy garrisons were not in the best of condition; approximately one-third of the Japanese troops were suffering from beri-beri, and they were acutely conscious of the propensity of the Ibans, whenever an occasion offered, to cut off a sickly Japanese straggler or lone sentry. Wooler's orders were to help clear the lower Rejang of the enemy. This he and a few other S.O.E. agents did with the indispensable help of the Ibans, who were a little bewildered by the reversal of the British prewar prohibition of head-hunting.

Now they were offered a Sarawak dollar for each Japanese head as well as medicines for their jungle ulcers (the Japanese would provide none). After decades of official discouragement by the British, all the traditional skills of the head-hunters were again in full play: the certain knowledge where the enemy was; the silent, stealthy approach through the thick jungle; the accuracy of the eight-foot blowpipe with its venomous dart; the decapitation with a finely balanced small sword (blades for the "parangs" were frequently beaten from old Ford spring plates, earned in return for occasional work on coastal rubber plantations). The small, black-haired, brown-skinned Ibans had adapted perfectly to their lush and unchanging environment; they could move effortlessly through either the dense jungle or along the sinuous river with equal skill. The Japanese gradually withdrew down the river, the head-hunters spreading terror among the debilitated enemy.*

Thanks to the Ibans' knowledge of all Japanese movements, Wooler and his team could move safely along the river by day. The canoes themselves were not, however, so reassuring. "They were slight craft, each hollowed from a single tree trunk, and usually...[with] only an inch of freeboard...above water. At every paddle stroke it seemed they must ship a wave, be swamped and sink from view. The danger was all the grimmer because a hungry crocodile might be swimming below. Yet the catastrophe never occurred. The oarmen's strokes were deft, the passengers sat with calm nonchalance on their frail seats, and the

*Less than a year later, visiting the small town of Kapit, where a brief but savage battle had occurred, Malcolm MacDonald found that "the Ibans had raised a flamboyant arch of welcome, decorated as always with palm fronds, orchids and other bright tropical blooms. Its principal adornments, however, were more unusual. They were two Japanese heads. Already one was almost a bare skull, but on the other, scraps of flesh still clung to the bone. The cropped black hair of a soldier sprouted from its pate, and eye-lashes grew in withered eyelids half closed over lack-lustre eyes. For the rest, little of the countenance remained. The nose had mostly disappeared and the face looked like the mask of a dead leper. These horrifying relics of the head-hunters' victory hung among flowers." (MacDonald, Borneo People, pp. 84-85)

canoe skimmed smoothly and safely forward."[3] The Ibans not only provided invaluable knowledge of the enemy's movements and of the river's shallows and rapids which made rapid advance downriver feasible; they also supplied rice, rice wine, eggs, chickens, and occasional small "mouse" deer and wild pigs which enhanced the team's diet. As Wooler moved westward down the Rejang, he was in radio contact with the headquarters of the Ninth Australian Division in Labuan, Borneo. Through it supplies were flown from Australia (including two mortars, light machine-guns, ammunition, money, drugs, and even food for a few Chinese Catholic sisters who had successfully hidden in the jungle with the Ibans for four years).

One month after his own arrival, Wooler learned that more Canadians were on their way to Sarawak. Sitting in his tree-trunk canoe, he noted, "Cat arrives tomorrow bringing Cheng and his party of Chinese-Canadians."[4] As we have seen, with the cancellation of Operation Oblivion, Roger Cheng and four wireless sergeants, Jimmy Shiu, Norman Lowe, Roy Chan, and Lewis King, had volunteered to remain with S.O.E. in either the Pacific or southeast Asia theatres. Yet more training had followed. The low, sandy Fraser Island on the Queensland coast was a major training camp of the Services Reconnaisance Department. Although it was opened only in late 1943, it trained almost one thousand students (at least twice that of S.T.S. 103) in a variety of subjects ranging from small-boat work to Japanese equipment. Aside from some instruction for Cheng's group in elementary Malay (a language useful along the coasts of many islands still occupied by the Japanese), his party was sent there for what Fraser Island excelled in: jungle training across the island and in the forests and sugar fields of the adjoining coast, and a ten-day medical course on what maladies were likely to await them in the jungle.

An R.A.A.F. Dakota carried them by stages from Brisbane to Morotai Island in the Netherlands East Indies where a holding and advance training camp had been established by the Australians two months before. Here final exercises were held and a little more Malay learned. As the official Australian history of special operations drily notes, since "The greater part of Morotai was occupied by small parties of Japanese, mostly ill-equipped and under-nourished, [the island] provided excellent facilities for training in realistic conditions without undue risk."[5] Finally, on 6 August 1945, Cheng and the four sergeants were landed by an R.A.A.F. Catalina on a wide stretch of the Rejang River, to join a small British team about fifty kilometres from Sibu, the second largest town of Sarawak.

Their task was to assist in gathering, collating and evaluating information about Japanese strength and intentions, this information to be radioed to the headquarters of the Ninth Australian Division at Labuan, to facilitate the planning of operations intended to clear the Sarawak coast and the Rejang delta of Japanese. A coastal tribe of Dayaks was trained in the use of small arms in preparation for a surprise attack on the Japanese in Sibu, an attack to be supported by the R.A.A.F. from Labuan. However, the morning before Cheng's team arrived, a U.S.A.A.F. Superfortress had dropped an atomic bomb on Hiroshima. It soon became evident that the assault on Sibu would be unnecessary.

No nation could face nuclear devastation. Eight days later, hostilities formally ended. Within a month Japan had surrendered. Unlike in Europe, however, where the war had ended promptly in May, it dragged on in parts of Asia for weeks and even months as isolated Japanese units refused to accept the humiliation of the defeat of their homeland.

The uncertainty about the intentions of local Japanese garrisons made more difficult the second assignment of the team which the Canadians had joined: the transmission of information about conditions in prison camps at Kuching, the capital of Sarawak. There the Japanese had concentrated about twenty-five hundred British military and civilian internees.[6] No one could be certain of their fate; their safety would depend upon the willingness of the Japanese guards to accept that their Emperor had indeed ordered them to surrender and to turn the camp over to

Australians from Labuan. The Australians were ready with troops and the United States navy with ships for the surrender of Kuching, a few miles up the Sarawak River, but first the readiness of the Japanese garrison to obey their Emperor's surrender order had to be determined. On 14 August 1945, news of the Japanese capitulation had reached the camps via concealed radio; on the 20th, R.A.A.F. aircraft had dropped leaflets promising the malnourished inmates early help. Food containers followed, but it was only on 11 September that the Australians were sufficiently confident that the Japanese guards would not slaughter the prisoners that they finally felt able to occupy the small capital and enter the camps. Following the successful transfer of the emaciated prisoners to the care of the Australians, the recovery of arms and equipment, and the concentration of Japanese units for repatriation, Cheng and the other Chinese-Canadian volunteers returned to Australia on the first stage of their long journey home.*

By then, however, they were far from the only Chinese-Canadians in S.O.E. Six were hard on their heels in Australia, and many more were being trained in India. When Cheng and the first four Chinese-Canadians had been en route to Sarawak, sixteen others (whom Legg had helped to recruit during a trans-Canada rail trip) were given clandestine warfare training at Park Orchards near Melbourne, which operated under the not very opaque cover of the "School of Eastern Interpreters." There, for the Chinese-Canadians, instruction in Cantonese was also provided. Orders were issued for the volunteers to be flown to Labuan by 30 August, but at the last moment the orders were cancelled when Japan had capitulated. The sixteen remained briefly in Australia, pending their return to Canada.

---

*Today Jimmy Shiu lives in California, Roy Chan in Victoria, Lewis King in Calgary and Roger Cheng in Vancouver. Norman Lowe is dead.

During August, as the surrender of Japan proceeded, S.O.E. teams had cleared the Japanese from most of the Rejang and the other principal rivers of Sarawak, they and their head-hunters and other tribes accounting for more than seventeen hundred Japanese dead. About twenty-five kilometres from Sibu, amidst the rubber plantations near the Rejang delta, Wooler first learned by radio of the atomic bombing of Japan; on 11 August he noted tersely in his diary, "Last night radio reported Japanese acceptance of Potsdam terms with provision that Emperor be allowed to remain."[7] The Japanese garrison in Sibu, however, would not accept such reports. It continued to hold out, awaiting orders from its distant commander-in-chief in Singapore before finally surrendering to the Royal Navy in September. Wooler, by then eager to return to a life more familiar than that among Sarawak head-hunters, nevertheless volunteered to assist in the repatriation of Allied prisoners of war and civilian internees in the Philippines, some of whom had been taken there from Hong Kong. He returned to North America on a hospital ship, taking P.O.W.s to Tacoma, Washington, and to Vancouver. While crossing Canada by train from Vancouver to Montreal, Wooler, who had survived so much during the war, barely escaped death in a derailment in a snowstorm in the Rockies. In February 1946, he was finally re-united in England with his W.A.A.F. officer wife whom he had not seen for four and a half years.*

Once having swallowed the extraordinary idea of Chinese-Canadians in the Canadian army, Ottawa had set about recruiting them with an enthusiasm that astonished those who had repeatedly and vainly sought to enlist. The initial Ottawa approval had been for the recruitment by S.O.E. of a maximum of thirty-five Chinese-Canadians. However, even before the first

---

*After discharge from the British army, Wooler lived briefly in Toronto before settling in Montreal where he was in business until he retired to the Annapolis Valley of Nova Scotia in 1973.

contingent had left Vancouver for Australia, S.O.E. requested an additional twenty-five. In December 1944, the Minister of National Defence approved a further increase to a maximum of one hundred and fifty.

A final total of one hundred and forty-three Chinese-Canadians were sent to Australia and India. Records of their recruitment are limited, but it appears that in mid-or late 1944, S.O.E. requested Ottawa to recruit them for loan to the British army, primarily to serve as wireless operators and as guerrilla instructors in southeast Asia. Again, approval had to be obtained from Ottawa. Moreover, "difficulties arose in shipping them direct to India,"[8] so three drafts totalling one hundred and twenty-eight were sent via Britain in February 1945. From there they sailed for India via the Cape of Good Hope in early March, finally arriving at the S.O.E. camp above Poona in late April. None, however, saw combat service before the Japanese surrender, except for ten whom we shall meet in the jungles of Malaya.

15

Burma

The Chinese-Canadian volunteers were not the only Canadians with Force 136 who lived through the turmoil and dangers of southeast Asia during the months both preceding and following the surrender by Japan. Of the seventeen Canadians with S.O.E. who survived their hazardous service in occupied France, ten volunteered for S.O.E. operations in French Indochina when that possibility was raised with them in London upon their return from France.* Following informal conversations with Felix

*More Canadians might have been in Southeast Asia Command had it not been for Prime Minister Mackenzie King's aversion to Canadians fighting for what he considered the restoration of Britain's colonies and, perhaps more importantly, his sensitivity to the likely domestic electoral impact. King noted in his diary, "No government of Canada, once the European war was over, could hope to send its men to India, Burma, and Singapore to fight with any forces and hope to get through a general election successfully." King, ever-suspicious of perfidious Albion, may have partly drawn this lesson from his mid-1941 error in sanctioning the despatch of two battalions to the doomed Hong Kong.

Nevertheless, Canadians had served with R.A.F. squadrons in Malaya even before the war with Japan began. An R.C.A.F. Catalina squadron was based on Ceylon between March 1942 and January 1945. Later, the crews of many R.A.F. Liberators were partly or even wholly Canadian. Squadrons 435 and 436 of the R.C.A.F. were formed in northwest India in October 1944 for Dakota supply drops in Burma. In January 1945, it was estimated that more than 3,100 Canadian airmen were serving in southeast Asia with R.A.F. or R.C.A.F. squadrons.

Walter at C.M.H.Q., S.O.E. formally asked, on 20 November 1944, for the services of Chassé, Labelle, Taschereau, Meunier, Thibeault, and Archambault.*Later, Benoit, Hunter, Fournier, and Caza joined them.

After the war had ended, Walter speculated on the reasons why the ten had volunteered for S.O.E. a second time. In his view, they

> found it very difficult indeed to return to regular army life. This was not only because of the excitement and the informality of the life which they had enjoyed as agents in the field but also because it was difficult, if not impossible, for the Army to re-absorb, into their parent corps, Majors and Captains who, when last heard of, had been infantry subalterns or R.C.C.S. privates. The prospect they faced was that of being sent back to Canada and demobilized. A number of them, therefore, were only too willing to volunteer for a fresh tour of duty in a field which showed every promise of making ample use not only of their operational experience but also of their language qualifications.[1]

The one Canadian S.O.E. veteran who volunteered but did not serve with Force 136 was the dynamic Guy d'Artois of Quebec City. The Toronto *Star* of 20 December carried a dramatic front-page interview with him in Montreal, following the arrival there of his wife, Sonia. D'Artois, on a month's leave before he was to return to Britain for passage to India,† described to the newspaper some of his adventures and those of his wife (now

---

*Sirois was approached informally in London in October 1944, but he declined the offer, given the uncertain state of his health. He returned to his native Saskatchewan, graduated in law from the University of Saskatchewan in 1950, and after many years of law practice became a Justice of the Queen's Bench in Saskatoon.

†The same issue of the *Star* carried rather more circumspect and briefer interviews with Benoit, Meunier, and Labelle. Four days earlier, a short interview with Chassé had been published. On 22 December, the newspaper ran posed photographs of the two ex-agents as if they were being parachuted. After the war, d'Artois continued his military career, serving in the Van Doos in Korea. He now lives in retirement in Quebec City.

expecting their first child). The article carried the enthusiastic headline, "She ate with the Gestapo. Killed some? Why, sure." Retaliation as sometimes practised by the *maquis* was described in more detail than S.O.E.—still very much at war with the Germans—found acceptable. D'Artois had in any case decided by then not to accompany the other nine French-Canadian volunteers to Asia.

Eight of the nine spent December 1944 on leave in Canada. They flew back to London in January, embarking together in Liverpool on January 24 on a trooper bound for Bombay where, after Benoit had won considerable amounts of sterling at poker, they arrived a month later. Upon arrival, Labelle had to be withdrawn: shell shock in Italy and the strain and exhaustion of his service in France caught up with him in Bombay, necessitating his removal and hospitalization in Poona.*

Archambault, Benoit, Chassé, Fournier, Meunier, Taschereau, and Thibeault† travelled by train from Bombay to spend February and March at S.O.E.'s Eastern Warfare School at Poona (where by now Kendall was second in command) and at the jungle training school at Horana, about thirty-five kilometres from Colombo, Ceylon. Caza arrived in mid-March, and by April, all eight veterans were on their way either to Burma or later to Malaya.

They were good candidates for service there, in the sense that they were brave, experienced, capable wireless operators or sabotage instructors, knowledgeable about the ways of clandestine warfare. Their principal shortcomings were that they knew nothing of life in the jungle nor of local languages and customs. Unlike many in Force 136, none had been in Asia before. Despite

---

*He returned by hospital ship to Scotland, and after recuperation at a Canadian army hospital in Britain, travelled home to Canada. At the time of writing, he is executive director of the Red Cross in Quebec.
†Gustav Duclos, the Frenchman who, disguised as a Canadian, had parachuted with Taschereau and Thibeault into France, also served with Force 136 in Burma. He became a Canadian citizen after the war and now lives in Toronto. His was a case of the wartime disguise becoming the postwar reality.

those handicaps, they were all to serve with distinction. The opportunity to employ their talents and experience might have been even greater if, given their language qualifications, they could have operated in French Indochina, the theatre originally envisioned for them.

As early as June 1940, the Japanese, anticipating an eventual move southward on Malaya and Singapore, demanded of the local pro-Vichy administration in Hanoi that a small Japanese mission be allowed to ensure that no supplies were reaching the Nationalist Chinese through French Indochina. This was the foot in the door. Additional Japanese demands gradually led to a *modus operandi* whereby the Vichy administration and a small Japanese occupation force lived more or less in peaceful co-existence, the French continuing to administer the country under the suzerainty of the Japanese who thereby saved themselves the trouble of sending large numbers of officials and troops to the colony.

The possibilities for sabotage and harassment of the Japanese in Indochina were not, however, entirely neglected by the Free French, despite their understandable preoccupation with the problems of their homeland. With the approval of de Gaulle, a small group of French officers with prewar service in Indochina and a few Vietnamese serving with the French army in North Africa were trained by S.O.E. in India and despatched to Chungking. There a group of French naval officers was also being briefed for a mission into Indochina. Disputes between the de Gaulle and the Giraud factions, however, eventually led to the disbandment of both teams before they crossed from China into the former colony.

More successful was an intelligence network in Indochina itself, the "Gordon-Bernard-Tan Group." In the immediate wake of the declaration of war with Japan, it began operations in early 1942 under Laurence Laing Gordon, a thirty-six-year-old native of Vernon, British Columbia, who was employed in Hanoi by a

U.S. petroleum corporation. Gordon had taken the first step toward the intelligence business more than two years before. On a visit to San Francisco during the autumn of 1939, he called at the British consulate to offer his services now that the British Commonwealth was at war with Germany. However, instead of service in the armed forces, Gordon eventually found himself back in Indochina, gathering intelligence about the Japanese forces there. The group included one Harry Bernard and a U.S. citizen of Chinese origin known as "Tan" (hence the network's designation of "GBT").

> The original purpose ... appeared to have been to bolster the morale of the employees' French friends in the country by maintaining contact with the outside world. However, what had originally been a casual arrangement began to assume the characteristics of an amateur intelligence agency. Subsequently, it developed into an actual intelligence network collaborating with Allied organizations.
>
> GBT began operations with couriers. It acquired a limited number of radio sets from the British in India and established stations at Hanoi and Haiphong, as well as a headquarters station at Lungchou in China, across the Indochina border. The Chinese Government supplied operators for the headquarters station on condition that all intelligence received would be sent to Chinese military intelligence in Chungking ....
>
> However, by 10 March 1945, the Japanese completed total occupation of Indochina. The result was the inevitable disintegration of GBT. Its headquarters were transferred from Lungchou to Kunming in China. From there, infrequent radio contact was maintained with Hanoi, Haiphong and Saigon.[2]

By 1944 the Japanese were becoming increasingly uneasy about their hold on French Indochina. Long-range U.S.A.A.F. bombers, operating from the interior of China, had already severely disrupted coastal shipping, leading to the Japanese occupation of the whole of the south China coast to secure their overland supply route to Singapore. In Indochina, unrest was mounting among both the French and the anti-French Vietnamese nationalists (who, as in Malaya, were largely communist). To the Free French, to the O.S.S. in Chungking, and to those of Force 136 in Calcutta responsible for operations in Indochina, the time appeared right to attempt clandestine assistance to the French army units still intact in Indochina, and to those planters and other Europeans willing to risk their necks against the Japanese. With the liberation of France and the disappearance of the Vichy government, the administration in Indochina would presumably be more willing to co-operate with Allied agents. From about October 1944 to February 1945, S.O.E., the Free French, and O.S.S. gave Indochina a higher priority.

Indochina was not, however, as promising as it looked. The idea of building a resistance there involving French agents or forces did not take fully into account the objections of the United States, which joined Chiang Kai-shek in opposing any help to a European power attempting to recover its prewar colonial empire. Moreover, Roosevelt deeply mistrusted de Gaulle, so he was in no mood to assist him in expanding his authority. Further, both Force 136 and the Free French, in surveying the prospects in Indochina, underestimated the determination of the Viet Minh, the communist-dominated nationalist guerrillas, to rid themselves of their colonial masters. Pledged as they were not to allow Indochina to revert to a French colony once the Japanese had departed, it became increasingly evident that, while the Viet Minh made occasional excursions against the Japanese, Ho Chi Minh was in fact husbanding his forces for an eventual showdown with the French. Nevertheless, at the beginning of 1945 the outlook appeared more promising. With the help of Force 136, and despite the chronic shortage of long-range aircraft and the opposition of the United States, de Gaulle's representative in Asia succeeded in parachuting at least twelve parties into Indochina, controlling them by radio from Calcutta.

The Burma offensive of the British Fourteenth Army was, however, given priority over operations into Indochina. In any case, prospects there gradually took a turn for the worse: several of the agents dropped into the Hanoi plain and Cambodia were captured and beheaded by the Japanese, allegedly betrayed by the Viet Minh. Nevertheless, a few air drops continued, for the plan was to build up dumps of arms and stores in the mountains to be used, whenever feasible, against Japanese land communications from China to Saigon, thereby further disrupting a vital link in the Japanese overland route to Malaya.

19.

The jetty and beach on Lake Okanagan, British Columbia, where the Chinese-Canadian volunteers trained during the summer of 1944 for Operation "Oblivion." *(Courtesy G. V. H. Wilson)*

20.

Lunch in one of the marquees at the small tent camp at "Commando Bay" on Lake Okanagan. Sgt. McLure, a demolition instructor, is on the left of the Chinese-Canadian volunteers while on the right are Mike Kendall, who was to lead Operation "Oblivion," his Cantonese wife Betty, and Hugh Legg, the wireless instructor whom S.O.E. transferred from South Africa to assist in the training. *(Courtesy G. V. H. Wilson)*

21

Using folding boats of the type that they would have employed to land from their R.N. submarine on the Japanese-held coast near Hong Kong, Chinese-Canadian volunteers train near Melbourne during the winter of 1944-45. (*Courtesy Tom Lock*)

Norman Wong, Roger Cheng and Jimmy Shiu talk with three Australian-Chinese girls in Melbourne in August 1945, shortly before the departure of the latter two for Borneo to serve with S.O.E. teams working with the head-hunters in Sarawak. (*Courtesy Tom Lock*)

22

Two Dakotas of No. 436 Squadron R.C.A.F. on a supply drop to a S.O.E. team in the Shan hills of Burma in August 1945. The guerrilla units, with which several French- Canadian veterans served, harassed the Japanese in their efforts to escape eastward from Mandalay into Thailand. The painting is by Robert W. Bradford of Ottawa. *(Canadian War Museum)*

24.

Charlie Chung parachuted into the Malayan jungles to work with the guerrillas near the Thai border with a team lead by Pierre Chassé, the veteran of S.O.E. operations in France and Burma. After the capitulation of the enemy, the team took on the responsibility for the civil government of the Sultanate of Perlis, one of the smaller states of Malaya. *(Courtesy Charlie Chung)*

25.

The nineteen-year-old Henry Fung of Vancouver, the first Chinese-Canadian to parachute into Malaya, who worked with a S.O.E. team in sabotaging Japanese communications and otherwise harassing the enemy. For his photograph, Fung wore a beret with the tiger-head cap badge of the Malayan Peoples' Anti-Japanese Army. *(Courtesy Henry Fung)*

26.

A photograph (damaged by humidity) of Bing Lee of Vancouver who parachuted with Alistair Morrison of the Gurkhas into Malaya in July 1945. On the right is Bill Lee who joined them in Kuala Lumpur a few weeks after the Japanese surrender. *(Courtesy Bill Lee)*

The disbandment of the communist-dominated Malayan Peoples' Anti-Japanese Army was a delicate problem for several S.O.E. teams in which Canadians were included. A ceremonial parade in Kuala Lumpur, inspected by the British general commanding the area, marked the contribution the guerrillas had made to Allied victory. *(Courtesy Bill Lee)*

27.

Harry Ho and Victor Louie in India following their operations in Malaya. In Meerut in early 1946 on the first stage of their long journey home to Vancouver, they paused long enough to be photographed with a camel outside the "Palace Talkie" cinema. *(Courtesy Harry Ho)*

28.

29.

The sword of a Japanese officer and a Japanese flag were popular trophies of Allied personnel in Asia. Canadians who had served first in occupied France and subsequently in Burma and Malaya were no exception; from left to right: Pierre Meunier, Paul-Emile Thibeault, Joseph Fournier, and Pierre Chassé on their arrival in New York on 20 February 1946. *(Public Archives Canada)*

30.

Motor Gunboat 503 was one of three used by the R.N. for the evacuation of evaders and escapees from the Brittany coast. Small rubber boats would ferry those arriving and departing. M.G.B. 503 survived the war but immediately following VE-day was lost with all hands upon striking a German mine. *(Courtesy Ray LaBrosse)*

31.

In the right foreground of a group of Canadian prisoners at Dieppe stands Robert Vanier, his head bandaged under his helmet. The Germans herded the captured Canadians onto trains to take them to prisoner-of-war camps. Within days Vanier had escaped to begin his career in helping others to escape. *(Courtesy Robert Vanier)*

32.

Robert Vanier, Conrad LaFleur and Guy Joly of the Fusiliers Mont-Royal, were captured at Dieppe, but escaped from the train taking them to Germany. In rough disguise in Montmorillon, near Poitiers, in early September 1942, the three escapers eventually made it back to England to join M.I.9. *(Courtesy Robert Vanier)*

34

Above: Most agents had available two or more forged identity cards to support alternative disguises: Ray LaBrosse of M.I.9 as Marcel Desjardin and Paul Coubet. *Below:* Ray LaBrosse, pistol in hand, walks alongside a farm cart bearing a German soldier mortally wounded in a counter-attack at Plelo which marked the completion of his and Dumais' service in Brittany. *(Courtesy Ray LaBrosse)*

The Chinese-speaking Arthur Stewart of Vancouver was photographed while with M.I.9 in the hills of northern Burma. A hard-driving, prewar police officer of great stamina, Stewart was later to serve in Malaya and the Netherlands East Indies, bringing help to the suffering inmates of Japanese prisoner-of-war camps. *(Courtesy Robert Stewart)*

Arthur Stewart and Bill Lee of Vancouver were parachuted into Malaya to make their way into Singapore in the uncertain days following the Japanese surrender. Stewart's team commandeered a truck at a pineapple plantation to drive to the nearest Japanese checkpoint where staff cars took them to the Allied prisoner-of-war camps in Singapore. *(Courtesy Bill Lee)*

37.

In Changi prison in Singapore, Stewart and Lee were shocked by the emaciated state of the Allied prisoners. Stewart was prompt in calling in air drops of food and medicines – and in raising the Union Jack over Changi. *(Courtesy Robert Stewart)*

38.

The Japanese, of course, became aware of the intensified Allied drops of arms and men during the winter of 1944–45. Their response was to warn the French governor general in February 1945 that unless such activities promptly ceased, they would assume complete control of the colony. By 10 March, the Japanese, fearful of an Allied amphibious landing, had interned all French officials and troops (those whom they did not kill) and occupied the whole of Indochina. In doing so, they incidentally made it much more difficult for Allied agents to move about the country. Moreover, the Japanese encouraged the establishment of a native Vietnamese government – admittedly a puppet one – a move which could incidentally cause additional dissension between the Free French and the United States. When fighting broke out between French units in Indochina and the Japanese, the French retreated into the mountains, suffering severe casualties from disease and deprivation and Japanese brutality. With the virtual elimination of organized French units and the readiness of the Viet Minh to betray to the Japanese anyone working with the French, drops of agents and arms to Indochina ceased. And so it remained until the end of the war when the British occupied Saigon and the Nationalist Chinese Hanoi. The re-establishment of French authority in its colony was accordingly delayed to the point where it was never again entirely firm – with all the consequences for the following decades. This opportunity of the communist guerrillas in Indochina to organize and equip themselves in the absence of Allied agents was in time to have far-reaching consequences, but for the nine remaining Canadian volunteers, it meant unexpected diversion to the more immediately promising theatres of Burma and, later, Malaya.

Following the defeat of the Japanese at Imphal as they attempted to thrust into India in mid-1944, the British Fourteenth Army had gone over to the offensive, beginning to move east and southward into Burma. By the middle of December, the army was across the Chindwin and approaching Mandalay. The lack of long-range Liberators limited the support Force 136 could provide before December 1944, but thereafter, especially after VE-day, increasing numbers of agents (both European and Asian) were dropped with their stores to help ambush and otherwise harass the retreating Japanese.

Japan had declared Burma independent in December 1943, establishing, as it was to do later in Indochina, a puppet government of nationalists, including communists, most of whom, however, gradually recognized that they were merely tools in the hands of the occupation forces. Presumably they and others also recognized, as 1944 passed, that Japan was losing the war. In any event, one faction put out feelers to the British. Concurrently S.O.E. also developed contacts with the virtually independent hill tribes, who were either pledged to or contemplating active anti-Japanese resistance. Many of the nationalists in Rangoon were not communists, but the prospect of collaboration with any communists was viewed with distaste, if not abhorrence, by the governor of Burma (then living in a sort of exile in northern India) and by some on the staff of Southeast Asia Command. Mountbatten, on the other hand, was quite clear that everything possible should be done to hasten the recapture of Rangoon and Singapore. Force 136 was accordingly given a clear mandate to train all those in Burma, communist or otherwise, willing to take up arms against the Japanese.

Bickham Sweet-Escott, a lively and observant senior S.O.E. staff officer, later summarized succinctly the challenge facing Force 136 in Burma during the first months of 1945:

> The contribution of Force 136 to the final assault on Rangoon was ... based on two major operations – Character in Kerenni, and the rising of the B.D.A. [Burma Defence Army]. The assault was to consist of two separate moves. There was first of all operation Dracula, the seaborne and parachute attack on Rangoon itself ... for which "D" Day was the 2nd May.
>
> Secondly the 14th Army was to drive down the narrow valley of the Sittang to reach Rangoon by land from the north. Meiktila, more than 300 miles north of Rangoon, did not fall till the end of March, so that 14th Army had less than six weeks to get to Rangoon ....
> Lord Mountbatten ordered both General Leese and General Slim to

"take all risks" to ensure their objective. The main risk consisted in the possibility that the two divisions which would have to push down the Sittang might be cut off, either by the two Japanese divisions west of the British line of approach, or by one [Japanese] division, [which] might well move from the valley of the Salween westwards along the road which led from Mawchi to Toungoo. If that division got to Toungoo airfields before 14th Army it might hold us up indefinitely. If it got to Toungoo after our two divisions had passed through to the south, it would cut them off and imperil their line of supply.[3]

As the Fourteenth Army moved southward, the Japanese would be pushed back on Rangoon or into the hills flanking the Sittang valley. There the Karens, loyal to the British, awaited them.

The Japanese forces that had been opposing the 19th Indian Division to the north had been obliged to withdraw east into the foothills of the Shan States. When our armoured thrust developed along the motor road running south from Meiktila ... to Rangoon the Japanese had not enough heavy equipment left in Burma to oppose it, and their troops escaped either westwards into the dense jungle-covered foothills known as the Pegu Yomas ... or eastwards across the Sittang River.

On the east of the Sittang there is flat paddy country for a distance of ten to fifteen miles and then the ground rises very steeply into the Karen Hills, which run as high as seven thousand feet in a few places and stretch beyond the Salween River into Siam. These hills grow enough rice to feed the Karen villagers who live in them.... There was really no reason for strangers ever to penetrate into that country and the people led a healthy life with plenty to eat and very little to trouble them. Some of the more adventurous Karens had penetrated into the Burmese plains at an earlier date, and in the way that hardy mountain people do had proved more than a match for the easygoing Burmese plainsmen. This penetration into Burma proper had not endeared them to the Burmese, and they would doubtless have been persecuted as a too energetic minority if the British administration had not been there to protect their interests.[4]

The Karens, people originally from eastern Tibet, had retained their language and traditions. As early as the campaign of

1826, they had been loyal allies of the British against the Burmese. Since the first days of the Japanese occupation, a British officer had been with the Karens. Although in March 1944 he voluntarily surrendered himself to the Japanese—and to certain execution—to prevent further bloody reprisals against the Karens, he had kept alive a sense of Anglo-Karen co-operation almost until the first officers of the Fourteenth Army and Force 136 began to arrive in early 1945.

By January 1945, S.O.E.'s Burma country section in Calcutta had placed several teams in the Karenni hills, but their principal task was to restrain the Karens' enthusiasm for the offensive. If a general uprising occurred before the drive southward of the Fourteenth Army, little more than widespread, devastating retaliation would result. However, by 3 February 1945 when Mountbatten was formally authorized to attempt the capture of Rangoon before the May monsoons, planning in Calcutta of Operation Character was well advanced. Two R.A.F. squadrons, one of Dakotas and the others of Liberators, began to fly in teams and supplies from Jessore and Comilla. By the end of February, sixty teams had been dropped into the mountains. The Karens were then unleashed, with complete success.

The Japanese did not reach Toungoo. The Fourteenth Army pushed southward down the Sittang without major hindrance along its flanks, entering the abandoned Rangoon as the rains began. The loyal Karens, assisted by the Force 136 teams, had contributed so much and had been so consistently loyal that "for a few weeks after the capture of Rangoon, the sun shone on the Karens. For once it shone on S.O.E. too."[5]

During March and April 1945, Archambault, Benoit, Chassé, Fournier, Meunier, Hunter, Taschereau, and Thibeault all parachuted into Burma, wearing the green jungle uniform, high canvas boots, and Australian-type bush hats of Force 136. Most went as part of Operation Character in the Karenni highlands.

All had received more than two months jungle training in Ceylon, learning how to survive and fight in the hot, humid, and dangerous forests. One student who passed through the jungle warfare school recorded his impressions of their training.

> We were given practical experience of the jungle's usefulness to the knowledgeable soldier. By moving and living in it, we came to appreciate its value as cover. Dummy ambushes taught us how to achieve the element of surprise. We went out in small groups, patrolling by day and by night. We were sent out individually without provisions, so that we were compelled to exist on the jungle's natural resources. We learned how to carve out paths where no paths were, to fashion our own snug habitations, to extract drinking water from what looked like black slimy ooze, to eat strange fruits and stranger flesh, to conceal ourselves so effectively that a man might approach to within a yard of our hiding-place without suspecting we were there. In time we could read the jungle like a book. Every tree, every creeper, every leaf had its message. We could interpret jungle sounds; we could identify jungle smells. We developed the quivering awareness of the beasts and reptiles of the jungle, for were we not sharing this tangled luxuriance with wild elephants, rhinoceroses, man-eating tigers, buffaloes, deer, monkeys, cobras, chameleons, and hamadryads twelve to fifteen feet long? We were still afraid in the jungle. The man without fear there is the man without caution and in the jungle it pays to be apprehensive. But our fear was no longer a vague, shapeless, illogical emotion. We had analysed it, reduced it to essentials, put it in its rightful perspective. Each combination of noises conveyed its appropriate message and we reacted accordingly. We knew when to relax and when to be on our guard.[6]

Taschereau was one of the first Canadians to go into Burma as part of Character. Exactly where he went and with whom is unknown. But Taschereau had the singular good fortune to be observed landing by an elderly Karen who emerged from the jungle to inform him that he had served as a batman in the British army during the First World War. After proudly showing to the astonished–and relieved–Canadian his carefully pre-served 1914–18 medals, he led Taschereau along the jungle paths to a remote Italian mission. Its Roman Catholic fathers warmly welcomed him, providing food and shelter and helping him to reconnoitre a nearby rail line and mountain paths used by Japanese.

Many enemy units, now disorganized and ill-equipped, were retreating along narrow, difficult jungle trails, ideal for ambush. In the face of the advancing Fourteenth Army, they sought refuge in attempting to cross the jungle mountains into Thailand. With the help of Karen guerrillas, Taschereau mined mountain routes with 100-metre lengths of cordex, detonating the explosives as convoys of pack animals and porters struggled along the trails and shooting the survivors before disappearing back into the jungle.

It was in such hit-and-run warfare that the one Canadian fatality in Force 136 occurred. With the onset of the monsoon rains, it was doubly important to keep explosives and primer cord dry, ready for use. On 17 May, Archambault, while preparing explosives for sabotage of a railway bridge somewhere in the Karenni highlands, discovered that moisture had begun to damage his limited supplies. In attempting to dry them in his tent, he accidentally detonated them. Mortally wounded, but while still conscious, he had the guerrillas prop him up against a tree so that he could write a final report of his activities against the Japanese. Without immediate medical treatment there was no hope. He died within two days.

Two Canadians, "Rocky" Fournier and Paul-Emile Thibeault, parachuted together to the Karens as Japanese units, withdrawing eastward, were hoping somehow to make their way through the jungle-covered mountains of the hostile Karens to Thailand. The diseased and exhausted troops were frequently reduced to small groups of stragglers attempting to pick their way along jungle tracks. Few made it; they were sitting ducks for ambush and starvation.

From an R.A.F. Liberator based on Calcutta, Fournier and Thibeault dropped on 20 April 1945 to reinforce teams in the "Hyena" area of Burma, led by H. W. Howell, a British lieutenant-colonel, who, during the First World War had been a pilot in a largely Canadian squadron of the Royal Flying Corps. Between the wars, he had been in business in China, but his knowledge of Burma was acquired through service with Orde Wingate's Chindits. The village headman in the area where Fournier and Thibeault initially served fortunately spoke a little English and certainly the Karens were willing students of clandestine warfare, but there was little time to train them before they went into action. The two Canadians were soon assigned to different outstations, living with tribesmen, sharing their repetitive diet of rice, wild pork, and chicken, and enduring the endless rain. Scouts warned of enemy movements, which generally consisted of units on foot, since gasoline and vehicles were scarce and, in any case, roads were few.

The Karens were adept at camouflage in the rain forests, and clever at hiding bamboo spikes along the path at the place of ambush so that the Japanese, diving for cover at the first shots, would impale themselves on them. But they too succumbed to the temptation of all half-trained guerrillas: they lingered at the scene of attack, presenting the Japanese with a fixed target. And it was not always the Japanese who were ambushed; they also sprang surprise attacks. Thibeault later recalled, "I was ambushed by the Japs and had to leave my rucksack behind and a week later one of Howell's men killed the little yellow bastard who looted my sack, and my pips and parachute wings were returned to me."[7]

Various jungle diseases also took their toll. Despite debilitating dysentery, Thibeault continued to instruct the Karens in the use of explosives (cautioning them to make certain that the ubiquitous red ants had not eaten the primer cord), while Fournier provided the essential wireless link with S.O.E.'s Burma section headquarters in Calcutta. Through radio contact with Rangoon (which had been recaptured in May), Howell was able to call up sudden fighter strikes against Japanese columns. He also arranged for drops to supply the Karens with rice, their pay of 30 rupees per month, and such other essentials as medicines and weapons, shirts, and shorts. The incessant dampness caused endless problems for Fournier in maintaining his radio and its generator in working order, but Howell recorded his success in a message to Calcutta. "I should like to call attention to the good services rendered by Lt. Fournier. He is a first-class operator and technician; he is capable of keeping any equipment in order. I consider him one of the best and most useful officers under my command."[8] Howell, a man of great energy and determination, visited as many of his teams as the terrain would allow: Fournier was generally with him while the radios of "Hyena" head-quarters on Mount Plakho were manned by three British N.C.O.s. With an aerial on a long bamboo pole, Fournier kept both Mount Plakho and Calcutta informed of what Howell and he had found.

But Fournier was not content to be only a radio operator; he went into action from one of the out-stations commanded by a young British prewar commercial artist named Wilson. Their part of "Hyena" was particularly dangerous: "Wilson had started off with a few spectacular ambushes along the main track, and then his entire area had been overrun and for a while he [and Fournier] had to go into hiding in the jungle and exist the best [they] could on bamboo shoots and roots."[9]

With the British in Rangoon and the Japanese either dead or struggling across the Karenni hills into Thailand, Thibeault and Fournier, despite their recurrent dysentery and malaria, walked out to the Fourteenth Army at Toungoo, a major town on the Sittang; from there they were flown to hospital in Calcutta.*

Pierre Meunier parachuted into the Pegu Yoma mountains on the opposite side of the Sittang from the Karens. He was assigned to a team led by John Harrington, a regular army major in the Rifle Brigade who had been with S.O.E. in Yugoslavia. The other members were a British sergeant radio operator and two S.O.E.-trained Burmese guerrillas.

Our party of five left the Calcutta airdrome one dark evening and, oddly enough, the entire crew of our aircraft were Canadians.

*Upon recovery, Thibeault volunteered for service in the Netherlands East Indies, but the war ended while he was being given further training in Ceylon. Today Thibeault is a security guard in a department store in his native Montreal. Fournier and his English bride settled in Trois Rivières where he was in the insurance business until his death in 1967 at the age of fifty.

Needless to say we had a good chat about Canada – which eased the tension considerably.

   Heavily loaded with containers of weapons, food and radio sets, we were told to stand in the bomb bay until we were fully airborne. This took about twenty minutes – the longest 20 minutes I've ever spent. The outward journey took about five hours before we baled out. Once landed we looked around for the enemy which, fortunately, were not around. We gathered our containers, contacted some Burmese who were waiting for us with a party previously parachuted and made our way into the jungle to a safe place where we were to organize, discuss our locations and plan of action. Two days later, an order came from . . . Calcutta telling our group that we were required to operate 150 miles southeast of Tangoo.[10]

This change in orders required the team to leave behind their heavier equipment with the other Force 136 team who had organized their reception. Carrying a minimum of supplies so as to reach their destination as quickly as possible, Harrington, who had travelled extensively in India before the war, had recruited only a few porters for the tiring ascent of the Pegu Yoma, the mountain range astride their route. After nine days in the jungle with little food or water – the monsoon was still two months away and riverbeds were dry and the few wells muddy – the team reached a point twenty-five kilometres from the Rangoon-Mandalay road, near the village of Letpadan (a few score kilometres northwest of Rangoon). Only occasionally had their few army rations been augmented by chicken curry in friendly villages, so it was with great satisfaction that the team received a substantial air drop of arms, ammunition, and food on a nearby rice field. Harrington had radioed Force 136 headquarters the exact location of his team and, two days later, the supplies, including a gasoline- driven, 6-volt battery charger for the team's radio, were dropped from two Dakotas.

With adequate supplies now in hand, Harrington and Meunier, assisted by the two Burmese guerrillas, set about the tasks for which they had been trained. Three weeks after parachuting, Harrington

started to send our guides to recruit Burmese among the hill tribes. In ten days, we had 150 men and a system of intelligence informing us of all enemy movements within a radius of 100 miles. Besides ambushing enemy convoys and patrols, we found large dumps of food and ammunition, the locations of which were wirelessed to base and within a matter of six to eight hours these dumps were bombed by R.A.F. medium bombers. This, I must say, was not an easy task for the pilots as these dumps were concealed in the jungle and they had to drop their loads blind, relying entirely on our map references and the assurance that mobile A/A could not fire at them. During my stay behind the lines, we had approximately twelve air strikes and not one missed its target.[11]

After two months of successful harassment of the enemy and with the rapid approach of the Fourteenth Army, Harrington decided to attack the small Japanese garrison in Letpadan. Meunier was to lead their best one hundred men on the village while he and the radio operator brought up supplies in the familiar bullock carts. Meunier divided his men, armed with automatic weapons, into small groups in order to avoid any major losses if enemy patrols were encountered during their advance. Halting his guerrillas a mile from Letpadan, he and one of the British-trained Burmese approached sufficiently close to the village to see Japanese soldiers destroying its small rice mill and gathering rice in final preparation for their withdrawal. Meunier decided upon an immediate attack, but it took him two hours across open fields (where few ditches offered shelter from enemy observation) to regain the safety of his guerrillas' positions. By then, the guerrillas had confirmation from villagers that the Japanese garrison, being uncertain of how close the Fourteenth Army actually was, had begun to withdraw toward Rangoon, using the sole remaining locomotive on the rail line running through the village. The withdrawal might be accelerated if the Japanese could be induced to believe that the guerrillas were in fact advance units of the British army. Before forming ninety of his men into a column to march to Letpadan, Meunier sent the other ten to cut the rail line about fifteen kilometres to the south, ensuring that the enemy retreat would be blocked.

Meunier's *ruse de guerre* of marching on the village in column order was entirely successful. The garrison hurriedly departed, leaving the village to the guerrillas without firing a shot. Although the precious rice stores were in flames, there was no other damage and Harrington was able to bring in the heavy supplies without hindrance. During the next days, however, enemy patrols remained in the vicinity and in several small clashes with them, Harrington's guerrillas killed a number of Japanese, including the officer commanding the Tharrawaddy district.

Harrington's British radio operator having become seriously ill with malaria, contact with Calcutta was lost. To re-establish contact, Meunier travelled northward with a few guerrillas for two days until he encountered British tanks supporting a Gurkha regiment. For a few weeks, Harrington and Meunier acted as advisers and intelligence officers and briefly as civil administrators for an Indian division, as it moved southward past Letpadan during the final drive on Rangoon. With some difficulty they repossessed the small arms which they had distributed (the communists of the Burmese Defence Army attempting to retain theirs for postwar purposes), paid off loyal tribesmen, and moved southward to Rangoon where they arrived in early May to be flown back to Calcutta.

Perhaps the most unusual of S.O.E. volunteers from Canada who served in Asia was Cyril Carlton Mohammed Dolly. His parents were Indian Moslems, from the Assam border region, who had emigrated to Trinidad, where Dolly was born. From 1934 to 1937 he had studied natural sciences at New York University before completing his B.Sc. at McGill in 1942. The son of a physician, he intended to study medicine at McGill University, but as a member of the McGill Canadian Officers' Training Corps, he was called for active service and commissioned in the Royal Canadian Army Medical Corps. While serving in England in 1944, the fact that Dolly spoke Urdu, Hindustani, Punjabi, and Arabic became known to C.M.H.Q. After determining his willingness to volunteer for "special duty," Canadian headquarters passed him on to S.O.E. which promptly flew him to Bombay for training in New Delhi and Ceylon. Little time was lost in training, however, as Dolly and Peter Goss, a British officer, parachuted into Burma in March to the Shan State, north of Shwebo. They were to report by radio to Calcutta on the movements of the Japanese Fifteenth Army and of the remnants of the Japanese-sponsored Indian National Army, observing especially if they showed any sign of moving westward to launch a flank attack on the Fourteenth Army as it advanced southward. Dolly liked Goss, but was pleased to see him depart on his separate assignment: "Let's face it, it would have been exceedingly difficult to get much done with someone of such a light complexion."[12]

Disguised as an Indian coolie, Dolly moved about freely, driving bullock carts – even occasionally for the Japanese army – from late March until August. In gathering intelligence, he had the help of local guerrillas, including members of the communist-dominated Burmese National Army, but generally he preferred the greater security of working alone. Even then, however, subterfuge was difficult: the Japanese had informants in many villages who reported on the presence of strangers. Dolly kept moving, spending only a few days or weeks in any one place. Once he was staying in a sort of cave village in the Shan hills when the Japanese, tipped off by collaborators, became suspicious of him. Two officers, disguised as Buddhist priests, set out to kill him. Fortunately for Dolly, the concealed weapons under their saffron robes made such a noise as they moved toward his cave that he was alerted and managed to escape.

Despite the Japanese surveillance, Dolly succeeded in his mission; he reported to Calcutta on the average of once every three days, relaying intelligence for the advancing Fourteenth Army. He did even more: he helped to sabotage Japanese rice stores and blow up wireless installations.*

---

*Following his return to Canada in 1946, Dolly moved back to New York City where he became a U.S. citizen and is employed as a chemist.

Little information remains of Ben Hunter's service in Burma. With a British Captain Wakefield, he parachuted in March 1945 into the Shan State near Mong Nai. Following two days' briefing at the area headquarters of a Lieutenant-Colonel Crosby, Hunter and Wakefield departed for their respective assignments among the hill tribesmen. Hunter was apparently highly successful in leading his team of Shan tribesmen and former jemadars and subadars of the Burma Rifles. His citation for the Military Cross records that "in April when on patrol with four sections he so successfully controlled his levies when they were attacked by a force of eighty Japanese that he not only extricated his men without loss but killed ten and wounded several."*

Unlike the other Canadians who went into the seclusion of mountain ranges, Chassé parachuted into the flatlands of the Irrawaddy delta near Bassein (a major town due west of Rangoon). With him were a British officer and two radio operators. The Fourteenth Army, having captured Mandalay at the end of March 1945, was now driving southward down the Irrawaddy, "taking all risks" as Mountbatten had ordered, to be in Rangoon when the monsoons broke in May. Discussions had been continuing between the Burmese National Army (formerly and paradoxically, the Japanese-sponsored Burmese Defence Army) about rising in open revolt to co-operate with the British advance down the Sittang valley and with Operation "Dracula," the seaborne assault on Rangoon planned for 2 May. The B.N.A. duly rose against the Japanese on 28 March. It was accordingly to a reception committee of the B.N.A. that Chassé's team parachuted in early April.

*I can learn no more about Hunter's service and I have been unable to locate him. About Benoit's work in Burma I know even less. He parachuted into the Shan State on 18 April 1945 and on 16 May returned to Calcutta. No records are available in London or Ottawa about his month in Burma, and I have been unable to trace either his widow or his four children.

The delta of the Irrawaddy is a flat fan of rivers and slow-moving streams. Upon landing, the guerrillas quickly placed Chassé and his British second-in-command and their radio operators in the bottom of sampans, stinking of fish but out of sight of Japanese or informers, and ferried them to their camp. Chassé's orders were to transmit intelligence about the defences of Rangoon and to carry out, with the B.N.A., sabotage of Japanese installations and communications as the Fourteenth Army and the amphibious fleet approached. However, by the time that Chassé's team and its equipment had been moved eastward from Bassein nearer to Rangoon, the British were already at Pegu, only a few score kilometres north of Rangoon. On the same day, 2 May, the seaborne Operation Dracula was launched against the city. Foot and Langley in their history of M.I.9 provide a graphic description of what happened next:

> Early on 2 May 1945 a Mosquito flew over Rangoon, high up, to make a final photographic check of the state of the defences; "Dracula," a large combined operation, was about to engulf the city. There was no anti-aircraft fire, so the pilot made a second run from a much lower level. Something out of the usual caught his observer's eye; they flew lower still. They read in large letters on the roof of the jail the clear if inelegant message EXTRACT DIGIT JAPS GONE. Emboldened, they landed on the deserted airfield and went into town, to find several prisoners just capable of walking who told them that the garrison had pulled out a few days earlier, taking all the fit prisoners with it. "'Dracula's" covering fire plan was thereupon cancelled, and the survivors in the jail could at least feel that they had saved their countries a large expenditure in ammunition.[13]

In the tropical rains several days later, Chassé and his team entered the liberated capital of Burma, their clandestine work having been overtaken by the sudden Japanese withdrawal. Within a few days, an R.A.F. Liberator flew the team back to Calcutta where possibilities of additional assignments – this time in Malaya – awaited both Chassé and Benoit.

16

Malaya

Following the British surrender of Singapore to the Japanese on "Black Sunday," 15 February 1942, the first substantial contact in more than a year between Malaya and the British in India was made by John Davis. A former Malayan police officer who had successfully sailed a small vessel to Ceylon following the capture of Singapore, Davis had volunteered to return to Malaya, was surreptitiously landed with five Malayan Chinese on a secluded beach by a Royal Netherlands Navy submarine in May 1943, and picked up a month later. His report of an active Chinese underground operating in the Malayan jungles was encouraging, even if the guerrillas were clearly communist-dominated. However, contact with them remained sparse and spasmodic. The Chinese-speaking Davis accordingly returned to Malaya in late July 1943. During the last days of the year, he succeeded in concluding a formal agreement with the Communist Party, placing its Malayan Peoples' Anti-Japanese Army (M.P.A.J.A.) under the general operational orders of Mountbatten's Southeast Asia Command in return for British instructors with arms, explosives, money, medicines, and other supplies.

One problem with this agreement – unwelcome to the British

Colonial Office because it was with communists presumably as committed to the expulsion of the British as of the Japanese – was that knowledge of it reached S.O.E. only in February 1945 when reliable wireless communication with Davis was finally established. As in the earlier cases of Yugoslavia, Albania, Greece, and Burma, the decision was taken to drop arms and instructors to the communist guerrillas as an expression of the priority given to the need to defeat the common enemy. As a result of a further agreement in March 1945, over one hundred Force 136 officers were sent into Malaya in June. On the basis of the information which they radioed back, Mountbatten authorized the drops of an additional two hundred and fifty men into the mountains and jungles during the few months remaining before Operation Zipper, the great amphibious landings planned by the British for early September to drive the Japanese from Malaya.

Among the units assigned to strengthen the guerrillas were ex-officers of the Malayan police, former civil servants and planters, several British S.O.E. veterans from Europe, a sprinkling of Australians, and an unlikely contingent of Canadians, including three of the French-Canadians with Force 136 – Chassé, Caza, and Benoit – and ten Chinese-Canadian sergeants who had joined the army a year earlier.* Their mandate was, broadly, to train the M.P.A.J.A. to disrupt enemy communications, ambush his troops, and collect information of value to Southeast Asia Command. The distances from their home base was vast, but long-range Liberators were available in growing numbers and, fortunately, few Japanese fighters were still flying. Air supply had accordingly become both feasible and frequent. Once Rangoon had fallen, and the R.A.F. had transferred its long-range supply squadrons from Calcutta to Colombo to escape the worst of the monsoon, "the air effort became majestic. Japanese opposition was so slight that all sorties, except the very southerly ones in the Singapore area, were coolly done by day. By the time the

---

*Meunier also served in Malaya, landing with an Indian division in Operation Zipper, but since his service there was after the Japanese surrender, it falls outside the ambit of this book.

Japanese handed over their swords, a very large force had been built up [by S.O.E. in Malaya], well armed and well trained."[1]

The S.O.E. teams were dropped to the M.P.A.J.A. which was divided into eight "regiments," two each in Pahang and Johore and one for each of the other four Malay states. Each M.P.A.J.A. regiment was in turn divided into five patrols. Generally, a Force 136 lieutenant-colonel acted as "group liaison officer" to each regiment and a team led by a major was assigned to each patrol. Their roles were somewhat similar to those of S.O.E. officers sent into France in 1944: the guerrillas were to be assigned targets, trained in their destruction, and then restrained from attacking until the landings of Zipper along the Johore coast.

The Japanese capitulation following the nuclear devastation of Hiroshima and Nagasaki in early August altered all such plans. No longer would ambush and sabotage be the task of Force 136 teams; now they were to emerge from the jungle to accept the surrender of Japanese units and to employ them in ensuring civil order, pending the eventual restoration of civil government. In Malaya, as elsewhere in southeast Asia, skirmishes persisted for weeks after the capitulation, as sporadic fighting continued between the guerrillas and the Japanese until the arrival in force of the British and Indian army divisions of Zipper. Among Japanese units prepared to surrender, there was a marked preference to trust themselves to Force 136 rather than to M.P.A.J.A. For more than two months in some areas of Malaya, all the tact and courage – and frequently bluff – of S.O.E. officers were required to gather in Japanese units for repatriation. Concurrently, the M.P.A.J.A. had somehow to be disbanded.

Although Singapore was reoccupied by the British on 9 September 1945, more than three years after they had surrendered it to the Japanese, it was at least a month before British military administration had spread throughout most of Malaya. During the autumn of 1945, the Moscow-supported M.P.A.J.A. were in virtual control of many areas, seeking to give the impression locally that it was their efforts – and not the atomic bomb or Operation Zipper – which had brought about the expulsion of the Japanese invader. This exacerbated the already tense relations between Malays and Chinese. The fear spread among the Malays that the Chinese guerrillas were moving into the political vacuum to such a degree that postwar Malaya would be dominated by its Chinese minority. Racial as well as political clashes occurred, leaving each community yet more suspicious of the other.

During the autumn of 1945, the situation throughout much of Malaya remained tense and uncertain as Japanese forces were concentrated for repatriation, guerrilla units disbanded, and civil order gradually restored. For S.O.E. teams, Malaya remained a dangerous, alien, and highly volatile place as they turned from making war to keeping the peace.

The challenge facing the few officers of Force 136 scattered throughout Malaya was formidable: how to disarm both the Japanese and the communist M.P.A.J.A. while re-asserting British authority over Malaya, pending the arrival of Zipper. The Malayan police could not hope to control the M.P.A.J.A. since they, having continued to function under the Japanese, were now demoralized and disorganized. In any case, they were many fewer in number. Further, a minimum degree of co-operation with the M.P.A.J.A. would be essential if civil order was to be maintained. During the early autumn of 1945, that co-operation was grudgingly secured by paying the M.P.A.J.A. as if it were a regular Malayan army. A bounty was offered to all those turning in weapons upon being demobilized. With the growing number of British and Indian army units in Malaya, the Communist Party eventually agreed that the M.P.A.J.A. should be disbanded at a series of ceremonial parades during December. Although over six thousand guerrillas handed in a weapon of one sort or another and received in turn a bounty, large numbers of British or Japanese weapons remained unaccounted for. They were to be taken up again in the 1948 uprising intended to drive the British from Malaya.

In addition to dealing with fanatical Japanese on the one hand and the recalcitrant M.P.A.J.A. on the other, a third task confronted several teams: the succour of Allied prisoners of war, many of whom were suffering acutely from disease and malnutrition following three and a half years of imprisonment. By August 1945 only limited planning had been completed by Southeast Asia Command about what should be done if Japanese resistance suddenly collapsed, the general assumption being that the war would continue through 1946 into 1947. In the wake of the Japanese capitulation, what little planning could be hurriedly done by a special section of Southeast Asia Command, the Relief of Allied Prisoners of War and Internees, was predicated on the assumption that Force 136 parties would be able to move at once to the nearest camps, radio back priority needs, and arrange for the dropping of food and medicines. On 28 August 1945, this plan was formally approved. During the following fortnight almost one thousand tons of supplies and one hundred and twenty physicians and other relief workers were flown to all known camps.

This was the changeable, unorthodox war to which Benoit, Caza, and Chassé parachuted – and the first taste of war which ten Chinese-Canadians experienced.

We have already noted the persistent efforts of young Chinese-Canadians to volunteer for the Canadian army and how that persistence was finally rewarded late in 1944. By the first months of 1945, there were several hundred Chinese-Canadian volunteers undergoing basic training, primarily at Chilliwack, British Columbia; Red Deer and Wetaskiwin, Alberta; and Maple Creek and Swift Current, Saskatchewan. When S.O.E. finally received the agreement of the Canadian government to their recruitment, Legg and two Chinese-Canadian sergeants from Vancouver began to interview possible volunteers. In their camps, the Chinese-Canadians assembled to hear the two sergeants describe the dangerous nature of "special duty." More than one hundred promptly volunteered, eventually to find themselves on the *Ile de France, Aquitania,* and *Nieuwe Amsterdam* in a January Atlantic convoy. A few weeks' training in southern England preceded three weeks on a trooper bound for Bombay, via Suez.* In India, rudimentary rail cars, with cockroaches "as big as your thumb" crawling about the woodwork, carried them to the S.O.E. Eastern Warfare School above Poona.†

During the following months, everything in India either fascinated or repelled the Chinese-Canadians: the hilarious tonga rides in Bombay; the fiery curries and the mangoes at almost every meal. At Poona some evaluation and sorting out was done; a few volunteers were found unsatisfactory for a variety of reasons, while others were assigned to psychological warfare or other non-combatant duties in India. Bing Lee and Bill Lee, who showed special aptitude for radio work, were trained at the wireless school at Meerut, while the remainder were given instruction in languages, sabotage, and small arms at Poona.

All underwent parachute training at Jessore, near Calcutta. There the Chinese-Canadians were astonished to meet more Canadians. A memorable party followed with the three French-Canadian volunteers for Malaya who, as we shall see, were on a brief refresher course. Jungle warfare, map-reading, demolition, small arms, and other courses were given at Horana near Colombo, Ceylon, where the final evaluation of all the volunteers was made.

Several of the Chinese-Canadians served in the state of Selangor (which includes Kuala Lumpur, the capital of today's Malaysia). One of the first into Selangor was Henry Fung of Vancouver, who parachuted from an R.A.F. Liberator on 22 June 1945. His team was headed by Ian Macdonald, a tall, thin, bespectacled

---

*Bing Lee and Bill Lee flew from Weymouth, England, to India in a Sunderland flying boat.
†The school had opened in March 1943; it closed in September 1945.

major, a prewar planter who spoke Malay. Mike Levy, his second-in-command, was a young, dark-haired captain who had been trained and commissioned in India after escaping overland from Shanghai, where his Jewish family had been interned after taking refuge from Nazi Germany. They went as one of four patrol liaison teams to serve under one of the most intrepid of S.O.E. colonels in Malaya, "Duggie" Broadhurst, an ex-Malay policeman who had escaped to Australia when Singapore fell. Broadhurst had spent the intervening years on secret missions in Portuguese Timor, Borneo, and the Philippines. Now he was back in Malaya as one of the first to return following the establishment of John Davis' radio contact with Force 136 headquarters.

Macdonald's team was dropped to an M.P.A.J.A. reception committee north of Kuala Lumpur. With its help, they made their way for four days and five nights through the hot, humid jungle to a camp near the town of Kajang, south of Kuala Lumpur. Once they had established their small camp near the guerrilla regiment, air drops provided badly needed arms, food, clothing, and medicines both for them and for the guerrillas (all of whom seemed very young to Fung, who was only nineteen himself). The team assisted in blowing up a railway bridge and tracks, destroying telephone lines and harassing Japanese road convoys, but left the assassination of collaborators to the guerrillas. Macdonald, who knew the area well from his prewar work as a rubber planter, also undertook a very different task: he radioed back, as ordered, reports on the state of local rubber plantations and nearby tin mines. The British had their eye on the availability of any scarce raw material which might help to speed their own postwar recovery.

With the formal Japanese surrender in early September, Macdonald's team cautiously entered Kajang to take over control from the local Japanese command (in the house of a senior Japanese officer, Macdonald was somewhat disconcerted to find his prewar Eurasian common-law wife expecting a child by the Japanese colonel). The situation in Kajang was anything but certain. The Japanese garrison understandably refused to surrender its arms until the British arrived in force; the guerrillas attempted to assert their authority, and a gang of bandits was a frequent problem until the arrival of an Indian Army detachment.

The experience of Macdonald's team during the uncertain weeks that followed the Japanese surrender were typical of those of the Force 136 teams scattered throughout Malaya. The co-operation of the Japanese was uneven and the attitude of the M.P.A.J.A. unpredictable, although they remained largely in their camps, understandably reluctant to intervene in what was no longer their concern. For the next few weeks, the S.O.E. team had its hands full, attempting to prevent the beating – or worse – of collaborators. Once the British forces arrived in the area of Kajang, Henry Fung moved with Macdonald's team into Kuala Lumpur where several of the other Chinese-Canadians had already congregated.*

Two of the other Chinese-Canadians with whom Fung was re-united in Kuala Lumpur had also served in Selangor: Bing Lee and Ted Wong of Vancouver. They had parachuted from a Liberator in July with Alistair Morrison (a Gurkha captain and son of the famed London *Times* correspondent, "Peking" Morrison and later himself an eminent journalist) and two British radio operators. They had also operated under Broadhurst ("always cool and calm" in Bing's recollection) who had parachuted in early May into Selangor where later he was joined by John Davis.

In the jungles, Bing Lee and Ted Wong worked with M.P.A.J.A. patrols in shooting up truck convoys and trains "and then beating it." Sacks of rice and Australian canned food were dropped to them, but the meat of monkey and wild boar relieved the increasing boredom of their rations. It was during this period that Bing Lee contracted malaria, which he suffered from intermittently until after his return to India in December.

---

*Fung returned with the other volunteers to India and to Britain, but jaundice and malaria kept him in a hospital near London for a month. He sailed for Canada later than the others on the *Lady Nelson*, a C.N.R. Caribbean liner converted to a hospital ship.

At first, little changed in Selangor as the news of the Japanese surrender spread. Despite the emperor's announcement, there was widespread uncertainty about whether the Japanese would continue fighting; one encouraging sign was that local units seemed to lose interest in the movements of guerrillas. As August passed into September, a sort of truce between the Japanese and the M.P.A.J.A. evolved in and around Seremban. The Japanese garrison showed no sign of surrendering, but they quietly relinquished control of the local police station and hospital to Morrison's team, now to his pleasure reinforced by a detachment of twenty-five Gurkhas. With the situation in Seremban more or less stable, Broadhurst decided to risk entering Kuala Lumpur itself. In a Japanese staff car borrowed in Serandah, he and Bing Lee drove into the future capital of Malaysia. After a night under surveillance in what was called a hotel, they were received by the officer commanding Kuala Lumpur, who politely told them that he had ordered his troops to remain where they were until they could turn control of the city over to British from Operation Zipper. (During the discussions, Broadhurst and Lee were disconcerted to see on the wall a map pinpointing accurately every one of the M.P.A.J.A.'s – and their – secret camps.)

Broadhurst's team and a few Gurkhas nevertheless moved into Kuala Lumpur, along with M.P.A.J.A. patrols which took up residence in the grandstand of the prewar race track. Broadhurst requisitioned the nearby large house of a Chinese millionaire physician, which was not only comfortable but also, since it overlooked the racetrack, allowed him to keep a wary eye on the M.P.A.J.A. An uneasy truce with the Japanese followed until the arrival of the British forces in mid-September, after Mountbatten's formal acceptance of the Japanese surrender in Singapore on 12 September. Pending their arrival, Broadhurst's team was kept busy discouraging the M.P.A.J.A. from summarily punishing real or imagined collaborators and encouraging them to prevent looting.

From the physician's house, Bing Lee helped to encode messages to Ceylon and later Singapore about the situation in Selangor. He joined also in supervising work parties of twenty or so Japanese, under a guerrilla guard, in cleaning up the wartime detritus and in maintaining peace between the Malays and Chinese in the city. Initial help was provided to Australian prisoners of war in the area, but the team's principal task remained to assist in keeping public order.

Despite having had severe malaria while training in Ceylon, Bob Lew, born in Nipissing, Ontario, parachuted on a July night onto a dry riverbed about forty kilometres north of Kuala Lumpur. He jumped with Robert Hine, a small, wiry Australian major on his second mission to Malaya, and Hugh Fraser, a British captain who, like Hine, had learned Malay as a prewar planter. A British sergeant radio operator accompanied them, as did a tracker dog which, unfortunately, was killed upon landing. During the seemingly endless flight from Ceylon, Lew was delighted to be able to chat with the pilot, who was from Vancouver.

The guerrilla reception committee collected their radio and other parachuted equipment and then led them for the next five days through the dense jungle to a camp near Serandah. There the team trained the guerrillas in the small arms and explosives dropped to them, although the first drop was missed when the guerrillas suddenly had to decamp at the approach of a sizeable Japanese patrol. But the movement was not all in one direction: Lew risked a visit to Japanese-occupied Serandah, to collect information about the garrison there. Dressed in a borrowed shirt and trousers, Lew went with several guerrillas so as to be able to report to Ceylon on the state of the local railyard and the size and appearance of the Japanese units. His training in Ceylon had included how to walk like a Chinese of Malaya rather than as a Canadian; the ruse worked, and the information would have been highly useful if the Japanese had not suddenly capitulated.

When Hine learned that the officer commanding the Japanese troops in Serandah wanted to surrender to him rather than the M.P.A.J.A., he found a truck and had himself and Lew driven into the town where they shared the austere rations – mainly rice and tapioca root – of the Japanese commandant. Again on a wall was a map pinpointing the guerrillas' camps. During the next few days in Serandah, where the Japanese reluctantly agreed to keep order until the arrival of the British forces, Lew and the others used their own meagre medical supplies to treat the endemic skin ulcers of the under-nourished Malays. Later, Lew joined several other Chinese-Canadians at the home of the physician in nearby Kuala Lumpur, supervising work parties of Japanese.

George Chin, another Chinese-Canadian who went to Kuala Lumpur as the war was ending, was part of a liaison mission led by a British Major Maxwell whose deputy was an S.O.E. veteran from Europe. The usual British sergeant radio operator completed the team. What was unusual about Maxwell's team was that it also included two Nationalist Chinese radio operators. Chin was never certain why they had been sent, but in any event, they did not last long. Once the team had established itself near a guerrilla camp, the Nationalist Chinese had been sent up a hill with their radio to attempt to contact Ceylon. There they were murdered by communist guerrillas. All Force 136 volunteers in Malaya had been cautioned before leaving Ceylon to keep well out of any political discussions or machinations; after the murder of the two Nationalist Chinese, Maxwell again warned the remaining members of his team, "Keep your bloody mouth shut or you won't be alive! And don't be too tough with the guerrillas."[2]

Chin, a demolitions instructor, found his guerrilla trainees generally inflexible and unimaginative; he was not impressed. Nevertheless, using explosives from several air drops, Maxwell's team and the guerrillas prepared an ambush for a Japanese truck convoy. They laid explosives, to be triggered by a wire, across a road and drove bamboo spikes into the verges of the road to keep the Japanese exposed. Despite repeated admonitions to the guerrillas hidden in the roadside bush "to fire three minutes and then get the hell out of there," the guerrillas nevertheless remained in place, firing at the Japanese long beyond the agreed three minutes. The Japanese troops quickly recovered from their surprise. The result of their superior discipline was soon evident; two of the guerrillas were killed and several wounded.

Once the Japanese had capitulated, Maxwell's team increased their para-medical activities. In the jungle, they had treated guerrillas for beri-beri and skin ulcers. Now they extended their healing efforts into the nearby town of Kuala Kubu Bahru. There the Japanese garrison was put to work cleaning up the town, before Chin joined his fellow Chinese-Canadians in the relative luxury of the racetrack villa at Kuala Lumpur.

One of the last of the Chinese-Canadians into Malaya with Force 136 – and the last out – was the large, irrepressibly cheerful Victor Louie of Vancouver. As a boy, he had been taken to south China for twelve years by his merchant father. Consequently, when Louie returned to Vancouver as a young man, he spoke fluent Cantonese, and had to relearn English.

The twenty-eight-year-old Victor Louie had been trained with the main body of Chinese-Canadians which included his cousin Ernie, but he was not dropped into Malaya until the first week of September, the week before the formal Japanese surrender. Originally intended to support Zipper, the small group with which Louie served was directed to the dangerous and frequently bewildering task of inducing Japanese units to obey the surrender order and to help restore civil government. Led by Allen Shaw, a former Malayan police officer, and consisting of a British captain, a sergeant radio operator, and a Nationalist Chinese sergeant, the team parachuted to a guerrilla camp in the mountainous central region of Selangor, northeast of Kuala Lumpur. Operating in the area of Kuala Pilah and Tampin, the team and the M.P.A.J.A. patrol encountered Japanese units still full of fight, despite disease and isolation. Sometimes alerted by collaborators, even at this late date, the Japanese would fight back fiercely. The guerrillas, themselves in need of food, raided the Japanese camps. On one such raid, Louie was captured and held in a Japanese camp for two days before he managed to escape in clothes smuggled to him by guerrilla supporters.

The effectiveness of the M.P.A.J.A. in its raids was enhanced by the S.O.E. team's instruction in the use of Bren and Sten guns and the much-admired U.S. carbine. Their leaders were supplied with binoculars and .45 revolvers, and supply drops of food, clothing, and medicines were organized, using an S-phone during the final approaches of the drop aircraft. On one such flight came a record of Bing Crosby singing "Don't Fence Me In," which the guerrillas played endlessly on an ancient gramophone, leaving Shaw and his team yearning for the peace of the jungle. Gradually an uneasy truce spread through Selangor, allowing Shaw and Louie to travel southward by car to the adjoining state of Malacca to attempt to induce the Japanese commander there to surrender. Assistance to the returning civil authority in and around Kuala Lumpur, particularly the disbanding of the 1st M.P.A.J.A. Regiment, kept Shaw's team in Malaya until early 1946.

Charley Chung and Harry Ho, both of Vancouver, parachuted into the torrid jungles with Pierre Chassé, who, upon his return from Rangoon in May, had volunteered for a third mission with S.O.E., this time to head a liaison team with an M.P.A.J.A. patrol. His team consisted of Derek Burr of the Royal Leicestershire Regiment, a British radio operator, and the two Canadian sergeant-interpreters. In a second Liberator flew another S.O.E. team led by Roger Landes, Al Sirois' erstwhile parachute companion and Pierre Meunier's circuit chief in Bordeaux.

After a two-thousand-kilometre flight from Ceylon, the two teams parachuted on 14 July 1945 near Alor Setar, the small capital of the northern state of Kedah. In their jungle green uniforms, they and all their equipment were dropped on a dry riverbed. Or at least that was the plan; in the event, Burr was caught at the top of a tall tree for almost eight hours. Working feverishly throughout the night and into the next day to free him and his parachute, which was all too visible from the air,* the two teams and their M.P.A.J.A. reception committee were finally able to lower Burr to the ground, using several of the 12-metre lengths of rope all parachutists carried for just such emergencies. Chassé's team, parting with Landes', began the long, difficult trek northward through the jungles of Kedah toward their final destination, the small sultanate of Perlis on the border of Thailand. Their orders were to carry out sabotage and collect intelligence in the sultanate, situated on that narrow point of the peninsula where all traffic between Thailand and Malaya must pass.

Rivers are the obvious way to move through jungle, but the Japanese and their collaborators remained more or less in control of them. Through the hot, humid jungle, Chassé's team could make no more than about ten kilometres a day (even with their supplies carried by Chinese porters who built them crude shelters each evening). After a fortnight of toil, weariness, and tension, the team finally reached Perlis and their principal target: the roads connecting Malaya with Thailand. With Japanese patrols searching for them, the team kept on the move through Perlis and northern Kedah, enduring the dysentery, sores, and monsoon rains that plague Europeans who attempt to live in the jungle, all the while ambushing convoys and sabotaging bridges.

For more than a month, Chassé's team evaded Japanese patrols, existing in part upon rations from occasional air drops. With the Japanese capitulation in late August, Chassé and his six haggard companions cautiously emerged from the jungle. Upon the formal Japanese surrender in early September, Calcutta

---

*Fortunately for the two teams, Japanese air surveillance was severely limited by petrol shortages which had grounded many of the remaining Japanese aircraft.

ordered Chassé to Kangar, the small capital of Perlis, to assume responsibility for local government until the prewar regime could be restored–a formidable task for a young officer with only a four-man team to support him. Before that, however, Chassé returned southward to be present, with Roger Landes, at the surrender of the Japanese around Sungei Patani in southern Kedah (Chassé must be the only Canadian officer who was present at the surrenders of both a German and a Japanese general).

Back in Perlis, however, pending the arrival of a promised Gurkha detachment, the only force capable of keeping civil order in the town was, ironically, Chassé's recent enemy. With the Japanese general commanding the area, Chassé successfully negotiated the surrender of his troops, but at the same time borrowing some to act as sentries and police during the food shortages and unrest which attended the end of the fighting.*

Chassé's second problem was one with which the surrendered Japanese could hardly be expected to help: in the jungles of Perlis and Kedah, fanatical Japanese continued to refuse to believe that their beloved homeland could have capitulated, despite frequent broadcasts in Japanese from Calcutta repeating their emperor's order to lay down their arms. Gradually some recognized the hopelessness of their situation and came out of the jungle; others died there of disease or, later, at the hands of Gurkha patrols.

Two other immediate problems confronted Chassé: Thai marauders and how to restore the rajah of Perlis to his throne. The young Syed Putra, the heir to the throne, had escaped across the border into Thailand following the Japanese occupation. There he spent the latter part of the war as a bullock-cart driver. Upon orders from headquarters, Chassé despatched Burr to Bangkok to find him, while he began to clear Kangar and eventually Perlis of those Thais (including a general) who, being collaborators with the Japanese, had been given administrative and commercial opportunities in the two border states.

Burr was successful in his bizarre mission to Bangkok, return-ing to Kangar with an amiable, slightly bewildered young man

*Chassé obtained from General Tomenaga a personal flag which is now in the regimental museum of the Royal 22nd Regiment at Quebec City.

who was promptly transformed from bullock-cart driver to rajah.* Now there was a tangible focus for the full restoration of civil government. From the British residency in Kangar (an admirable house except for the rats) and aided by infusions of Straits dollars flown in from Calcutta, Chassé and Burr set about advising the rajah on civil government programs (in this role Burr was especially enthusiastic, being a confirmed Fabian). They were assisted by a British army paymaster who acted as a sort of minister of finance. With the assistance of a small detachment of Gurkhas, Japanese were sent home and a number of disgruntled Chinese communist guerrillas were warned to remain across the border in Thailand. Civil administration was gradually restored.

Chassé, a professional officer whose ambition was to emulate both his father and brother by commanding the Royal 22nd Regiment, decided by October that it was time to return to more orthodox soldiering.† Surprisingly, he was replaced at the residency in Kangar by another Canadian, Colin Munro of Montreal. A former member of the McGill University Canadian Officer's Training Corps, Munro was an artillery officer who had already seen considerable fighting in Normandy, Belgium, and the Netherlands.

While artillery-spotting one night in Normandy, Munro had taken a wrong turning and briefly found himself behind German lines. He made his unexpected nocturnal visit to the enemy a useful one, radioing back valuable tactical information. Canadian Field Security noted his exploit, but in any event Munro's quick intelligence, wireless skills, and good knowledge of French would have made him a possible candidate for S.O.E. In November 1944, while on the Maas River in the Netherlands, Munro was inexplicably ordered to report to the War Office in

---

*In 1961 the rajah became the king of Malaysia for a period of five years in accordance with the Malaysian constitution which rotates the monarchy among the traditional heads of the various states.

†Eventually Chassé realized his ambition. Following the completion of his service in Perlis, Chassé drove to Singapore, flew to Ceylon, and sailed from Madras for Britain. As a retired colonel, he has now made reality of his disguise in occupied France by becoming an art dealer.

London, which in turn sent him to an interview at the Victoria Hotel, just off Trafalgar Square. There the pipe- smoking Munro, measured, courteous, and even courtly, evidently made a good impression on his S.O.E. interviewers.

Yet for sometime thereafter nothing happened. Having volunteered in December 1944 for a secret mission about which he was told nothing further, Munro remained for the next six months at the School of Artillery in Seaford, Sussex. Suddenly in June 1945 he was ordered to London. The war with Germany had been over for more than a month, but during interviews at the War Office Munro confirmed that he was willing to volunteer for a minimum of one year's service in Asia, despite the impending arrival in London of his Canadian fiancée. Without further training, special briefings, or even detailed instructions, Munro was flown across the Middle East to Colombo. At nearby Horana, he was given accelerated jungle training and parachute instruction at the R.A.F. station at Jessore, north of Calcutta. Munro was originally destined for French Indochina, along with the Canadian S.O.E. veterans and several Free French officers with whom they trained at Horana; but by the time Munro reached Ceylon, it had become abundantly evident that to drop teams into Indochina was almost tantamount to sending them to their death. Bali, in the Netherlands East Indies—which the British had undertaken to occupy pending the return of the Dutch—was briefly and tantalizingly substituted before Munro was finally ordered to Malaya.

In early September, when Munro departed on his new assignment, the war with Japan had already ended. No longer was there a need for surreptitious parachuting: Munro flew into Singapore in a Liberator. In his khaki tropical kit, he made his way alone northward by rail and road to his first assignment in Kedah. During the next month, Munro, with a Gordon Highlander of the same surname who had served with S.O.E. in Albania, kept order in Klang Lama in Kedah, where racial tensions between the Chinese and Malays had been aggravated by food shortages which followed the sudden surrender of the Japanese. Here, as elsewhere in Malaya, S.O.E. officers had to rely upon their erstwhile enemy to provide the necessary guards (and the Japanese proved to be excellent guards) for stores and camps.

In late October 1945, Munro was ordered farther north to Perlis, to replace Chassé as principal adviser to the rajah. In taking over in Kangar, Munro's main tasks were similar to those he had performed in Kedah. Japanese troops had to be repatriated (other than those guarding the precious rice) but there remained renegade and fanatical Japanese in the jungle who continued to refuse to surrender. Gurkhas and Malay police also fought marauders from across the border in Thailand (including Thai pirates whom Munro captured by using ex-guerrillas in sailing tonkins). It was not, however, only the Japanese and Thais who threatened the peaceful restoration of civil government. Perlis was largely peopled by Malays, but the 8th Regiment of the M.P.A.J.A. had operated there along the border with Thailand. Some were loathe to surrender their arms, anticipating the day when they would rise against the British, as they had done against the Japanese.

Munro collected many of their arms by the simple device of inviting a number of ex-guerrillas to a tea party at the residency in Kangar. The Gurkhas not only surrounded its gardens, but put on a chilling

> demonstration charge ... with their kukri [knives] drawn [which] certainly sobered the cocky Chinese. I then took them to a "victory parade" in Alor Star where they found the town surrendered by the 16th Indian Division. For good measure, a flight of Spitfires just happened to swoop low over the parade which ended in the Chinese reluctantly handing me their weapons.[3]

A senior civil servant finally arrived to run the small government office at Kangar. Like Chassé, Munro got along well with the amiable young rajah, informally advising both him and the senior civil servants in a variety of areas, including the distribution of food, until civil order was fully restored.*

---

*With the full restoration of civil administration by December 1945, Munro sailed from Port Swettenham to Madras, the first step of the long return journey to England (where he arrived at the beginning of March 1946). Munro was briefly in the film industry in Canada before rejoining the army in 1948. Following service in Vietnam and Cyprus he retired in 1965 and has since lived part of the year in Ottawa and part in his ancestral homeland of Scotland.

On 5 August 1945, the day before the U.S.A.A.F. obliterated Hiroshima with an atomic bomb, Joe Benoit, the thirty-nine-year-old father of four, led the one all-Canadian team of Force 136 on Operation "Tideway Green" to work with an M.P.A.J.A. patrol in the northern region of Johore. Four months after he had first gone to the Siamese border region of Burma, and following a brief respite and additional jungle training in Ceylon, Benoit parachuted with his fellow-Canadians from a Liberator to a reception committee headed by the British lieutenant-colonel who was the group liaison officer with the South Johore regiment of the M.P.A.J.A.

With Benoit dropped John Elmore Hanna, the son of a Toronto-born mother and an Irish Baptist missionary father, who had spent many years in northern China. There until the age of sixteen, Hanna had learned to speak Mandarin fluently. His parents having both died, Hanna arrived in Canada in 1931. Until he joined the army in February 1941, he was a bookkeeper for, successively, the Dominion Bank, McDonald Currie, and eventually Dome Mines at Tyanite, Ontario. Hanna was tall, well over six feet, but his weak eyesight would be something of a drawback in front lines. He was, intelligent, mild-mannered and, in keeping with his bookkeeper background, meticulous and, as his army reports noted, somewhat pedantic; in short, administrative officer material. After a year as an N.C.O., it was from the School of Canadian Army Administration that in September 1944, when twenty-nine years old, Hanna volunteered to use his knowledge of Chinese on special duty in Asia. The S.O.E. liaison office in New York informed London and New Delhi that Hanna had been strongly recommended by the Canadian army and, late in November 1944, arranged for him to be flown from Montreal to New Delhi to begin seven months of training, concluding in a parachute course at Rawalpindi.

The third Canadian on Tideway Green was a sergeant-interpreter, Ernie Louie, the cousin of Victor Louie. Before parachuting with Benoit and Hanna on 15 August, Louie, who spoke fluent Cantonese and was popular with everyone, had completed his training with the team at Horana. The fourth Canadian was, like Benoit, a veteran of S.O.E. in France: the former journalist Roger Caza of Ottawa. He was dropped by a Liberator two days after the other three, having been delayed by a training accident which had left his ankles swollen to twice their normal size.

On 9 August, two days after Caza's drop, the all-Canadian team was ready to trek through one hundred and twenty kilometres of Malayan jungle to its final destination in northern Johore. The trip was estimated to take three days, but with heavy loads of equipment and a dearth of porters, it took six – three in torrential rain. The team arrived suffering from the sores and leech bites inseparable from jungle treks. Its original instructions had been to collect information about Japanese movements in northern Johore; to instruct and supply local guerrillas; and to attempt to block three major roads when Zipper landings took place. However, during the ten days between the parachuting of the team and its arrival at its assigned territory, the Japanese had surrendered.

Little co-operation could now be expected from the M.P.A.J.A., so Benoit had to use his own team to search for a dropping zone to which additional men and supplies could be parachuted to assist prisoners of war known to be in the area. On 30 August, Tideway Green was reinforced by an Australian captain and corporal. For their reception, Benoit had to send Hanna and Louie to seek a safe landing zone, the Chinese guerrillas being reluctant to carry out any reconnaissance in the face of the mounting hostility of the Malays (who feared postwar domination by Chinese). Benoit later reported that Hanna and Louie had "showed much courage in carrying out their task by setting out alone on unknown jungle trails, marching by compass."[4] With the arrival of the Australians, Benoit's team was ordered on 1 September to move to the town of Batu Pahat, where they arrived two days later. The next day, they reached nine hundred near-starving and diseased prisoners of war in a camp at nearby Kluang. Food and medical drops were organized for them on 12 and 14 September, and arrangements begun to return them home.

Although hostilities had officially ceased, the dangers for Tideway Green were far from over. Its six members faced the same hazards confronting all S.O.E. teams emerging from the jungle. Benoit and his team found Batu Pahat in a state of panic, Malays having allegedly killed two hundred Chinese a few days before the mission's arrival. When Benoit learned of Chinese on the outskirts of the town still being killed and their houses burned, he sought assistance from nearby Singapore where British forces were arriving. A company of Punjabis helped to restore order, but some Japanese troops, so recently the common enemy, had also to be employed in patrolling the area. Between mid-September and 18 October, when Benoit turned over his command to a British officer, Tideway Green was based on Muar, engaged in essentially police work and civil administration.

Benoit, Hanna, Caza, and Louie (who won an enthusiastic commendation from Benoit) completed their Malayan tour on 12 November and returned to Meerut in the case of Louie, and to Colombo in the case of the others, on their way home to Canada.*

All the Chinese-Canadian volunteers, whether in Sarawak or Malaya, had served well. All had gone to war as light-hearted young men, eager to make the best of their assignments. They embarked for their destinations halfway around the world without a care for the morrow. In volunteering for clandestine warfare, the spirit of adventure was as evident in them as it had been in those Canadians who went into occupied Europe. But for the young Chinese-Canadians, their service meant something more. For them, it was also an affirmation of equality. Their parents or even grandparents, as well as themselves, had been second-class Canadians, deprived of the full privileges of citizenship. They were ready, even eager, to fill all the obligations of citizenship so that in return they might receive all those rights which other Canadians took for granted. Sarawak and Malaya were two exotic way-stations on their route to full Canadian equality.

*Most of the Chinese-Canadians embarked in Bombay for England on 8 March 1946 in the *Moreton Bay*, a cargo vessel en route from Australia for Southampton where it arrived on 28 March. They disembarked in Halifax from the *Ile de France* in late April, among the last of the Canadian veterans to return home.

PART THREE

M.I.9

17

Escape and Evasion

As early as the summer of 1940, the first Canadian soldiers and airmen found themselves inadvertently behind enemy lines, either cut off from their retreating units in the case of the army or on the run after having baled out or crash-landed in the case of airmen. Occasionally, especially during the confused months of the *Blitzkrieg* of 1940, some Canadians simply drifted back to England without much assistance or, in a few cases, without much desire to return to the routine of training in southern England. One such soldier, who was with a Canadian unit sent to France in the vain effort to halt the swift German advance, has left a memorable description of his carefree attitude during the summer of 1940.

> We disembarked at Brest. We had all the food supplies, the petrol supplies, all the ammo and it was our job to get it up to the front. So there we were, with the Germans maybe only a hundred miles ahead and the whole of France had collapsed, and we were going on our merry jaunt.
>
> We marshalled in a vineyard and proceeded to get good and gloriously drunk. We got loaded on to a cattle train and were unloaded at a little place called St. Denis, I think about 22 miles

outside Paris. A suburb. All our trucks were there. All lined up. Brand new. Ford trucks. About 150 miles on each. Everything for the division was on them, the works....

We didn't have any orders. We just sat there. This was the time of Dunkirk.

And then they say to get the hell back to Brest. Get back any way you can. That's when we scattered, every truck for itself. So my partner and I headed back and I think the Germans were only a few miles up ahead and these refugees, it was tough going past them. Thousands, and they didn't know where they were going. Where were they going? Where was there to go? It was lucky there was no strafing by the Germans.

To show you how stupid it was, we'd pass British troops going back toward Brest – but we'd also pass British troops moving up to the front! There was no communication. Nobody was directing us....

We followed the road right back to Brest and hung around there a couple of days and still nobody knew what was going on. I remember my buddy and I went in to a little square and bought some wine and bread and we're sitting on the curb and drinking and I said, "Hell, it's a pretty day and look at all the great broads walking around and I like France. I don't want to leave it. Let's stay," and we kind of decide to stay. To hell with going back to England. That's how little we knew about the situation....

Finally somebody must have said we should get the hell out of there and we sailed. Not in a convoy, but by ourselves. We just went. Somebody said go. Landed at Southampton, and that was the end of that jaunt in France.[1]

This was in 1940. During the subsequent five years of war, most Canadians who found themselves inadvertently in enemy-held territory did not view their situation in quite so light-hearted a manner. Those who had been able to evade capture or who, against the most daunting odds, managed to escape from a prisoner-of-war camp, generally had only a single thought in mind: to return to Britain and to resume the fight. It was their duty to do so. But what were they to do, once they were fugitives on the run?

During the latter half of 1940, in London, the Lowlands, and France, a secret network capable of sustaining men on the run slowly emerged, but what was it like to be on the run? What happened when a soldier or airman made his way out of a P.O.W. camp or landed at night from a damaged aircraft, undetected and not seriously injured? Most airmen shot down over occupied Europe would have agreed with Ray Sherk, a Toronto school-teacher who escaped twice while serving with the R.C.A.F.: "When we went into hiding after baling out or a crash-landing... we were more or less just trying to postpone what we considered to be our inevitable capture."[2] Nevertheless, like Sherk, many airmen recalled their M.I.9 briefings which had taught them to get clear at once of the landing area, avoid towns, and seek an isolated farmhouse or church. These first movements in enemy-occupied territory were the crucial ones. "'We did not grasp until it was too late,'" one escaper recalled, "'that the moment we hit German soil was the moment for which we were afterwards to work so sweatily, bitterly and ingeniously, and often with such terrible disappointments, to re-achieve.' In other words very few men grasped that their arrival on enemy soil was really a state of freedom. It was only from behind the barbed wire of compounds that they looked out and planned with such meticulous care and risk the business of getting back to the very point from which they had started."[3]

Cautiously and full of foreboding, the downed airman would make his way to what he hoped would be a sanctuary. Occasionally he would be denied entrance or even betrayed to collaborators or to the occupying forces, but such cases were rare. Much more frequently, the generally bewildered airman would soon be passed to a local priest, schoolteacher, or railway worker, the people most likely to be scouts for somebody in the resistance who in turn might know something of an escape network. There is no record of a priest in occupied Europe ever betraying an evader or escaper. "Failing a priest, the next best hope was a railwayman; not a station-master, who might well have been picked by the occupying régime, but a porter, whom one might hope to intercept on his way home as he came off shift.... Failing a priest or a porter, one could try a schoolteacher; but this was more risky. Teachers were not stupid, but might well be opinionated; or, even worse, sympathetic to the régime."[4]

If the fugitive airman in Europe was fortunate, he soon found himself clothed in whatever civilian garments could be hurriedly collected – or had already been collected – by the network. Before beginning his dangerous journey to Switzerland, Sweden, the Spanish frontier, the Mediterranean or, later, the Brittany coasts, the escaper or evader would generally spend several days in one or more local "safe houses," while the necessary arrangements were made to pass him along the line to a central collection point. While beginning the long journey, guides sometimes learned to their consternation that a few of the Canadians and many of the Americans, unlike R.A.F. airmen, could not ride bicycles. Angus MacLean (a future federal cabinet minister and Premier of Prince Edward Island) after having baled out of his bomber over the Netherlands, was to be taken into Belgium by a Dutch priest to whom he was to be introduced by a young girl in the underground.

> MacLean was to rendezvous with the priest at the railway station, twenty miles away. Jane and he would cover this distance on bicycles, carrying fishing tackle to complete their disguise as an average young couple on an outing. A hitch arose when MacLean confessed that he had never learned to ride a bicycle. The slim, teen-aged girl carried the tall, raw-boned and husky aviator the entire distance on her handlebars. It was twenty miles of sheer mental and physical torment, and, as they wended their way along the back roads in the roundabout route selected to avoid German patrols, the sight of little Jane chauffering the heavily-built flier drew questioning looks and grins from passers-by.[5]

The guides for the fugitives during their rail journeys across occupied France were frequently Frenchmen and women, but among the most successful were young Belgians (generally girls) who earned for themselves an unparalleled record for bravery in this novel form of underground warfare. The guides would make their hazardous trips by always-crowded trains to the Spanish frontier with one or more – and sometimes many more – Allied airmen who had been shot down over Belgium, the Netherlands, or northern France on the bomber routes to Germany. Despite the often ill-fitting civilian clothes of their charges and their all-too-obvious unfamiliarity with their surroundings and local language, the resourceful guides would somehow manage to shepherd them unnoticed as far as the Pyrenees. There, for a price, hardy Basque guides (often prewar smugglers) risked capture by French or Spanish police to conduct their charges across the mountains by gruelling forced marches, lasting as much as forty-eight hours. Once in Spain, the dangers of arrest were less than in occupied France. But many airmen can attest to the squalor of typhus-ridden Spanish internment camps until their release was arranged through the intervention – and generally bribes – of British diplomatic or consular officials.*

As early as July 1940, Donald Darling, the handsome young British businessman whose intimate knowledge of the Franco-Spanish frontier had made him a prewar recruit of M.I.6, went to Lisbon and Madrid to link the incipient escape organizations in the Low Countries and France with certain officials in the British embassy in Madrid and the consulates in San Sebastian and Barcelona. They would be responsible for passing the men on to the safety of Gibraltar or Lisbon, from where they could be returned to Britain.

It all sounds orderly, perhaps even simple, an oft-repeated routine calling above all for steady nerves, the capacity to sustain long periods of intense strain, and a strict sense of security. It was, in fact, a complex and dynamic form of resistance, highly dangerous because it was more visible than most and particularly vulnerable to enemy penetration.

The provision of even the most rudimentary needs of all humans – food, clothing, and shelter – became a complex challenge for those assisting strangers on the run. Food and clothing in occupied Europe were strictly rationed, increasingly so as the war dragged on. Boots and shoes were especially difficult to come

---

*Descriptions of conditions in the largest and one of the most notorious Spanish camps are in Madeleine Duke, *No Passport* (London: Evans, 1957) and George Langelaan, *Knights of the Floating Silk* (London: Hutchinson, 1959), pp. 177-90. At one point, the Allies bartered wheat for the release of airmen held by the Spaniards.

by, but all kinds of clothing became so scarce that the networks were hard put to provide adequate disguises for the airmen. And so it was with food. To feed the airmen, French, Belgians, and Dutch often gave up their own meagre rations or ran the risks inherent in purchasing food at exorbitant prices on the black market, sometimes bought with local occupation currency parachuted or otherwise sent to them by M.I.9. And there was always the problem of providing the airmen with false identification papers, a task which in itself required a sub-network of skilled forgers and printers.

Houses in the countryside frequently had more food and were more secure for considerable periods. In Paris and other major cities, the anonymity of crowds did not adequately compensate for the omnipresent enemy garrisons and the higher risk of informers. And it was also in cities that lines might be most readily penetrated by agents, usually by English-speaking Germans and in a few cases Dutch and Scandinavian collaborators who posed as R.A.F. personnel seeking to return to Britain. In these efforts, the Germans were persistent and sometimes successful. Many agents or even a whole network would then be on a one-way journey to a German concentration camp.

In messages to and from London and along the escape lines, the airmen were frequently called "parcels." They were, however, anything but parcels. They were young men with the full spectrum of human traits and needs that any large group will invariably display. Some were passively co-operative, others aggressively independent; some were cautious, others careless to an unbelievable degree; some were manifestly highly intelligent, others decidedly less so. Some could cheerfully bear confinement for weeks on end; others became impossibly restless and depressed in a day or two. A silly, careless error – and there were so many that the airmen were sometimes referred to as "the children" by the guides – could cause disaster: a package of British or American cigarettes unthinkingly brought out in a crowded rail compartment; an obvious lack of knowledge of a continental language or of everyday practices; a chance expletive in English.* Or any one of many human weaknesses could betray the airmen and their guides: the urge to find sexual release, to walk in a town, to go to a cinema after weeks and sometimes months of seclusion. Ray LaBrosse, a Canadian organizer of an escape line, found occasional mavericks among his charges.

> A few were unwilling to follow instructions and stay put. Some attempted to convince their local helpers to take them out on the town, to a cafe or something. You know what would happen with those guys – they'd be picked up. They would start to speak English in public or something. One arrest would lead to another. This did not happen very often, but you had problems with four or five young men living together under the same roof, perhaps for weeks, perhaps for months. The safe house might be kept by a woman whose husband was perhaps in a concentration camp. So you had some problems. This was not surprising when dealing with people who were hemmed in, unable to go out, unable to exercise. And yet local people were finding ways of feeding them better than they were feeding themselves.[6]

M.I.9 in London could not expect to control in any detail the courageous local volunteers who established or ran escape lines. It could, however, send them money, arms, and other supplies, provide them with training and advice, attempt to co-ordinate their activities, and send its own volunteers to occupied countries in the hope of setting priorities or asserting an influence which it could not otherwise hope to achieve. M.I.9 could also organize, through its own agents, its own lines whose security might be greater than that of the home-grown variety. What the historian of S.O.E. in France, Michael Foot, has written about its escape lines for its own agents is equally

---

*It was not only airmen on the run who were capable of thoughtlessness which could betray them: Pierre Meunier, the S.O.E. agent, recalled at the end of the war, "Once I forgot myself and went down the street whistling 'It's a long way to Tipperary'. A few French civilians stared at me. I caught on and stopped whistling. It was an awful strain to watch every move I made night and day." (Toronto *Star*, 20 December 1944).

applicable to those under the co-ordination of M.I.9. All these lines, Foot writes,

> worked with the usual appurtenances of secret service in fiction, except for the excitement, the gunplay, and the easy women; most of the time most of the agents led an extremely dull life, existing as calmly and discreetly as they could, busied with their cover employment as commercial travellers, booksellers, doctors, laundresses, of whatever it might be ....
>
> The moral foundations of all escape lines are the same: steady nerves and complete discretion. The physical foundations lie in two things familiar to all who have worked underground: "safe houses" and "cut-outs." Safe houses explain themselves: in them escapers could be hidden by twos and threes between the stages of their journey. Their essentials were thickly curtained spare rooms, no inquisitive neighbours, and access to extra ration cards .... A secluded garden was a luxury; but more than one exit was advisable, and a telephone was a necessity, for the working of the cut-out.
>
> A cut-out is the nearest thing to a safe device in underground warfare: it is a means of establishing contact between two agents which, if it works properly, affords the minimum for the enemy security services to bite on. One agent passes a message in a simple code to the cut-out; it might be to a bookseller, saying, "I have two volumes of Anatole France that need binding; can you arrange it for me?" The cut-out holds the message till approached by the next agent down the line, who rings up to ask, "Have you any Anatole France in stock?," and will infer from the answer "Yes, two volumes have just come in" that there are two escapers to be collected from the circuit's safe house in the Boulevard Anatole France; while the reply, "Sorry, Mademoiselle, we're right out of stock" means there are no passengers that day.
>
> ...[some lines had] a series of cut-out rendezvous, which divided each line into watertight compartments. Passengers would be taken from one section of the line by a guide who would leave them at a pre-arranged spot, usually a park bench, and go away. A quarter of an hour later a guide from the next section would arrive and collect them; never meeting her predecessor, whom the passengers would take care not to describe. This exposed nervous passengers to a series of *mauvais quarts d'heures* and depended on strict timing and discipline; but it worked well.[7]

Such were some of the practices of clandestine escape lines. Whatever the specific techniques, however, all workers on the lines required courage, coolness, an ability to act a part, and a capacity to sustain fear and loneliness for prolonged periods. It was not an easy life. It was all too often a short one.

All possible escape routes were kept under constant review by M.I.9. Although the difficult route across the Pyrenees into Spain offered the greatest chance of success, understandably the appeal of evacuating escapees and evaders directly across the English Channel always remained strong. The possibilities of such a short if highly hazardous route had been contemplated by M.I.9 soon after its inception. The coast of the Lowlands was, however, far too closely guarded to offer any chance of success. More promising was the rugged Brittany coast. Early attempts, in co-operation with Free French naval officers, had come to nothing.* By late 1942, however, action became pressing as a result of intensified Allied air raids on submarine ports of Brittany. Increasingly large numbers of airmen were hidden throughout the province. Further, the principal line based on Marseille had been successfully infiltrated by the Gestapo as the result of disclosures by a French traitor. What was needed now was a new line totally divorced from its remnants. On the other hand, Channel embarkations were highly dangerous; the coast was increasingly heavily guarded in anticipation of an Allied invasion.†

---

*From the autumn of 1940, the "Helford Flotilla" was operated by S.O.E. between Penzance in Cornwall and Brittany to transport agents and stores; in that sense, M.I.9's operations were following a precedent.

†On the Mediterranean coast of France, S.O.E. operated two feluccas, manned by Poles, and M.I.6 operated H.M.S. *Fidelity,* a 1,500-ton ex-French merchantman which, until she was lost with almost all hands, was also used by S.O.E. and M.I.9.

An incipient organization to support sea evacuation existed in a local resistance unit based on the Breton coastal village of Plouha. It had already been contacted to help open a line to Spain for the airmen bottled up in Brittany. With the collapse of the Marseille organization, the essential link between London and Brittany was broken. An agent being needed to re-establish the link, M.I.9 somewhat hurriedly settled upon "Val Williams" to attempt it.

Val Williams, born Vladimir Bouryschkine in Moscow in 1913, had emigrated with his family from revolutionary Russia, first to France and then to the United States, where he became a noted basketball player and physical training instructor. In France in 1940, as a volunteer with the American Red Cross, he had worked with Donald Caskie, the British chaplain to seamen in Marseille, who did so much to pass Dunkirk evaders into Spain. Under the unlikely cover of coach to the Monaco basketball team, Williams had later joined the extensive Marseille organization led by Albert-Marie Guerisse, an escaped Belgian army medical officer who posed as "Pat O'Leary," a French Canadian serving in the Royal Navy. Williams assisted in the evacuation of the first group of escapers by the disguised trawler *Tarana*, and was himself brought out on its second voyage on 13 September 1942, shortly before the betrayal and arrest of O'Leary and the subsequent collapse of his organization.

With the need for a cross-Channel line becoming pressing, M.I.9 decided, despite mounting evidence of careless security on Williams' part, to recruit him to return to France. He would be the link between the survivors of the O'Leary net in Paris, which would collect airmen from across northern France, and the resistance in Brittany, which would provide local support for the evacuations. Early in 1943, when Donald Darling, now in Gibraltar, had been informed by London headquarters that Williams was being trained to organize sea evacuations from Brittany, he recalled his impressions when Williams had first arrived at the Rock aboard the *Tarana:*

> He was likeable, open, almost baby-faced yet very sophisticated . . . .
> He seemed something of a "smart alick" [sic] . . . though clearly a

man of courage and determination, I had thought him somehow
unproved and I was therefore not enthusiastic about [the] scheme. I
knew that [London] was irritated by my criticisms of their
agents...[so] I kept quiet, knowing the shortage of agent material to
be acute, but I...[was] near the mark in my assessment of brave,
but rash Val Williams.[8]

Williams, having eagerly volunteered to return to France, soon
completed his training, including special instruction in the
organization of beach embarkations and the reception of Lysanders on night pick-ups. By this time, however, the survivors of
the O'Leary net in Paris were also betrayed to the Germans. That
meant that Williams would have the additional challenge of
organizing a new group to collect, feed, shelter, and guide airmen
to Brittany. "Oaktree," the code name for Williams' mission,
would have been dangerous and difficult enough if restricted to
its original assignment. When the task of creating a new support
organization in Paris was added, the risks of Gestapo penetration
were compounded.

During his final weeks in England, Williams was given intensive briefings by the Admiralty about the Brittany beach tentatively selected for the evacuations. It was near Plouha, not far
from the small port of Paimpol and twenty-five kilometres from
the rail line at Guingamp. Le Cornec, who had become the *patron*
of the Plouha café upon his demobilization from the French
army, would be responsible for hiding the airmen prior to their
embarkation. It was Williams who would have to ensure their
safe delivery from Paris to Plouha and, equally dangerous, to
help carry out the beach operations below the German-patrolled
cliffs.

During his final briefings in London, Williams met for the first
time the radio operator who would go to France with him,
Raymond LaBrosse of the Royal Canadian Corps of Signals, a
tall, dark-haired soldier of twenty-two, with a strong jaw, clear
and observant eyes and an engaging sense of humour. Like
several young French Canadians with S.O.E., he had volunteered
for the army soon after Canada entered the war. As a signalman,
LaBrosse went overseas in 1940. Before long, M.I.9 joined S.O.E.

in seeking French-Canadian signalmen for clandestine warfare.* All secret organizations were chronically short of good wireless operators in the field, especially those fluent in French. LaBrosse was just such a *rara avis*. War Office wheels were then set in motion and, as a result, one day in the summer of 1942 LaBrosse was invited to walk with a British officer in the garden of a large country house near Three Bridges. He questioned LaBrosse at length about his background and opinions. That interview soon led to a second, this time with M.I.9 in London in early August. Did he like sports? As a boy, what games had he played? How did he feel about the war? The British? The French? A further interview led finally to the question: would he be willing to volunteer for secret and highly dangerous work in occupied France, helping Allied servicemen on the run? LaBrosse replied that he would.

When he returned to his camp in Sussex, LaBrosse was questioned by his fellow signalmen about where he had been. To all their questions and to later queries when some chanced to meet him on a London street in civilian clothes, he returned the answer that he had been instructed to give: he was working at a secret radio station in Scotland. When staying at the Regent Palace Hotel in London during his training, LaBrosse read the headline in a morning newspaper, "Canadians Land at Dieppe." He jumped to the conclusion that the invasion of the continent had begun. "My morale went right down. I said to myself, 'Well, that's it. Hardly am I involved in something and the war is over.' "[9]

LaBrosse need not have worried; the war was far from over. During the next days, the Dieppe raid began to be seen as the disaster it was. In any case, LaBrosse would not want for danger

---

*Some Canadians in Britain had already had some contact with M.I.9; in May 1942 instruction in escape and evasion techniques were given to the Canadian Second Division (units of which were already earmarked for the Dieppe raid) and subsequently to most Canadian soldiers and airmen. While LaBrosse was the first Canadian to serve with M.I.9, another Canadian was recruited and trained about the same time, but was returned to Canada for security reasons.

and excitement. Oaktree was a difficult and dangerous mission; when the O'Leary line was penetrated some agents might have been intentionally left free by the Gestapo so that they might be followed into any new line.

The mission's beginning was at one with the problems to come. Having been rushed through parachute and other training and given their final briefings, Williams and LaBrosse had the harrowing experience of departing from the R.A.F. station at Tempsford nine times, only to return when the pilots were unable to find the assigned dropping zone. The dangers of being shot down over France were bad enough, but almost worse was the nervous strain of preparing to jump from a Halifax bomber night after night, only to return for another day or more of fitful sleep and watchful waiting. Williams did not help matters by his restlessness. Langley at M.I.9 had the unenviable task of trying to control him.

> Keeping Val happy during the day nearly drove me mad. The "secret house" at Godmanchester, where agents spent the hours before leaving and slept if the parachute operations was unsuccessful, rapidly bored him and he insisted upon making a tour of the local pubs. His vociferous complaints of the inefficiency of the R.A.F., to all and sundry at the bars, soon attracted the attention of the local security authorities and through them [Sir Claude Dansey], who vented his wrath on me and threatened to send Val to Wormwood Scrubs for the rest of the war.[10]

Finally, on 28 February 1943, the volatile Williams and the phlegmatic LaBrosse were successfully parachuted near the Forest of Rambouillet, on the outskirts of Paris, where Williams was to establish the new organization for the collection, care, and feeding of evaders and escapers, drawing as necessary upon the large amount of francs which they had brought with them.

Their reluctant host for the remainder of their first night in occupied France was a farmer who, at great peril to himself, agreed to hide their supplies until they had organized their Paris base. To assist Williams and LaBrosse in entering Paris with a minimum risk of detection, two specially packed bicycles, complete with yellow French bicycle licences, had been parachuted with them. LaBrosse's bicycle had been badly damaged upon landing, so Williams pedalled to the nearest rail station to catch the first train to Paris while LaBrosse remained at Rambouillet, trying repeatedly and vainly to contact London on his equally damaged wireless set. His inability to do so during the following days meant that M.I.9 knew nothing of their successful landing. In Paris, Williams, as instructed, contacted a lawyer from Corsica who had earlier been involved in helping to send escapers and evaders southward to Marseille and across the Spanish border. While Paul-François Campinchi began to organize volunteers to move evaders from Paris to Brittany, Williams paid a hurried visit to Brittany where, in the Château de Bourblanc, the Count and Countess de Mauduit (who was an American) were secretly housing no less than thirty-nine of the estimated one hundred airmen in the area. The problems of feeding such a large number were rapidly mounting and, in any case, the longer they stayed the greater were the chances of their being detected.

Williams visited the château on 10 April 1943, envisaging a sea evacuation in May from the Brittany coast, as soon as he and LaBrosse could make radio contact with London to arrange the date. LaBrosse contacted London through a Free French intelligence group – a dangerous procedure since crossed lines frequently caused problems or even disaster but London had somehow to be contacted if Oaktree was to achieve anything. LaBrosse arranged with London for a new radio to be smuggled in from Spain and, at great risk, he duly collected it at the left luggage office at the Bordeaux railway station. LaBrosse would certainly have been tortured and at least interned for the remainder of the war if he had been caught with his cumbersome and not very well-disguised set,* but he successfully made his way with it by train to Brittany. From there, London agreed to organize an evacuation of the airmen by R.N. motor gunboat on the night of May 29. However, LaBrosse's second set was also unreliable, and M.I.9 decided that without dependable com-

---

*Only later in 1943 did the more compact and better-disguised sets become available to M.I.9.

munications for last-minute arrangements, the risks of error and detection were too high. London cancelled the proposed evacuation. As LaBrosse later summarized their situation, "We ran into a lot of problems and had a lot of difficulties."[11]

"Roger le Légionnaire," an early French volunteer who had changed sides and was now working for the Gestapo, had caused the downfall of the O'Leary line, personally assisting in the arrest of O'Leary himself in a Toulouse cafe. Now it had become known that he was working with the Gestapo in Rennes, taking a great interest in Brittany. Further, it had become evident to M.I.9 that Williams was again dangerously careless about security. Agents who knew France and had already served in an escape line were so rare, however, that M.I.9 had swallowed its misgivings and hoped for the best. LaBrosse soon fully recognized the nature of the man with whom he had been paired:

> My experience with Val Williams, whom I respected highly, was an unfortunate one, because he was in my view – and the view of everybody – the worst type of individual you could select for that job. Whereas he was very courageous, from the security point of view he was extremely careless and lived on expediencies . . . . He was hopeless from the point of view of security, just hopeless.[12]

Campinchi later recalled Williams' penchant for talking about his mission to anybody and everybody, "The only thing he didn't do [in France] was put an ad in the papers, asking for British intelligence workers." In these risky circumstances, London's decision to cancel the evacuation was understandable, but it left Williams, LaBrosse, and the airmen in yet greater danger.

With eighty-six airmen collected in Brittany and no secure way of evacuating them by sea, Williams now had no alternative but to attempt the hazardous overland route to Spain. Despite strict orders to the contrary, he sought assistance from former agents of the compromised O'Leary line. The Gestapo had become increasingly well informed about Williams' own not-very-covert activities. Their net began to close on him. With two Polish and two American airmen in tow, Williams was seized by the Germans on a train near Pau on 4 June 1943. Eight days later, the Count and Countess de Mauduit were also arrested, along with a number of airmen at their château in Brittany.

La Brosse was more fortunate. With Williams imprisoned, there was nothing further that he could usefully do in France. Williams had their code, and, in any case, by then the Gestapo probably had a clear idea of who LaBrosse was. He told the local resistance that he intended to escape to Spain, but that the incipient Brittany organization would probably be needed in the future. LaBrosse's escape—with twenty-nine airmen—through Toulouse, Andorra, and Barcelona during August 1943 was successfully organized in part by Georges Broussine, a tough and volatile Jew, an agent of the Free French Intelligence Service who was working jointly with M.I.9. Oaktree had clearly not been a success, but in Gibraltar, before LaBrosse returned to England on 3 September 1943, he and Donald Darling discussed the possibilities of beach embarkations in Brittany which, despite the Williams fiasco, LaBrosse was convinced could be made to work.

18

Dieppe and Beyond

The slaughter of Dieppe has entered permanently into Canada's military history. Much has been written – and no doubt more will be – about the raid in which about 3,900 Canadians landed on the Channel beach that summer morning in 1942. By noon, when the last landing craft were withdrawing, 3,367 Canadians were casualties, of whom almost one thousand were prisoners of war. The Dieppe raid had a number of unforeseen consequences on the subsequent course of the war, but one of the most unexpected was that it produced three of the best operators the Allied escape lines in Europe had during the four years of their hazardous work.

Among the Dieppe prisoners were four French Canadians, all of the Fusiliers Mont-Royal. They were Conrad LaFleur of St. Jean d'Iberville, and Robert Vanier, Guy Joly, and Lucien Dumais of Montreal. Of the four, Joly saw no further service behind enemy lines. But Dumais, LaFleur, and Vanier were all to play major roles in the risky business of assisting Allied escapers and evaders in occupied France – after they had first escaped themselves. Dumais made his way alone across France; LaFleur, Joly, and Vanier travelled together.

In the hand-to-hand fighting on the Dieppe fortifications near the casino, Vanier had been severely wounded in the back by a German soldier lunging at him with his bayonet. LaFleur had shrapnel wounds in one leg. Joly was mistakenly believed to be seriously wounded as well. All three were moved from Dieppe to a German military hospital at Rouen and from there, along with other walking wounded, were soon placed on a train to carry them to a P.O.W. camp in Germany. Vanier "didn't feel like going to Germany," and later LaFleur, a short, powerfully built young man of straightforward opinions, enquired rhetorically, "What the heck would we have done in Germany?"[1] Despite their wounds, all three managed to jump from their guarded train into the unknown darkness, as the train slowed to round a bend shortly after leaving Rouen.

The next morning, a beautiful late August day, they warily approached elderly peasants harvesting hay. From them they obtained old work clothes to replace their dirty, blood-stained uniforms. They were passed on to a Dr. Beaumont who was in contact with a line assisting escapers and evaders southward to Paris and across the demarcation line to Toulouse in Vichy France. In Paris itself, however, Vanier, Joly, and LaFleur were virtually on their own.

> Strangers in German-occupied Paris . . . [they] found a room in a slum hotel where visitors for one night were asked no questions. Vanier, weak from shock and loss of blood, [was] left in the bedroom while his companion went out to try to acquire some disinfectant with which to attend to the other's wound, which he had assured him was a "mere scratch." In LaFleur's absence, Vanier managed to get off the bed and inspect his back in a mirror. To his horror he saw a long, angry wound apparently running down his spine. He fainted and was on the floor in this condition when LaFleur returned with disinfectant and make-shift bandages.[2]

To be in occupied Paris was a bizarre, unforgettable experience for three soldiers who had so recently been in action against the Germans. Vanier never forgot the sensation of sitting next to three German soldiers on the Metro as a guide took them to the Gare d'Austerlitz for the Toulouse train. It was not many days before that he had been bayoneted by one such soldier. A few days later, the three Canadians successfully crossed a secluded part of the demarcation line assisted by French police who were, in fact, resistance workers pretending that they had the three Canadians under arrest. For three weeks in Toulouse, a woman physician, whose name had been given to them by Dr. Beaumont, treated Vanier's now severely infected wound while Joly and LaFleur waited, hidden elsewhere in the city.

From Toulouse, the three escapers were taken eastward to Marseille, the principal collection point for escapers and evaders. Canadian, American, Australian, South African, and British airmen were already hidden there, awaiting transport to Gibraltar. The demands of keeping a large number of airmen fed and hidden required the help of more than two hundred and fifty French volunteers. Despite the many dangers involved in moving about the countryside, Vanier, LaFleur, and Joly all offered to act as local couriers in an effort to keep knowledge of the existence of the O'Leary organization as restricted as possible.

Under O'Leary's direction, Allied soldiers and airmen were gradually assembled at Pau and Perpignan for transport to Gibraltar on the *Tarana*. As soon as the *Tarana*, in its warship grey, cleared Gibraltar and the prying eyes of Spanish workers, it was quickly repainted to resemble a colourful Portuguese trawler and the crew donned motley Portuguese shirts. When the three Canadians arrived in Perpignan in the first days of September 1942, the *Tarana* had since July successfully embarked a large number of escapers and evaders at night from the rocky beach at nearby Canet. While awaiting their embarkation, the Canadians were housed with a courageous Jewish family and were taken to the cinema in Perpignan for diversion. To their delight, they saw in a German newsreel of the Dieppe raid a column of Canadian prisoners and recognized themselves. The three Canadians were among more than forty evacuees (including an R.C.A.F. sergeant and Val Williams) who waited with increasing impatience for the rendezvous date. They need not have worried. The *Tarana* arrived on schedule on the clear Mediterranean night of 13 September to convey them safely to Gibraltar. From there, Joly, Vanier, and

LaFleur sailed in the battleship *Malaya* (the crew of which treated them "like kings"), arriving in Greenock, Scotland, on 6 October 1942.

On the *Tarana's* next voyage, planned for 5 October, came a fourth survivor of Dieppe: Lucien Dumais. A "short, articulate and very tough" sergeant-major in the Fusiliers Mont-Royal, whose "forceful personality contrasted with that of the quiet, unflappable LaBrosse,"[3] Dumais had been with his regiment on the beaches of Dieppe in August 1942. In the murderous cross-fire which the Germans had concentrated upon the Canadians and in the fighting in the casino, Dumais had organized his men, directed their return fire, tended their wounds and successfully evacuated many of them. He himself was eventually captured after having been, in effect, left behind amidst the carnage of the beaches. Dumais was, however, totally unwilling to accept that his war was ending when it had barely begun. At thirty-eight, with long prewar service in the Canadian army reserve, from the moment when he was first captured, he was determined to escape. Like Vanier, Joly, and LaFleur, he succeeded in jumping from a heavily guarded train taking Dieppe prisoners to Germany. With the help of friendly French he made his own way across northern France into Vichy and eventually to Marseille. There the U.S. consul surreptitiously passed him on to a French contact of Pat O'Leary. Dumais was added to sixty-five other Allied escapers and evaders successfully carried to Gibraltar on H.M.S. *Tarana's* third voyage. From Gibraltar, Dumais was flown to London, arriving a fortnight after the other three Canadians.

It was not surprising that all four Canadians from Dieppe were seen by M.I.9 as prospective workers on escape lines. Shortly after they were back with the Fusiliers Mont-Royal from a period of leave and interviews with M.I.9, Joly, Vanier, and LaFleur were interviewed by a Canadian intelligence officer from London. To each man his questions were basically the same: Do you wish to be loaned to a secret British organization for training in helping Allied evaders and escapers in occupied France? LaFleur understood that they had the choice of secret service in France or a desk job in southern England (where he had been since 1940, following six months in Scotland). Escapers and evaders such as himself, he further understood, were unlikely to be sent into action again because if captured, torture might force them to reveal who had helped them. Moreover, since all three had been in Britain since 1940 and were still privates, there were few immediate or alternative prospects of much excitement. As Vanier said later, "To tell the truth, I was fed up being in England doing nothing."[4] Finally, all three were grateful to those who had helped them and wanted to repay the debt by helping others. They volunteered.

In a small group which also included French, Dutch, and Italian volunteers, intensive training in wireless, small arms, disguise, and evasion followed. At Ringway, they all qualifed as parachutists; but before completing their M.I.9 training, which was similar to that given to S.O.E. agents, but without the sabotage instruction, illness and other factors forced Joly to withdraw. Final briefings for Vanier and LaFleur revealed that they were destined for different areas of France, but both were being sent to assist in the evacuation of important British or Free French agents who were either under German suspicion or whose assignment had been completed and, to a lesser extent, of Allied airmen on the run.

Vanier was assigned as a radio operator to a sub-circuit led by one of the Free French volunteers in M.I.9, Yves le Henaff. The circuit itself was headed by the same Georges Broussine, the Free French officer working jointly with M.I.9 who had been instrumental in spiriting LaBrosse out of France. Henaff, the son of the owner of a large fish cannery at Quimper in Brittany, was going home, in the sense that one of his assignments was to help Broussine develop cross-Channel escape routes.

Le Henaff and Vanier were parachuted into the Brittany woods one night in May 1943. From a nearby village the next morning, le Henaff simply telephoned his astonished brother, a former French army officer, to ask him to collect them and give them rooms while they began their work. From his brother's house, le Henaff travelled with Vanier across the demarcation line to choose an isolated field suitable for night pickups by Lysanders, their first task. From this journey, Vanier soon recognized that the forged identity papers given him in London were wanting in several details. The underground quickly forged new papers for him, this time giving Vanier the guise of a "de-wormer" from the Auvergne. This was an excellent cover; a de-wormer was a sort of veterinary assistant whose specialty was removing worms from cattle, an unusual skill and hence one in demand and clearly requiring extensive travel.

Vanier made several trips from Paris with his radio set, crossing the demarcation line on several occasions with South African, American, and British airmen. Twice during his service in France, Vanier was detained by the German police while his papers were carefully scrutinized, but each time the Germans ignored his large suitcase containing the wireless set. Once he was arrested by German police, but got away from them, leaving a bicycle which the Germans were fortunately unable to trace.

Le Henaff and Vanier were successful in arranging several Lysander pickups, but these were mainly to remove S.O.E. and other Allied agents. The number of passengers who could be flown out was limited. Broussine had already organized several successful Channel crossings from the south coast of Brittany, and it was clearly necessary to make another attempt. Another reason appeared in the shape of Pierre Brossolette, an eminent prewar Socialist Party journalist and broadcaster and now a leading figure in the Free French. Another senior Gaullist, Emile Bollaert, was with him. The Gestapo were on their trail, and, in any case, they were eager to report to de Gaulle on the readiness of the French resistance to support an Allied invasion. During the previous weeks, disguised B.B.C. messages had repeatedly notified them of cancellations of their planned pickup, the severe winter weather having made night landings impossible. With no early prospect of a successful pickup, Broussine, using money parachuted from London, purchased a Breton fishing vessel, *Le Jouet des Flots.* Such vessels were both scarce and closely watched by the Germans, so the best boat available was a small wooden vessel which had been on the beach for two years. During that time, its seams had opened and the owner had thoughtfully closed them again simply by placing the vessel back in the sea until its planks became swollen with water. It had never been properly repaired. "Ce n'était certes pas la meilleure unité de sa catégorie, il venait d'être désarmé depuis quelques temps....De toutes façons, ils n'avaient pas le choix."[5]

Both le Henaff and Vanier, who were to undertake the voyage, were unaware of the true state of the vessel. They began their preparations in the belief that they had acquired a seaworthy boat. A more evident problem confronting them was the winter weather. They proposed to put to sea near Cap Finisterre, gratifyingly isolated but one of the most treacherous and stormy areas of the English Channel. To that end, they assembled twenty-six Allied airmen from Paris and Brittany, and six Frenchmen, including Brossolette and Bollaert, all eager to cross to England. They sailed from a secluded beach on the night of 3 February 1944, one of the worst months in the Channel. A leaky, unreliable boat, a dangerous stretch of coast, winter gales and crowded passengers violently sick from the storm; it was not a combination that augured well. It was soon evident that in the mountainous seas, the seams of *Le Jouet des Flots* were again opening and that the faulty pump could not keep pace. In the gale, the fishing boat's engine failed. She began to lose way and drift, half-sinking, onto the rocks.

> *Le Jouet des Flots* limped safely past [Cap Finisterre], unbelievably missing the rocks. In the east appeared the first streaks of dawn.... With infinite patience... the captain edged them into Plogoff, south of the promontory. They were now close inshore, and finally the anchor held. There was no time to lose, for daylight was fast approaching, and they were visible to German lookouts. In the comparative calm they were seen bobbing at anchor, but the enemy paid scant attention to the large fishing vessel, obviously so battered by the storm.... They got down the sail, and then the mast, that fell grotesquely athwart the deck. They up-ended it into the water so that a clumsy bridge was formed inshore.... They could wade ashore now. Carefully they made their way into the tiny fishing village of Plogoff.[6]

All thirty-two crew and passengers managed to scramble ashore, although several were battered on rocks by the surf. However, without shelter at hand or even identity papers in the case of the airmen (Vanier had also lost his, plus his radio transmitter and money), it was not long after daybreak before several evaders were found by German patrols. To reduce the chance of capture, the would-be evaders had separated, but the Germans soon pieced together what had happened during the night and captured most of them within the next few days. Brossolette and Bollaert were arrested late on 4 February because they had no permits to be in the forbidden coastal zone.* Le Henaff was also arrested and interrogated. Through resistance workers, Vanier learned that le Henaff was being held at a prison in Brittany. A rescue attempt was planned which, given co-operation from prison guards, had a good chance of succeeding. One week before, however, the Germans suddenly moved le Henaff to Paris. Eventually he was put aboard a prison train to Germany. Short of rail cars, the Germans simply packed the prisoners into the boxcar one on top of another. En route to the concentration camp, le Henaff died of suffocation.

Following the wreck of Le Jouet des Flots, Vanier had made his way along the coast, wet, without shoes and near freezing. Avoiding German patrols, he had survived three days in hiding without food. Fortunately, he knew several resistance workers in the area and through them learned of a mysterious "captain" who operated an escape route across the Channel. Le Cornec, the leader of the Plouha resistance group, in turn heard of Vanier from one of his men and was persuaded to meet this "agent of British Intelligence" who was staying at a small hotel in Guingamp. With le Cornec went Dumais who, as we shall see, had returned to France by a different route. With pistols at the ready (since there was always the possibility of a Gestapo trap), Le Cornec and Dumais met two men in the hotel corridor, one of whom was the near-destitute Vanier. Dumais and Vanier were equally astonished to see each other, and the two comrades from the Fusiliers Mont-Royal joyfully embraced. By chance, an evacuation from the beach at Plouha was scheduled for the following night. A little more than twenty-four hours after

---

*In mid-March the Germans finally recognized whom they had stumbled upon. Yeo-Thomas had returned to France to join in a desperate attempt to rescue them, but before it could be organized, Brossolette and Bollaert were moved to the Gestapo prison in Paris at 84 avenue Foch where Brossolette managed to kill himself.

meeting his fellow-escaper from Dieppe, Vanier was safely on his way back to England by motor gunboat.

Conrad LaFleur was an unsophisticated twenty-seven year-old who asked few questions during his training. He was not told until completion of his instruction that he would be part of a major rescue operation with the code name of "Marathon," conceived as a response to circumstances that it was assumed would follow the Allied invasion of France. Though the exact date of the invasion was, of course, unknown to Langley, Neave and others in M.I.9 headquarters, they began planning during the summer of 1943 for events following D-Day. It was expected that they would have to help the large numbers of Allied airmen and soldiers who, unlike their predecessors, would presumably be unable to reach Switzerland or Spain because of widespread railway disruption. They would need to remain approximately where they already were in the country-side or be sent there from the cities. In the countryside they could be more readily fed and hidden than in urban areas. Neave

> was sure that the safest plan was to evacuate the men, especially from Paris and Brussels, and hide them as far as possible away from German troop concentrations. The places selected should be sufficiently near railway stations to bring them to the camps, in regions where well-organized Resistance groups were known to exist....It was therefore necessary to train the special teams for "Marathon" and begin preparations well in advance....Their duties would be to keep the escape lines in operation until the time came to form the camps.[7]

The ideal sites of such camps would be northeast France, on the bomber routes to Germany and near railyards which would be among their major pre-invasion targets. Moreover, between Brussels and Paris many escapers and evaders were already hidden. Accordingly, Reims, near the Belgian border, was se-lected as a base for an additional escape line in northeast France to parallel the existing "Comet" line. Both Comet and the new line were run by Belgians, the former by the de Jongh family, who for two years had shown outstanding courage and daring; the latter was largely operated by Belgian air force and army officers sent from Britain.

With one such Belgian officer, the high-spirited Count Georges d'Oultremont, Conrad LaFleur jumped from a low-flying Stirling bomber on the night of 21 October 1943. D'Oultremont had worked with the "Comet" line as a guide from Brussels to Paris, but he had become known to the Gestapo. He himself had to cross the Pyrenees into Spain in December 1942. In Britain he was trained, commissioned, and assigned a new role in the escape business. Well armed with both guns and whisky, the sophisticated d'Oultremont and much more direct LaFleur landed near the village of Fismes, near Reims. Their final briefings in London had stressed the need to find suitable fields in the region for Lysanders to collect agents and airmen, to contact the "Comet" line, and to begin the planning of a secure haven for airmen in the forests of northeast France as the invasion approached. Allied bombings and sabotage of rail lines across France would make the route to Spain impossible. Accordingly, Allied airmen were to be gathered from various hiding places in the Low Countries and northeastern France and hidden in the forests of Fretteval and the Ardennes where they would remain until their liberation by advancing Allied forces. Having received special instruction in flare paths and other signal procedures for guiding pickup aircraft, the first task of d'Oultremont and LaFleur was to arrange for the safe reception of two Belgian officers sent to augment their own network.

LaFleur soon "came up on the air," reporting their safe landing and first contacts with local volunteers. In Paris, d'Oultremont arranged for several French women to act as guides for Allied airmen before returning to the northeast to choose a secluded landing field near Coucy-le-Château in the Aisne. LaFleur radioed a description of the field, confident that two Lysanders could safely land there in the same night. In early November, two Lysanders successfully evacuated three U.S.A.A.F. and two R.A.F. aircrew, but the hazards were high for such a small return.

Pickups were risked for political leaders or S.O.E. or M.I.6 agents on the run, but they were unusual for airmen. The Spanish and Britanny routes were relied upon to bring out aircrew in any numbers.

So d'Oultremont and LaFleur devoted their energies mainly to developing their parallel escape line to Comet and preparing possible sites for camps. While d'Oultremont was improving the line and arrangements were being made with London to receive more Belgian agents near Fismes, LaFleur's radio messages suddenly ceased. The husband of one of their couriers had become a collaborator, betraying LaFleur's hiding place in Reims. The Gestapo suddenly burst into the house, surprising LaFleur at his radio set. LaFleur did not hesitate; he shot two of the Germans, raced downstairs and out at the rear, pausing only long enough to throw a grenade into the corridor where other Germans had followed him.

By exercising great coolness and courage, LaFleur got away. At a hotel, friendly waiters quickly provided him with a black suit, hat, and glasses. In that slight disguise, he was driven in a carriage to the rail station where, despite the presence of German police on the platforms, he managed to board a crowded train for Amiens. Boldly sitting in the same carriage as Germans, his successful escape was suddenly jeopardized by an R.A.F. bombing of Amiens. Through Dr. Beaumont, the physician who had treated him and Vanier after their Dieppe escape, he managed to contact a physician near Amiens who hid him while the "Comet" line arranged for him to be escorted to Paris and on to San Sebastian on the Spanish frontier. Once in Spain, LaFleur was taken in hand by M.I.9 staff from the British consulate in Barcelona and eventually flown to England and a well-deserved Distinguished Conduct Medal.*

*During postwar years, LaFleur was a truck driver in Toronto where he died in 1979.

19

The Cross-Channel Ferry

Ray LaBrosse did a particularly valorous thing upon his arrival
back in Britain from his escapade with the theatrical Val Williams; he volunteered to return to France. And his partner in a
new M.I.9 team would be Lucien Dumais.

Unlike his fellow escapers after Dieppe, Dumais had declined
to volunteer for service with M.I.9. He wanted to return to his
regiment of which he was so proud. From there, he wrote a letter
to a London newspaper taking issue with an account of the
Dieppe raid that it had carried. Although Dumais had used a *nom
de plume*, his identity as the writer was soon discovered after
interception of the letter by censors. After what was considered a
breach of security, he was ordered to North Africa for combat
training. There, Dumais spent four months with the British First
Army, sometimes on horseback reconnaissance behind enemy
lines. Back in southern England by mid-1943, the routine of
camp life seemed dull and uneventful. He recalled the M.I.9
invitation and decided to volunteer through C.M.H.Q. in London. In turn, M.I.9, after again checking his background carefully, introduced him to a fellow Canadian over lunch in a
London restaurant. Dumais and Ray LaBrosse, only back a few

weeks from his abortive mission with Williams, were housed together in London for a week, each warily attempting to take the measure of the other. LaBrosse recalled,

> We shared the same room and I spoke about my experiences and he about his. We sized each other up. I wanted more or less to run my own show, but wireless operators were at a premium. So I agreed to go in with Dumais. I felt it was a natural and that we couldn't miss. We formed a very close-knit team right from the beginning which lasted throughout... in all humility our network was certainly not the biggest, but was a most productive one. From the point of view of technical operations and security, it was really letter perfect."[1]

During their subsequent training, each learned to have confidence in the courage, common sense, and caution of the other. Their personalities were almost antithetical: the fast-talking Dumais who quickly decided on all occasions exactly what he wanted to do was a good foil for the more reticent and reflective LaBrosse.[2] The chemistry worked; they were soon to prove to be one of the best teams M.I.9 sent into occupied France.

LaBrosse was already a qualified parachutist, so while Dumais was sent to Ringway, he received intensive training in cryptology and in the new, compact wireless equipment which M.I.6 had issued to M.I.9. Additional instruction followed for both in the rapid use of pistols in confined spaces, hand-to-hand combat, forcing locks, and shaking a pursuer. New identities had to be learned in detail: Lucien Dumais of Montreal became a mortician, "Lucien Desbiens" of Amiens, and Raymond LaBrosse of Ottawa became "Marcel Desjardins," a salesman of electrical medical equipment—a disguise which might provide a superficial explanation if he were caught travelling with his radio. Each was also given the necessary identity papers for several other disguises. As in the case of most agents, if they were compromised under one false identify, they could promptly adopt another, but details such as birth date of each disguise were related to others to simplify problems of memory.

As the day of their departure approached, detailed briefings were given by the Royal Navy about what its motor gunboats could and could not be expected to do in taking "parcels" off the coast of Brittany, if Dumais and LaBrosse succeeded in establishing a line there. As the designated night arrived for Dumais and LaBrosse to depart for France, codes were provided on microfilm and their pockets filled with an assortment of old Paris Metro tickets, road maps, and false fountain pens containing tear gas.

Only on a third attempt did the R.A.F. succeed in delivering the two Canadians. LaBrosse, recalling his earlier mission, was not surprised when weather and flooded fields caused again the harrowing experience of nerves stretched taut for a hazardous night landing and then the anticlimax of return to base. Finally, on 19 November 1943, a landing was successfully made. In a meadow near Chauny (eighty kilometres north of Paris) only five minutes after landing,

> the aircraft flashed their landing lights, turned, and taxied to the other end of the field, where some flashlights were blinking. They swung into wind; the leading aircraft put on its lights, the others did the same, and then they were racing down the field in perfect formation...we knew that now, after all the weeks of postponement, we were on our own.[2]

Operation "Shelburne" had begun.

The manager of a local sugar factory had arranged for the initial shelter of Dumais and LaBrosse. As soon as it was evident that their landing had been undetected, he put them on a train to Paris. There the two Canadians successfully made the contact assigned to them: a young woman working as a hairdresser in the rue des Capucines who had already been instrumental in arranging for several Allied airmen to be taken to the Spanish frontier. Her assistant in the shop provided a safe house for Dumais and LaBrosse, and both women volunteered to help find temporary shelter for escapers and evaders as they passed through Paris en route to Brittany. Dumais later recalled the essence of his instructions to them on his first night in Paris: "You and your friends will gather all the airmen you can and look after them in Paris. Later on you will be told where to take them. We will also set up mobile groups that will pick up airmen in the north of France."[3]

The two women were of undoubted courage, but in the view of Dumais—who never trusted anyone—they had little real idea of security. Dumais and LaBrosse in any event told them the minimum, both being deeply convinced of the "need-to-know" principle: tell even the closest colleagues only what is essential for them to do their jobs. The two Canadians had taken the first step to set their new network in motion, but it soon proved to be in vain. The two women were arrested the next day, along with several Allied airmen—the last from their earlier network—whom they were putting aboard a train at the Gare St. Lazare.

With the women on their way to a concentration camp, Dumais and LaBrosse had to start again. LaBrosse approached Paul-François Campinchi, a clerk in the Prefecture of Paris who had been Williams' helper during LaBrosse's earlier service in Paris. London had necessarily questioned whether Campinchi had somehow been involved in Williams' arrest or had been otherwise compromised by it, but LaBrosse had in fact little choice. M.I.9 had not given them the names of any other contacts in Paris; at least LaBrosse knew Campinchi. It was risky, but it proved to be a fortunate decision. Campinchi not only arranged for them to be housed safely in Paris (where his own wife and children were secluded), but he soon became the admirably efficient Paris chief of their network.

The next step for Dumais and LaBrosse was to establish wireless contact with London to keep headquarters informed of what they were doing. After one abortive transmission from Paris, LaBrosse risked carrying his wireless set, disguised as a suitcase, on a train crowded with German soldiers. From a small hotel in Normandy he was successful—to their own and London's great relief—in exchanging brief messages.

With both a Paris base and contact with London established, the whole Shelburne network had now to be developed. Campinchi, still employed at the Prefecture, undertook to find a "lodging master" able to organize safe houses; an interpreter to work with him; physicians willing to treat the sick or wounded; a sort of quartermaster responsible for finding food and suitable clothing (a formidable task in wartime France); and printers able to produce false identity papers quickly. These volunteers and others would also be called upon frequently to teach the airmen the most common mannerisms of French labourers whom they would impersonate. The most careful security, Dumais insisted, must be observed by all. To enhance their own security in Paris, Dumais, LaBrosse, and Campinchi split up, avoiding all but essential contacts. LaBrosse had been burned once by bad security; he was not going to take that risk again.

The Paris net was beginning to take shape. It was now the turn of Brittany. To establish a reliable line from Paris to the heavily guarded beaches of Brittany would obviously require local contacts of a high order. The problem facing them was that many local residents had been forced to move and access to the Channel was strictly controlled.

Travelling to Brittany with false papers especially prepared for entry to the restricted zone and carrying their wireless set, Dumais and LaBrosse ran great risks to reach the same small coastal village of Plouha which Williams and LaBrosse had intended to use before. Fortunately, LaBrosse recalled that a young physician, who had been a medical student in Paris during his first clandestine tour, had subsequently purchased a practice on the Brittany coast. LaBrosse contacted him and, reassured by him, also contacted a former French soldier, François le Cornec, whom he had known on his "Oaktree" mission. With him, Dumais and LaBrosse examined the secluded beach about eight kilometres north of Plouha, which had already been identified by the Admiralty as a likely embarkation point. They now described it in a detailed wireless message. Although there were German blockhouses nearby, the shingle and sand beaches appeared ideal for small-boat landings. Behind the isolated beach, however, rose a steep cliff seventy-five metres high, down which the escapers and evaders would have to scramble. Three days before an evacuation, the evaders would be brought by rail from Paris to Saint-Brieuc, a nearby market town where the local wheat controller (an official in the food rationing system) would ensure their safe lodging in the area around Plouha. On the small coastal train from Saint-Brieuc, le Cornec's men would then guide the evaders to Plouha. Le Cornec also assumed the dangerous task of billeting the airmen in barns and farmhouses in the area, as well as training a small special group to manage the embarkation on the beach. It now remained only for LaBrosse to contact London, obtain approval for the date of the first operation, and request that weapons, money, and a more powerful wireless set be sent by the R.N. motor gunboat that would pick up the evacuees. They then returned to Paris to set their first operation in motion.

In Paris, Campinchi already had twelve U.S.A.A.F. and four R.A.F. "parcels" waiting. On the train to Saint-Brieuc most pretended to be exhausted workers fallen into deep sleep. The short distance to Plouha they covered at night on the local train in groups of twos and threes so as not to arouse suspicions. Many were delivered to their billets by François Kerambrun, a mechanic who had to drive his truck for the Germans by day, but by night carried Allied airmen. (On one trip he carried as many as nineteen; when cautioned about the personal risk involved, Kerambrun replied, "Nineteen or one, what's the difference? The sentence will be the same if they catch me.")[4] This first embarkation was set for 15 December 1943, but a gale in the Channel delayed it. For ten days the gale blew, preventing the operation during those few moonless nights when the tides were right. The embarkation was accordingly postponed for more than a month, until 28 January 1944. The sixteen now bored, restless, and increasingly worried airmen were scattered among a half-dozen farmhouses to await the darkest phase of the January moon. During the interim, Dumais and LaBrosse returned to Paris where, for security reasons, they continued to see as little of each other as possible.

On the evening of 29 January, fair weather brought a go-ahead signal on the B.B.C. French Service to Dumais and LaBrosse: "Bonjour tout le monde à la maison d'Alphonse." A further confirmation on the B.B.C. news at 2.30 A.M. meant that a motor gunboat was leaving its base at Dartmouth. Now the sixteen airmen and two outward-bound British agents could be brought together for embarkation, as the M.G.B. crossed the one hundred and forty kilometres to Brittany. While a sleepless Airey Neave paced the floor at M.I.9 in the War Office and kept telephoning the naval duty officer at Dartmouth for news, le Cornec's armed guides moved the airmen by various routes across the fields from their hiding places to converge near the small beach. There Dumais briefed them on how they would be led Indian-file in complete silence down the steep cliff to the beach, each clutching the coat of the preceding airman. Tense with suppressed excitement, the agents and evaders waited impatiently, acutely conscious of the enemy patrols in the area. Punctually at 1.15 A.M. three small rubber boats arrived in response to the agreed flashlight signals. Agreed words of recognition were exchanged in the dark. Arms, money, and then stores were silently landed, and within fifteen minutes the airmen were on their way out to M.G.B. 503 and Dartmouth.* Dumais and the French, shivering from the cold water, turned their backs on the safety of England and clambered to the nearby farmhouse to await six o'clock, the hour the German curfew lifted, before dispersing. "It was a tremendous triumph, after so many failures, and messages of congratulations came in [to Neave] the whole day."[5] The uncertain reputation of M.I.9 perceptibly improved among the intelligence establishment in London.

Back in Paris, beginning preparations for their second evacuation, LaBrosse and Dumais ran the risks of detection familiar to all Allied agents. A random police inspection of identity papers came close to catching Dumais carrying a large sum of money in a suitcase – a highly suspicious act in wartime Paris. LaBrosse was picked up several times in Paris; once, on leaving a cinema, he was herded with others into trucks for interrogation at a German police centre. But each time his false papers passed scrutiny. Like all wireless operators, LaBrosse was also always in danger of detection from German radio direction-finding equipment (which had pinpointed Beekman and Sabourin). Transmissions

---

*The MGB's were 120-feet long, carried a crew of thirty-six and were powered by three diesel engines, with a six-pound gun aft and a two-pound gun forward and twin machine guns aft of the bridge. S.O.E. and M.I.6 had both operated small flotillas a few miles apart in Cornwall, working into the same coastal waters of France. Finally, in June 1943, they had been amalgamated at Helford from where M.G.B. 503 carried out the Shelburne evacuations. M.G.B. 503 survived the war in Europe, but was blown up by a mine in the Channel in late May 1945, with loss of all her crew.

were kept to an absolute minimum, but until LaBrosse received additional sets from London, he risked being picked up when carrying his suitcase transmitter. At first LaBrosse, an excellent and punctual operator, transmitted from the Gare LaChapelle where the stationmaster allowed him to use his office.* Later he had two sets, one of which he operated from Paris and the other from Brittany, thereby avoiding the many hazards involved in travelling with a transmitter.

Both Canadians were also in great, if briefer, danger when they somewhat reluctantly agreed to a request from Campinchi to spirit Val Williams across the Channel, following a spectacular escape from Rennes prison. Aided by a captured Russian officer, Williams had made his way to Campinchi in Paris, despite a fractured leg and an intensive Gestapo search. Yet Williams had apparently learned nothing about security. While on the train to Saint-Brieuc, he carelessly smoked English cigarettes with the Russian officer whom he wanted to take with him across the Channel. The danger of Shelburne being detected was seldom greater.

The second evacuation was on the night of 28 February 1944 by which time the Channel coast had become even more closely guarded by a German army increasingly on the alert for an Allied invasion. More arms and other stores were landed and a total of nineteen evaders and two agents (including Williams) were evacuated in even shorter time than the first group. The airmen were mainly U.S.A.F., but they would have included the first R.C.A.F. pilot to use the route if he and an R.A.F. fighter pilot had not by chance been arrested by French police on the platform of the Saint-Brieuc station. The whole operation nearly miscarried when Kerambrun, the mechanic, drove his truckload of evaders through a partially erected German roadblock. While dismantling it, Kerambrun was accosted by two gendarmes. Fully intending to kill them both if they were unco-operative, Kerambrun told them the truth and the gendarmes readily waved him on his way.

*LaBrosse married the stationmaster's daughter in 1945. He continued his military career during the post-war years, retiring as a lieutenant-colonel in 1976 and becoming a member of the Canada Pension Commission.

With the completion of this second operation, Shelburne had now dispatched thirty-nine "parcels" to England.

We were very busy, engaged in rounding up the airmen from wherever we could lay a hand on them. For example, we'd receive a message from an agent in the north that he had learned through the resistance of airmen hiding in a particular place. We would send one of our interrogators who would go to screen them on the spot, since the Germans were constantly attempting to penetrate the lines and no "airman" would be passed down it unless his identity had been clearly established. A local agent would guide the airmen to the nearest large city, another would take them on a train to Paris where others would take them to "safe houses" for anything from a week to several months.

Once you got the airmen you had to feed them; obtain identity papers for them; recruit more agents; keep up their morale; the tension, the waiting, the uncertainty was very hard on us. The airmen were, in a sense, captives, and did what they were told. They were given three meals a day and perhaps a little exercise. You had trouble ... you would wake up one morning and so-and-so was arrested. Why the hell had that happened? You were constantly trying to plug holes and avoid the consequences of an arrest.

It was a risky business. You were not going into France to blow up a bridge with only a few people in the know. You were dealing with bodies, human bodies with human problems, "problèmes de la vie." How do you keep, say, seventy-five airmen tucked away in Paris for a considerable period of time? How do you do it without anybody knowing about it and how do you move them from there to point A or B? You're always out in the open, subject to enemy control. You had to depend upon other people for help in feeding, clothing, guiding the airmen. It had therefore to be a big organization but the bigger it was the more likely it was to be penetrated. If one link in the chain couldn't resist and succumbed, you had to be able to toss away that link and rejoin the chain.[6]

Good weather and the dark phase of the moon had to coincide to mount an operation. During the winter months, this was infrequent. But as the Normandy invasion approached, more and more Allied aircraft were in the skies over Europe, both day and night, and increasingly large numbers of evaders awaited transfer to Britain. Dumais began to search for a way to supplement his hazardous Brittany route with an escape line through the Pyrenees, the traditional route which both he and LaBrosse had themselves followed in 1943. Through a young French civil servant in Paris whom Dumais had recruited, they contacted some Basque smugglers in the Pyrenees willing to guide thirty airmen whom Campinchi and an agent in Beauvais had collected. The operation was a success, and having been liberally paid, the Basques were eager to guide more – and larger – groups. But having reduced his backlog by the circuitous Spanish route, Dumais and LaBrosse concentrated upon improving their more direct Brittany line.

Still the flow of Allied airmen increased. At one point during the spring of 1944, Campinchi had seventy-five hidden in Paris, a dangerously large number to house safely and feed adequately. "In 1944 there were Flying Fortresses being shot down right and left. With ten to a crew, we were getting lots of Americans," LaBrosse recorded. Clearly something more had to be done to keep the pipeline clear. The only satisfactory solution was to intensify the operations of Shelburne. The Admiralty agreed to Dumais' bold proposal that three operations of approximately twenty-five airmen each be mounted from Plouha within eleven days: 18, 24 and 30 March. A coastal alert by the Germans greatly complicated the already difficult task of transporting undetected seventy-four airmen and two agents from Paris to the coast of Brittany. The three operations were, however, a complete success. By the end of March, a total of 115 airmen and agents had been returned to England. In London, Neave "was able to report to the United States [Army] Air Force command that a substantial portion of those who baled out of their aircraft on these raids [Bremen, Ludwigshaven, Kiel and flying-bomb sites] were being returned within a month, and sometimes within a few days, of being shot down."[7]

The increased traffic placed a severe strain on the resources of Shelburne and multiplied the possibilities of betrayal by rendering it more vulnerable to penetration (one effort by a young Dane working for the Gestapo only just failed). Dumais recommended to London that no further evacuations from Plouha be undertaken for a few weeks while he tightened security. With the help of local resistance, he cycled along the Brittany coast searching for a small, secluded harbour where airmen might safely be placed aboard a French fishing trawler for offshore transfer to a larger British vessel. The search was however in vain; all possible bays and inlets were too heavily guarded.

On 16 June, a sixth operation was successfully carried out at Plouha, despite the fact that by then the Germans had planted mines along the top of the cliffs. A former captain in the French merchant marine, Joseph Mainguy, was responsible for finding a path through the mines: "We...put a small piece of white cloth on a stick close to the mines, but we never removed the mines, because then the Germans would know what we were doing."[8] The passengers on this operation were only incoming; six agents, three British and three French, were hurriedly deposited on the beach and quickly assisted on their way to their assignment.

Dumais and LaBrosse, having spent more than six months in occupied France, could have returned to England, having accomplished their mission with outstanding success. Instead, they both agreed to remain with their volunteers. Their decision was not easy; each time that they had placed evacuees on the motor gunboat they had understandably wanted to go themselves.

> We used to put the airmen on the ship in pitch darkness...and we'd shake hands and away they'd go and they would be in Dartmouth in a few hours and we'd go back up the cliff, through the mine fields and back to work among the Germans. This little farewell was, for us, emotional, because we had the urge to get in the boat too and say, "I'd like to rest for a while."[9]

With the Normandy invasion on 6 June 1944, London ordered Dumais and LaBrosse to move from Paris to Brittany. The Allied air forces had so damaged the rail lines and yards across northern France that travel by train was now virtually out of the question for civilians. Dumais and LaBrosse would be more useful in Brittany than cut off in Paris. Accordingly, they bought bicycles on the Paris black market and began to cycle the four hundred kilometres to Saint-Brieuc. En route, Dumais was suddenly stopped by a German artillery sergeant who demanded his bicycle. Dumais waved LaBrosse on and, with incredible *sang froid*, complained at a nearby German military police post that the sergeant had stolen his bicycle. Eventually, after much shouting on both sides, the military police agreed to drive Dumais the remaining distance to Saint-Brieuc. There he arrived several hours before the exhausted, astonished, and relieved LaBrosse.

Brittany was by-passed by the Allied forces driving eastward from Normandy toward Paris, the Lowlands, and ultimately Germany. German units in Brittany had been reduced by the demands of the invasion front, but they were increasingly edgy and suspicious. Shelburne was, moreover, increasingly known among the resistance. Of its two final operations from the beach at Plouha, Dumais recalled that

> London was now using us as a ferry-boat service, and sending us all kinds of people who needed passage back to England. Some of them we had to go out and fetch ourselves, under directions from London; others made their own way....All our previous operations had been carried out under the cloak of secrecy; now we were working more openly, and were prepared to use force. This was due to the fact that the enemy was fully engaged on the Normandy front, and moving all available troops there. Even the Gestapo were becoming less effective in tracking down saboteurs, for they could not rely on as many troops for large-scale raids.[10]

Nevertheless, Shelburne came as close to detection as it ever did when shortly before the final evacuation, a small and apparently drunken German patrol—actually a mixed patrol of White Russians and Germans—burned the farm house near the Plouha beach where airmen had usually stayed on the suspicion that it was a hiding place of the resistance or of escapers.

No fighting occurred, but Dumais and LaBrosse and their workers, armed partly by cross-Channel supplies, were determined, if necessary, to fight it out if the Germans attempted to interfere with their final evacuations. On 13 July, eighteen passengers were embarked, mostly fighter pilots who had been shot down during daylight sweeps against enemy ground transport. On these two final operations at the end of the month, agents also passed on their way to or from assignments behind the retreating German lines.

The work of Dumais and LaBrosse was now complete. With Allied armies moving eastward across France, the few German units left in Brittany were isolated. The danger was not over, however. They were soon working with a *maquis* which suddenly and unexpectedly became well armed, as LaBrosse later explained.

> For security reasons, when a beach operation was taking place, I remained behind with my wireless set so that I could immediately inform London if things went wrong and also to ensure continuity. On the night of the sixth operation, I kept a rather lonely vigil back at the "command post." Suddenly I was alerted by the throbbing sound of a Halifax bomber, flying low and seemingly looking for a signal from the ground. My hunch was right. The plane was one of two aircraft circling the area in search of a pre-arranged drop zone, several kilometres away. Pointing my flashlight in the direction of the approaching aircraft, I signalled the letters "OK" in morse code. This improvised signal caught the pilot's eye, because a short while later the first aircraft returned, followed by the second. By this time I knew that I was on to something. With mounting excitement, I resumed my signals. Lo and behold, two ghostly black silhouettes suddenly streaked low overhead and quickly faded in the distance, leaving in their wake thirty containers which came parachuting down in the now quiet night. Thanks to this unexpected "manna from heaven," we were able to equip a 170-man Breton *maquis* with arms and ammunition. It was while serving with this *maquis* that we were overrun by American troops in August 1944, having helped liberate several localities in the area and having inflicted severe casualties on the enemy.[11]

The supplies were in fact intended for a nearby *maquis* which soon arrived to demand the arms and other equipment; only when LaBrosse promised to request another shipment from London did the Plouha *maquis* succeed in keeping its "manna from heaven" for their harassment of the Germans.

LaBrosse and Dumais fought in the final engagement of the local underground. With the rapid advance of the U.S. army into Brittany following its breakthrough at St. Cloud, an American tank squadron suddenly arrived in Plouha. The night before, the Germans had surrounded a resistance unit in nearby Plelo.

LaBrosse persuaded the tank commander to divert his squadron to Plelo to help rescue the beleaguered *maquis*—and to take Dumais and himself to join in the counter-attack.

Even then, however, Dumais was not finished with his assignment in Brittany. His final challenge was to help restore civil order and identify collaborators in the confused days following the liberation of the area by the U.S. army.

> In company with an American Town Major who spoke not a word of French and hadn't the foggiest idea of what he was supposed to be doing, I spent my time trying to sort out the fearful vendettas that followed the four years of enemy occupation. Accusations of collaboration and treachery were accompanied by arbitrary imprisonment and cold-blooded murder, with the communists denouncing as traitors political opponents whose only crime was that of not being communist.[12]

With the Saint-Brieuc region gradually restored to order, Dumais moved on to the S.H.A.E.F. Intelligence Headquarters where he soon became involved in helping to mount an overland rescue operation of more than one hundred and fifty Allied servicemen whom d'Oultremont, LaFleur, Campinchi, and others had directed toward the Forest of Freteval. They were brought to safety through enemy lines in a daring rescue by the British Special Air Service, using cut-down automobiles and French buses.

The one casualty among the Canadians recruited by M.I.9 was Georges Rodrigues of Montreal. Having enlisted with the Royal Canadian Corps of Signals in May 1941, he volunteered in November 1942 for service with M.I.9. A twenty-five-year-old signalman, he was given instruction in England and sent to Algeria for final clandestine warfare training and briefing early in 1943, prior to being dropped on the island of Corsica to help organize an escape line and provide it with an essential radio link to Algiers. The plan was abandoned, however, and Rodrigues instead parachuted into northern France in August 1943 on a mission about which there are now no details. Two months' service as a wireless operator with an escape network based in Paris—there are also no details about it—was brought to an abrupt end by his arrest on 15 October. After being tortured, Rodrigues was sent to Buchenwald in late 1943 or early 1944, and hence was there when Macalister, Pickersgill, and Sabourin were executed. In the early spring of 1945, the survivors in the camp were hurriedly evacuated in the face of the rapidly advancing Russian army. By then, Rodrigues had been in that hellish place for more than a year; not surprisingly, he was gravely ill from both malnutrition and tuberculosis. After Buchenwald was captured, he died in an Allied field hospital near Schwerin on 26 May 1945, three weeks after the German surrender. His citation for a posthumous Mention in Despatches records that when the anonymous French head of his circuit visited London following the liberation of France, he reported that "he was unable to find words adequate enough to describe his admiration for Rodrigues. From a technical point of view he gave complete satisfaction, but what was far more important, in spite of terrible treatment at the hands of the Gestapo, he never disclosed any compromising information about his organization."

20

The Mediterranean and Asia

The Canadians in the escape and evader business were primarily in France. But several saw service in the unlikely, and much less risky, venue of the Vatican.

Sam Derry, a major in the Royal Artillery who had been captured in North Africa in January 1942, escaped from a prisoner-of-war train in Italy and, with great difficulty, made his way into the Vatican under a pile of cabbages on a farmer's cart. Gradually, with the covert support of the British Minister to the Holy See, Sir Francis D'Arcy Godolphin Osborne, and with the unstinting help of an Irish priest, Monsignor O'Flaherty, Derry co-ordinated from his Vatican hiding place an extensive network to assist escapers and evaders which O'Flaherty had initiated. The British Legation to the Vatican could itself do little to help.

> Sir D'Arcy made it quite clear that because of his delicate diplomatic position [as British Minister to the Holy See in German-occupied Rome] he would be able to give little direct assistance beyond arranging a supply of funds from British government sources for . . . there was little doubt that the Vatican Secretariat of State would jealously preserve its neutrality, even to the extent of

withdrawing its hospitality to the British Legation if it had any suspicion of abuse. "I think I may be able to help you in one way, though," said the British Minister. "There is no reason why we should not arrange for some of the British officers interned in the Vatican to do whatever clerical work you may find necessary.... They have plenty of time on their hands."[1]

Sir D'Arcy was right. Among nine British and Commonwealth escapers housed in the Vatican were three officers interned there since they had escaped while being marched with other prisoners of war through back streets of Rome. A friendly physician had driven them to the Vatican where they were taken in shortly before the Holy See declared that it would accept no more combatants from either side seeking refuge, since it might thereby compromise its neutrality in the eyes of the Germans. The three escapers were "furiously impatient, and annoyed with themselves for having voluntarily become internees in the mistaken hope that they would be freed within a few weeks by a rapid Allied advance.... They welcomed any activity which might assist the Allied advance in Italy."[2]

One of these three officers, Captain Henry "Barney" Byrnes of Langley, British Columbia, had served in the prewar militia, gone overseas in 1940, and been a "Canloan" officer in North Africa from January to April 1943, when he returned to England. He was back in the Mediterranean theatre almost immediately with the First Division, part of the invasion force for Sicily. There he was captured in July 1943, soon after the landings. In September he made his escape in the back streets of Rome when the Italians surrendered.

Once in the Vatican, Byrnes began to compile lists of all known Allied escapers or evaders at large in Italy. After meeting Derry, Byrnes accelerated his efforts to prepare a reliable and comprehensive index. New sources of information were opened to him. "Byrnes tackled his mammoth task with enthusiasm, and it was largely through his work that we were able, not only to ensure that the assistance we were giving went into the right channels, but also to set at rest the minds of worried relatives of missing men much sooner than might otherwise have been possible."[3]

When the Italians surrendered in September 1943, hundreds of Allied prisoners of war simply walked out of their suddenly unguarded camps before the Germans could seize control of them. Many more Allied troops would have been guided safely to Allied lines if escape plans had been made and promptly carried out and especially if the senior British officers in camps had not been ordered by the War Office (via clandestine radio) not to permit any break-outs, pending the expected early arrival of Allied forces. The general expectation was that amphibious forces would land near Rome, quickly secure the city, and push rapidly northward. In fact, the Allied advance up the boot of Italy was a slow, bloody affair as the well-entrenched Germans proved themselves again to be among the most skilful and dogged of soldiers. Although many Allied P.O.W.s remained in their camps as ordered, some did break out, only to find themselves stranded in the countryside, aided by sympathetic Italians if they were fortunate. Derry and Byrnes, the several British officers in the Vatican, Monsignor O'Flaherty, and hundreds of Italian partisans faced a complex, daunting challenge in keeping such multitudes hidden, fed, and sheltered. A few made their way through German lines or even to Partisan units in Yugoslavia, and on three night operations, British landing craft took several hundreds off the Adriatic beaches where they had been quietly assembled. But even evacuations of this magnitude did not reduce substantially the logistics tasks facing Derry and Byrnes in attempting to assist thousands of Allied personnel scattered through northern Italy. Feeding such a large number was a problem considerably greater than that confronting the escape lines in occupied France and the Lowlands. On the other hand, the situation in Italy was more fluid and the possibilities of moving about a little easier after Italy's surrender than was ever the case in northwestern Europe. In November 1943, on microfilm which Osborne's resourceful butler had hidden in a loaf of bread, Derry managed to smuggle to an M.I.9 agent in Taranto in Allied-held southern Italy a list of almost two thousand P.O.W.s known to be hiding in German-occupied northern Italy. By the end of the war, almost four thousand escapers had been identified by the "Rome Escape Line," and many had received direct or indirect help from it. This was no small achievement for a few secluded men working surreptitiously from the Vatican.*

In the Mediterranean theatre, two Canadians served with M.I.9. Sergeant Rudolph Bozanich, a short, stocky, forty-year-old Yugoslav-Canadian shoemaker, had been conscripted in Canada in November 1942. He had volunteered for service in Yugoslavia when S.O.E. had raised the possibility with him. At the end of February 1943, after brief training at S.T.S. 103, Bozanich sailed from New York, passed through the Panama Canal, changed ships in Australia, sailed for the Persian Gulf, and finally arrived in Cairo in May only to fracture his spine while on parachute training in Palestine. He spent the next three months in a cast before finally reaching Bari in southern Italy in October. An R.N. motor gunboat ferried him to the sunny Partisan-held island of Vis in November. His spinal injury was so great, however, that despite his determination, he could not continue and had to be returned to interrogation and interpretation work in Bari where he spent the whole of 1944.

Bozanich was replaced on Vis by Corporal A.D. Yaritch of Toronto, who was recruited from the Corps of Military Staff Clerks in London in December 1942, given initial training by M.I.9, and then sent to the Middle East to receive additional training. He went on to the south of Italy in November 1943 and from there to Vis. In early January 1944, he was killed in a German strafing of the small boat taking him to the Partisans on

*Byrnes was briefly on leave in London in April 1945, when Derry assumed command of M.I.9 from Norman Crockatt. Byrnes agreed to Derry's request to return to Italy where he spent the remainder of the year with a small Allied unit attempting to determine which Italians deserved a reward for assisting Allied escapers or evaders. During the immediate postwar years, Byrnes lived in British Columbia, but he rejoined the army during the Korean War. Today he lives in retirement in British Columbia.

the island of Dugi Otok. He is buried in the Allied cemetery at Foggia, Italy.*

We have noted the formidable obstacles in the way of S.O.E. agents of European race attempting to move through Japanese-occupied Asia. Those same obstacles were even more intimidating for aircrew or escaped prisoners of war – invariably undernourished and diseased – attempting to make their way across the vast terrain of Asia to the safety of Allied lines. Very few prisoners of war did in fact successfully escape. Of these who tried and failed, many were beheaded by their Japanese captors. Nevertheless, M.I.9 did establish an advance base in India as early as October 1941, two months before the war with Japan. Its aim was to succour P.O.W.s or evaders to whatever extent the terrain, co-operation of local people, and courage and perseverance of the escapers and evaders themselves allowed.

From the autumn of 1943 M.I.9 operated in Asia under the cover name of "E" Group. Fully aware of the virtually insurmountable problems confronting any would-be escapers in the jungles of Asia, "E" Group's headquarters in New Delhi (and its liaison office at Mountbatten's headquarters in Kandy, Ceylon) concentrated on gathering information about the exact location, size, and conditions of prisoner-of-war camps, partly in an attempt to avoid Allied bombings and partly to be ready to send assistance as soon as the war ended. Concurrently, jungle training at S.O.E. camps in Ceylon and Assam helped to prepare aircrew for what they might expect to encounter if they were shot down.

With the turn of the war's tide in Burma, "E" Group began to

---

*Another Yugoslav-Canadian, Sapper J. Maystorovich, after having been vetted at S.T.S. 103 and trained by S.O.E. in England, was assigned to work with M.I.9 in Italy, assisting in the recovery of Allied airmen and escaped prisoners of war in Yugoslavia.

place rescue teams in frontline areas to assist in the recovery of aircrew and to encourage local tribes to help airmen return. Later still, as the defeat of the Japanese appeared increasingly likely, planning began on how relief teams might best be sent to P.O.W. camps. Many of the one hundred and forty thousand British Commonwealth, sixty thousand Dutch, and twenty thousand American internees might, it was feared, be massacred by Japanese guards rendered more fanatical by the shame of defeat.

It was as head of such a team that Arthur Stewart of Vancouver won the gratitude and admiration of thousands of Allied prisoners of war. Stewart was born in 1909 in Tientsin in northern China where his grandfather, a Scottish sailor, had founded a prosperous lighterage business and his father was Assistant Inspector of Salt Revenues for the Chinese government. Stewart spoke both Mandarin and Cantonese, a skill he was able to employ in the Vancouver Police Force which he joined shortly after arriving in Canada in 1929 at the age of twenty-one. Having briefly served in the North China British Volunteer Corps, Stewart also joined the Irish Fusiliers, a Vancouver militia regiment, transferring to active service in May 1942 as a senior N.C.O. By then, two brothers were in Japanese concentration camps in China (his seven sisters were safe in Canada, Australia, and Britain). Stewart embarked for Britain at the end of August 1943. There his language expertise led him to volunteer for "special duty" in Asia. Following interviews at Canada House and the War Office, Stewart was commissioned and given Intelligence Corps training in Britain. Additional instruction followed at the Intelligence School in Karachi and at the R.A.F. parachute school at Chaklala. Stewart was initially seen as a promising recruit for S.O.E.'s small China section. By May 1944, however, its needs for Chinese-speaking officers had dwindled, given the combined refusal of Chiang Kai-shek and his American advisers in Chungking to countenance British clandestine operations in or based upon China, especially any which might facilitate the resumption of British rule in Hong Kong or its other Asian colonies.

M.I.9, however, was delighted to have a recruit with Stewart's skills and background. By the time Stewart joined "E" Group on 30 May 1944, the Japanese were at the gates of India. But that same month their offensive against Imphal faltered, and from that point on, the initiative transferred to the British. By then, "E" Group's early work had largely been completed. It had instructed soldiers and airmen in what they might expect in the jungle if they evaded capture or escaped from a P.O.W. camp, supplied them with various escape aids (silk maps, tiny compasses, compact radios, etc.), and organized search and rescue groups equipped with light aircraft to seek evaders and escapees in Burma. Now the need for the accurate pinpointing of the camps had become more pressing and the methods for protecting and succouring prisoners more detailed. "E" Group's headquarters sent Stewart into Yunnan, that province of China which borders on Burma, to obtain information about P.O.W. camps in Burma and any aircrew who had escaped capture. "E" Group had assured Stewart that he "would have a lot to do with the Chinese guerillas in that area so your Chinese would stand you in good stead. The job is an active one and sometimes hazardous as it may mean moving in enemy occupied territory."[4] Many of "E" Group's problems in mounting operations from China were, however, mainly with the U.S. and Nationalist Chinese forces at a time when, in Stewart's terse words, "British efforts were not encouraged in this theatre of war."[5]

Nevertheless, in July 1944, Stewart reported to "E" Group's Number 1 Forward Headquarters at Paoshan on the Burma Road in the mountainous Burmese-China border area. There he joined Captain Bruce Bairnsfather, the popular British cartoonist of the First World War. Now over fifty, he had served in the Chinese Maritime Customs between the wars. Together, Bairnsfather and Stewart organized operation "Vancouver," an astonishing rescue feat about which details are today unfortunately few. Somehow, with the help of Chinese guerrillas, they managed to retrieve a total of five hundred and fifty Indian troops. Some may have been captured by the Japanese during their vain drive on Imphal, but although the records are frustratingly vague on the point, it is more likely that many were deserters from the Japanese-supported Indian National Army division which had been sent into action against the British Fourteenth Army near Imphal. They had earlier been captured in Malaya where they had been induced by bribes and threats to join the Japanese puppet forces. Once in action against the British, however, many had deserted at the first opportunity; it may have been some of them whom Bairnsfather and Stewart assisted.

Stewart, lean and tough from work in the mountains, transferred southwest across the Chinese border into Burma in December 1944, operating along the Salween River in the Shan State until February when he moved closer to the now-advancing Fourteenth Army. There he contrived to assist escapers and evaders, mainly U.S.A.F. and R.A.F. aircrews and remnants of Orde Wingate's Chindits, until he was withdrawn to India in May 1945 after almost a year in the Yunnan and Burmese mountains.

Stewart's stamina and love of irregular warfare was such that he volunteered to go into Malaya on a further mission of succour: Operation "Celery." To do so, he had first to be given intensive briefings about what he might expect to find in Malaya, particularly in the prisoner-of-war camps on Singapore island. Stewart's assignment was succinctly, if austerely, described in a postwar citation:

> To organize a team of "E" Group and Force 136 personnel in the field
> and, immediately on receipt by wireless telegraphy of the
> appropriate codeword from SACSEA [Supreme Allied Command
> South East Asia], to leave the jungle, proceed to Singapore, contact
> the Japanese commanders, visit and report on all prisoner-of-war
> and internment camps on the island and arrange for their
> immediate vital needs.[6]

At first light on the morning of 24 August, Stewart and his team took off in an R.A.F. Liberator with a Canadian crew from China Bay aerodrome in Ceylon, passing over the British fleet amassing for Operation Zipper. The original plan had been to drop the team on to Singapore island itself, but two Liberators which had preceded them had been fired upon while dropping leaflets proclaiming the Japanese capitulation. Stewart's team was accordingly diverted to the neighbouring Johore State, but even there their night landing did not go quite as smoothly as planned. To avoid enemy patrols, the reception committee had moved from a large to a smaller drop zone. Further, for some reason Stewart paused for a moment when the young R.C.A.F. despatcher gave him the signal to jump. The aircraft had there-fore passed over the drop zone by the time that Captain Ross of the Royal Army Medical Corps was able to follow. Major Clough, Stewart's second-in-command, preceded Bill Lee of Vancouver who recalled that

> Colonel Stewart made a beautiful target silhouetted against a full moon rising above the horizon. The drop zone appeared to be of postage stamp size... and guided by the glow of flares and occasional glimpses of flashlights, I controlled the lift shrouds of my chute towards the field. Just as I'd thought that I'd landed safely, a large tree loomed out of the darkness and I crashed through the branches, protecting myself by reflex action. Captain Ross was the only one to make it to the field. Major Clough was found through shouts and lights about ¼ mile further back from the drop zone while Colonel Stewart and I were close enough to be spotted in the trees. Major Clough and I ran out of rope freeing ourselves (40 feet of rope), which gives one an idea of how high we were hung up. Force 136 personnel in the receiving party helped guide us back to the main camp after the aircraft had made several free drops (no chutes) of supplies and equipment.[7]

The reception committee, carrying torches of raw rubber, con-veyed the team safely to a camp of the Malaya Peoples' Anti-Japanese Army–the nearest to Singapore–where, for almost a week, they awaited orders to cross the causeway to the island. Already with the guerrillas were a Force 136 team of two British officers, a Malay medical student commissioned in the British army, and a British and a Nationalist Chinese N.C.O. wireless operator.

The teams temporarily merged when orders were radioed from Ceylon to proceed to Singapore. It seemed likely that the Japanese there were willing to surrender and to facilitate the release of the Allied prisoners, but there was only one way to be certain. The two teams made their way through the dense bush for two days before reaching a pineapple plantation near Kulai where they commandeered a dilapidated truck. Its steering was dangerously erratic, but they somehow managed to tame it sufficiently to careen along the main coastal road to a Japanese control post. Their apprehension was only increased by seeing in the gathering dusk that the N.C.O. in charge had a machine-gun trained on them while he awaited a reply from the somewhat disconcerted captain commanding the small garrison. A passing ammunition convoy carried them a brief distance toward Singapore before they met two staff cars sent to take them to the headquarters of Japanese intelligence at Johore Bahru on the mainland side of the causeway leading to Singapore island. There a colonel emerged in a kimono to tell them that they would be taken across the now silent and dark northern roads of the island to the prison at Changi on the eastern side. Before their departure, however, the colonel took a moment to chat with the astonished Bill Lee about his prewar days in Vancouver, about Stanley Park and the Chinese community along Powell and Pender streets. "It was almost like talking to someone from home."[8]

The team arrived at the gates of Changi about ten o'clock on the night of 1 September to find that the prisoners had already assumed virtual control of the camp. The Japanese were still about, but they made no further effort to restrict the prisoners. While Stewart talked with a welcoming group of senior officers – British, Australian, Dutch, and French – Ross began to identify the most pressing medical needs of the skeletal prisoners, most of whom were suffering from malaria, malnutrition sores, skin ulcers, and other diseases. At several other camps on Singapore island and at Changi where ten thousand had been held in space originally intended for a maximum of two thousand, a number of prisoners were fatally ill, but all 32,578 surviving prisoners in the various camps were eager for news from the outside world, having been able to receive only limited news through hidden homemade receivers. "E" Group in Colombo was equally anxious to know of the conditions of the prisoners. Lee had been told that electrical storms over the Bay of Bengal would probably prevent nighttime transmissions from reaching Ceylon. It was not in fact until 2 September that Ceylon was able to reassure itself by Lee's first message, however garbled, that "Celery" had made it safely into Singapore. For the next ten days, the highly competent Lee worked twenty hours a day, coding and decoding and transmitting the flood of messages about conditions in Singapore – and a sixty-fifth birthday greeting sent to the Queen of the Netherlands from four thousand Dutch prisoners.

During 3 and 4 September, Stewart was the senior Allied officer in Singapore in contact with Southeast Asia Command, rapidly establishing his ascendancy over the Japanese. He visited all the camps, assuring the British, Indian, Dutch, and Australian prisoners and civilian internees, most of whom had been incarcerated for three and a half years, that the Japanese had indeed surrendered, that the Allies were everywhere victorious, and that a major British amphibious force would soon land in southern Malaya.

Stewart obtained nominal rolls of all the P.O.W.s and Lee radioed to Colombo the general conditions of the camps, of the airfields (to receive relief flights) and of Singapore generally. The culmination of Stewart's energy came at noon on 3 September with the raising of the Union Jack over the camps and several major Singapore buildings. The local Japanese, who had still not formally surrendered pending the arrival of the British fleet, protested in vain.

Parachute drops of food and medicines arranged by Stewart soon followed; Lee was pleased to see Canadian Red Cross packages among the supplies. After Stewart and the senior Allied officers in Changi had worked out a *modus operandi* with the Japanese headquarters in Singapore to govern the city until the imminent arrival of the Royal Navy, Lee moved with Stewart to a small guest house in the grounds of the Goodwood Park Hotel. There he was later joined by two Australian N.C.O. wireless operators, ending the initial period when Lee alone had provided the only radio link with Ceylon, laboriously coding and decoding all confidential messages himself.

Stewart's citation for the Order of the British Empire neatly summarized his achievements in Singapore:

It was due to Lieutenant-Colonel Stewart's leadership, and gallant and distinguished services that the urgent vital requirements of many thousands of prisoners of war and internees were so quickly and efficiently organized and dealt with and the general situation regarding camps and the conduct of the Japanese forces in Singapore kept well under control until the landing of British troops by sea. Innumerable expressions of sincere gratitude and admiration have been received from prisoners of war and internees themselves for Lieutenant-Colonel Stewart's splendid work.

Following the arrival of the British fleet on the night of 4 September 1945, and the beginning of the repatriation of the prisoners of war by both sea and air, Stewart no longer needed to remain in Singapore. Leaving Lee still transmitting messages from the hotel, Stewart flew the few kilometres to Sumatra and later to the more distant Java and Borneo with teams sent from Ceylon to ascertain the condition and the most pressing needs of the Allied prisoners and internees.

The Dutch, preoccupied with the myriad problems of deprivation and reconstruction at home during the harsh winter of 1944-45, were incapable of reasserting their authority over their huge colony in the Pacific. Under the benign eye of the United States, Indonesian nationalists were working – and arming – to prevent the return of the Dutch. The Japanese, still in large numbers throughout the scattered islands, wanted no more than to return home. Into this administrative confusion, British forces began to arrive on several of the main islands of the Netherlands East Indies, fulfilling an earlier British pledge to the Dutch to help them regain their colony. The many emaciated and diseased Allied prisoners and Dutch civilian internees had been left in a state of limbo in their camps, pending the clarification of who was actually in control. It was a volatile, dangerous situation, full of uncertainties for those few Allied officers such as Stewart who made their way to the camps in Sumatra and Java. To some degree, they were able to reassure and succour the internees by arranging air drops and medical teams; but in the uncertain and confused circumstances, Stewart and others could do little before the British arrived in force, pending the eventual, brief return of the Dutch.*

Lee was almost a month in Singapore, relaying Stewart's messages to Colombo. During early October, with his M.I.9 tasks completed, he was ordered northward to Kuala Lumpur where he rejoined several of his comrades from Force 136, helping them to disband the 1st Regiment of the M.P.A.J.A. With the other Chinese-Canadians he finally sailed for home on 7 December 1945, four years to the day since the war with the Japanese had begun.

*Stewart returned to Vancouver in August 1946 as a lieutenant-colonel in the Royal Canadian Artillery. He rejoined the Police Force as a senior officer and died in Vancouver in 1955.

Epilogue

We have reviewed acts of bravery, ingenuity, and perseverance by volunteers, which were of a character and magnitude that the passage of time cannot lessen. We have seen how Canadians joined with men and women of many nationalities in sabotage, subversion, assistance to escapers, and a multitude of other activities embraced by the phrase "underground warfare." The net impact of their efforts on the course of the Second World War and on the morale and skill of all who joined in widespread acts of resistance, large and small, will probably be debated as long as the War itself remains a subject of study. In any such review, the cost effectiveness of a single successful saboteur versus a bomber (with its air and ground crew) will remain a matter of debate. What cannot be disputed is the encouragement to individuals in occupied countries which assistance from outside brought with it. The will to resist or the determination to escape was frequently augmented by the knowledge that someone outside was working to help. How are such benefits to be measured? Intangible and ultimately immeasurable though such assistance to resistance may have been, it was an essential element in the conflict which eventually vanquished the tyranny of Hitler from Europe and that of the Japanese militarists from Asia.

Canadians shared in that achievement—Canadians from all the races, but particularly French , central European and Chinese Canadians. Their personal backgrounds and political convictions embraced a wide spectrum, but all gave unstintingly of themselves in Europe and Asia—as saboteurs, arms instructors, radio operators, and guerrilla leaders, sometimes employing the language of their ancestors' homeland or the skills that they had themselves learned in the new world of Canada. However diverse their backgrounds, aptitudes, foibles, and interests, all had one fundamental characteristic in common: courage. And they gave that without measure.

Appendix: Frogmen in Burma

Canadians with Force 136 were not the only ones to serve behind Japanese lines. Throughout the Second World War, unconventional warfare was practised by all three conventional services. Allied navies were no exception. By 1942 the Royal Navy was developing irregular units, among them Combined Operations Pilotage Parties skilled in the reconnaissance of enemy-held beaches, and a variety of units of surface or underwater raiders, including frogmen and small-boat crews.

Independently, Bruce Wright, a junior officer in the Royal Canadian Navy Volunteer Reserve, put forward in 1942 his own ideas on using expert swimmers to penetrate enemy harbour defences and attack shipping. Wright had been captain of a prewar University of New Brunswick swimming team. During the long watches on North Atlantic convoy escorts, he had mused on the possibilities of harbour sabotage by expert swimmers. Wright's inchoate proposals eventually reached Ottawa where they aroused sufficient interest for him to be sent on a hurried visit to Combined Operations Headquarters in London. Out of this meeting, Wright was given command of a small Anglo-Canadian unit stationed in the warm, clear waters of southern California where they could develop the equipment and techniques necessary to give substance to what had originally been little more than a gleam in his eye. Wright's team included Burton Strange, another lieutenant in the R.C.N.V.R., and Flight-Lieutenant Harry Avery, an R.C.A.F. radar technician. What Strange and Avery had in common with Wright was an exceptional ability to swim.

With the completion of their long periods of training in California, the Bahamas, and finally England, Wright and his team were ready for duty by the winter of 1943. Yet they spent almost all of 1944 in England, awaiting orders to join – somehow – in the invasion of Europe. But Commandos and Royal Engineers cleared the Normandy landing beaches with great courage and success. Wright was frustrated.

> In vain I tried to reconcile myself to the fact that we were a tropics team and not equipped for cold northern waters . . . . Nevertheless, the greatest military show the world had ever known had been successfully concluded without us . . . . The summer of 1944 was long and tedious for us . . . . By now I had abandoned all hope of employment in our operational role in Europe . . . I bent every effort to have us transferred to Admiral Mountbatten in Ceylon at once.[1]

Wright was eventually successful in his efforts: his unit was suddenly ordered to Ceylon.*

Arduous exercises along the beaches and in the jungles of the northern tip of Ceylon marked the arrival of 1945 – but still no action. More than two years had passed since Wright and his frogmen had begun training in southern California for warfare against enemy shipping. Now the Japanese had withdrawn their ships from the Bay of Bengal. The only remaining possibility of going into combat seemed to be in an army-support role.

By the end of 1944, the Fourteenth Army had begun to move southward through Burma toward Mandalay and Rangoon. The Japanese defending Mandalay were entrenched behind the broad, treacherous Irrawaddy River. If Mandalay held, the capture of Rangoon would be delayed by the May monsoons,

---

*In early 1943, Mountbatten, as head of Combined Operations, had interviewed Wright in London about his proposals for "The Use of Natatorial Assault and Reconnaissance Units in Combined Operations."

rendering air supply impossible. The prompt crossing of the Irrawaddy and the capture of Mandalay was an essential element in the strategy of Mountbatten, who, as we have seen, ordered his local commanders to "take all risks" to achieve their objectives. Amphibious landings were also planned on the Arakan coast of Burma to help ensure that no major Japanese units were left to threaten the flank of the Fourteenth Army during its drive on Rangoon. Thus it was that in February 1945, Wright and Strange, the naval officers, and Avery, the airman, found themselves in the front lines of an army.

Three of the four Sea Reconnaissance Units were now far from the sea, assigned the task of charting, in the night, the shoals and depths of the Irrawaddy (the fourth unit was to assist the amphibious landing on the Arakan coast). The north bank of the Irrawaddy near Mandalay was a sort of no-man's-land where Japanese patrols occasionally moved at night; the south bank was firmly held by the Japanese. Several crossing points had already been tentatively selected; it was for Wright and his men to establish where exactly the British crossings could most safely be attempted.

> The next job was to have a detailed look at the channels between the sandbars of the main stream and to examine the landing beaches on the Japanese bank. The sandbars were constantly changing, and the muddy water made depth determination from aerial photographs impossible. Also it had been decided not to photograph the assault beaches closer than ten days to the crossing date for the sandbars might change drastically. Hence the call for us.
>
> ... We had charted the best approaches through the ever-shifting sandbars to all five of the assault beaches; now we were preparing to cross ahead of the assault wave and mark the way for them. This was to be the major thrust of the 14th Army across the Irrawaddy. It was designed to close the pincer on Meiktila, the vital rail, road and air junction whose fall would split the Japanese army in Burma in two. But before all these good things could happen, we must face and complete the longest opposed river crossing ever attempted in any theatre of World War II.[2]

Night after night, a contingent from the Special Boat Section of the commandos and the Sea Reconnaissance Units carefully surveyed the crossing routes, sometimes within a few yards of enemy sentries or patrols and occasionally under fire from alert Japanese. All three units, using paddle boards or only rubber fins, crossed and recrossed the river, noting the sandbanks on which the assault boats could ground, testing the depth of the water, gauging the effect of the current on assault craft, obtaining reliable information about possible landing beaches and, on the nights of the crossings, acting as guides for the lead assault boats. On 16 February Mountbatten noted in his diary, "I was fascinated to see what a beach-head looks like on a river crossing, and found that it bore a fairly close resemblance to a beach-head in an amphibious assault, except that the soldiers run all the craft themselves. The Irrawaddy is now in the process of being crossed at four widely separated points.... The casualties in the crossing have to date been surprisingly light."[3]

With vital bridgeheads established, thanks in large measure to the courage of the commando's Special Boat Section and of the Sea Reconnaissance Units, the Indian and British divisions of the Fourteenth Army poured across the Irrawaddy, capturing Mandalay, and thirty-nine days later, just before the monsoons, entering Rangoon. Avery and four of his men were then ordered to Calcutta to prepare for their next and even more hazardous assignment: they were to be landed behind the Japanese-held island of Singapore, somehow cross the city at night, and swim about the harbour identifying Japanese warships for the approaching British fleet. The dropping of atomic bombs on Japan, however, suddenly ended any need for such a suicidal mission.

The work of Wright and his unconventional units on the Irrawaddy was completed in less than a month. More than two years of training had helped to ensure that there were no casualties on their dangerous surveys. It was not a long war for Wright, Strange, Avery, and the others, but for a brief period behind enemy lines along the Irrawaddy River, it had been dangerous enough.

The men of the Sea Reconnaissance Units had volunteered and trained extensively for their assignment. For another lieutenant in the R.C.N.V.R., two months' service with M.P.A.J.A. guerrillas in Malaya was accidental. Ian Alcock of Victoria had been loaned to the Royal Navy following convoy duty in the North Atlantic. Alcock had been trained in the techniques of amphibious landings, the reconnaissance of beaches, and other aspects of combined operations. Following participation in the invasion of Sicily, he was given further training, beginning in December 1943, and, a year later, from the R.N. submarine base in Ceylon, he participated in a total of seven beach reconnaissances along the coasts of Thailand, Burma, Malaya, and the Netherlands East Indies. Launched at night in small rubber boats from an R.N. or Dutch submarine, Combined Operations Pilotage Patrols had from 1943 been surveying beach gradients, natural obstacles, and Japanese defences, checking depth soundings and beach samples. Collapsible canoes were employed and occasionally members of the C.O.P.P. swam close to enemy-held shores (for one such exploit, Alcock received the D.S.C.).

It was Alcock's eighth reconnaissance that almost ended in disaster. On 8 June 1945, he and a naval rating shared one of four rubber boats launched from a submarine on the Malay coast about two hundred and forty kilometres north of Singapore to survey it prior to Operation Zipper. Detailed reconnaissance required swimming near the beaches, but on this occasion, the survey took longer than anticipated. Both Alcock and the sailor and, independently, another two-man boat crew concluded that, given the ocean currents, it would be impossible to return to the submarine before daybreak (when it must submerge to avoid Japanese patrols). Instead, the two boat crews, unknown to each other and full of apprehension, hid their rubber boats near the beach. In a drenching night rain, they pushed into the black jungle. For the next two days and nights, Alcock and the sailor forced their way through jungle and swamps, living on the meagre food of their emergency rations. A Chinese finally took them to a guerilla outpost where the other boat crew had also been led.

In this country of jungles, swamps and paddy fields, where Chinese and natives carried on a secret, unremitting struggle with the Japanese, spies abounded and were given terribly short shrift. The

four strangers in green-daubed battledress who claimed to be
sailors were received with the greatest suspicion; and their urgent
requests to be taken to a post from which they could send out a
wireless signal only added to the doubts already held about them.[4]

During the next fortnight, Alcock and the three Englishmen
were passed on from one jungle camp to the next, constantly
being assured that they were being taken to headquarters. When
they finally reached it, a senior M.P.A.J.A. officer subjected them
to intensive questioning before agreeing to arrange for a message
to be sent on their behalf to Ceylon. Partly as a test of their *bona
fides*, the agent asked them to include a request in their message
for a major air drop of arms for his poorly equipped troops.
Some arms were eventually dropped by Liberators, but not
before Alcock and the other three sailors were moved from the
headquarters camp near which Japanese patrols were becoming
increasingly active. As generally happened to all those unaccus-
tomed to the dense Malayan jungle, they soon became ill,
plagued by jungle sores. Unable to keep up with the main body
of guerrillas, they had to be helped along by small rescue parties.
The jungle routes of the Chinese guides – almost all of whom
spoke little or no English – seemed to the feverish Alcock so
circuitous that he began to wonder whether they were, in fact,
intending to avoid Japanese patrols or were merely leading him
about aimlessly before finally disposing of him.

After weeks of toiling through the jungle at night, living on a
little rice and whatever other scant food became available, a
Malay suddenly appeared with a message for Alcock from a
Force 136 team ordering him to the coast at Negri Sembilan.
There on 23 August 1945, a thirty-year-old "red-haired, scrawny,
fever-ridden spectre...staggered out of [the] jungle...[to] a
waiting British ship. Through the haze of semi-delirium he
learned that the last unyielding detachments of Japanese were
being mopped up and that the war had been officially over for
more than a week."[5]

Notes

(For full bibliographical details of sources quoted, see Bibliography.)

PREFACE

1. Howarth, *Undercover,* p. 136.
2. From the Foreword by Lord Mountbatten to Trenowden, *Operations Most Secret.*

CHAPTER 1: THE BEGINNINGS (pp. 1 – 10).

1. Quoted in Cookridge, *Inside S.O.E.,* p. 6.
2. *Ibid.,* p. 5.
3. "The Distant Future," extract from Joint Planning Staff's Review of Future Strategy, 14 June 1941, JP (41) 444 in CAB 79/12, quoted in Stafford, *Britain and European Resistance,* p. 239.
4. Quoted in Hugh Dalton, *The Fateful Years* (London: Muller, 1957), p. 368.
5. Quoted in Foot, *S.O.E. in France,* p. 12.
6. *Ibid.,* p. 13.
7. Cavelcoressi and Wint, *Total War* (London: John Lane, The Penguin Press, 1972), pp. 275-76.
8. Bickham Sweet-Escott, quoted in Auty and Clogg, *British Policy,* p. 15.
9. Stafford, *Britain and European Resistance,* p. 78.
10. Langley, *Fight Another Day,* p. 138.

CHAPTER 2: RECRUITMENT OF CANADIANS (pp. 11 – 24).

1. Buckmaster, *Specially Employed,* p. 18.
2. *Ibid.,* p. 29.

3. Felix Walter, "Cloak and Dagger," C.M.H.Q. file 760.013 (D1) 1946, p. 3. In the foreword to his 1946 report, Walter wrote: "It differs from other historical narratives in that it has not been possible ... to buttress up factual statements by a mass of footnotes and chapter and verse references. The reason for this is that while the author of this report was given free access to many of the relevant files, it was understood that no direct reference would be made to them. In addition, the special organizations concerned make it a practice, for security reasons, to keep paper work to a minimum and voluminous records do not, in fact, exist."
4. Foot, *S.O.E. in France*, p. 49.
5. War Office letter of 12 March 1940, quoted in unpublished history of the Canadian Intelligence Corps by Robert Elliot.
6. R. H. Berry, "Resistance: Aid from the Outside," *History of the Second World War*, vol. 2, no. 6, p. 607
7. Porter, "Sonia Was a Spy." p. 44.
8. Michel, *Shadow War*, pp. 127-28.
9. Major-General Sir Colin Gubbins left, unfortunately, few records of his remarkable wartime career which began with a hazardous mission to Poland on the eve of the German invasion. For his comments, see *Journal of the Royal United Service Institute*, vol. 93, pp. 221-23, May 1948, and his article in M. R. Elliott-Bateman, ed., *Fourth Dimension of Warfare* (Manchester: Manchester University Press, 1970).
10. Letter to the author, 17 February 1979.
11. Buckmaster, *Specially Employed*, p. 70.
12. F. Ippecourt, *Chemins en Espagne* (Paris: Gaicher, 1964), pp. 187-88.
13. Conversation of the author with LaBrosse, 3 September 1976.

CHAPTER 3: THE FIRST CANADIAN AGENTS INTO FRANCE (pp. 27 – 43).

1. From a report by the Commanding Officer of the Wanborough Manor school in Bieler's S.O.E. file, quoted in Foot, *S.O.E. in France*, p. 268.
2. Reader's Digest Association, *Canadians at War*, p. 221.
3. Walter, "Cloak and Dagger," p. 8.
4. Statement by Mrs. Dale in the possession of Bieler's daughter, Jacqueline Bieler-Briggs.
5. Quoted in Reader's Digest Association, *Canadians at War*, p. 221.
6. *Ibid.*, pp. 223-24.
7. Michel, *Shadow War*, p. 213.
8. *British Official History of the Second World War*, vol. 9, pp. 165-66.
9. From an unpublished interview of Chartrand by Douglas How, Montreal, c. 1965.
10. Interview in *La Presse*, Montreal, n.d. (probably autumn 1945).
11. *Ibid.*

CHAPTER 4: VICTIMS (pp. 44 – 56).

1. Quoted in Ford, *Making of a Secret Agent*, p. 46.
2. *Ibid.*, p. 93.
3. *Ibid.*, p. 157
4. *Ibid.*, p. 174.
5. *Ibid.*, p. 180.
6. *Ibid.*, p. 208.
7. *Ibid.*, p. 188.
8. *Ibid.*, pp. 197-98.
9. Unpublished letter to the editor of *Saturday Night*, 13 August 1952, in the possession of J. H. Yocom, Toronto.
10. Conversation of the author with Alison Grant Ignatieff, 10 September 1976.
11. *Ibid.*
12. Quoted in Ford, *Making of a Secret Agent*, p. 238.
13. From a final training report on Pickersgill quoted in a 25 June 1965 note prepared by the Foreign and Commonwealth Office.
14. Conversation of the author with Alison Grant Ignatieff, 10 September 1976.
15. Quoted in Ford, *Making of a Secret Agent*, p. 255.

CHAPTER 5: PLAYING THE RADIO GAME (pp. 57 – 64).

1. Quoted in Giskes, *London Calling North Pole*, p. 184.
2. From information supplied by J. W. Pickersgill to the author.
3. Quoted in Foot, *S.O.E. in France*, p. 348.
4. *Ibid.*, p. 347

CHAPTER 6: THE EXECUTIONS (pp. 65 – 74).

1. Walter, "Cloak and Dagger," p. 11.
2. John Wheeler-Bennett, *Nemesis of Power* (London: Macmillan, 1954), p. 662.
3. Quoted in *Sun Life Review*, Montreal, October 1945, p. 15.
4. Quoted in Reader's Digest Association, *Canadians at War*, p. 226.
5. Foot, *S.O.E. in France*, p. 425.
6. From a letter from Buckmaster to Mrs. Bieler of 5 July 1945, quoted in *Sun Life Review*, Montreal, October 1945, p. 15.
7. Yeo-Thomas quoted in Porter, "The Last Days of Frank Pickersgill," p. 47
8. Marshall, *The White Rabbit*, pp. 182-84.
9. Porter, "The Last Days of Frank Pickersgill," p. 49.

CHAPTER 7: SURVIVORS (pp. 75 – 85).

1. Walter, "Cloak and Dagger," p. 8.
2. Michel, *Shadow War*, p. 108.
3. Christopher Sykes, *Four Studies in Loyalty* (London: Collins, 1946), p. 183.
4. Foot, *S.O.E. in France*, p. 366.
5. From Caza's citation for the M.B.E.
6. Buckmaster, *Specially Employed*, p. 27.
7. Letter to the author, 9 March 1979.
8. Sirois, "Liaison Officer Reports," p. 7.
9. *Ibid.*, p. 42.
10. *Ibid.*, pp. 45-47.

CHAPTER 8: THE TRIUMPH OF THE AGED AND REDUNDANT (pp. 86 – 104).

1. C.G.S. memorandum to the Minister of National Defence, 22 September 1943, P.A.C.
2. D.N.D. file Special 25-1-1, vol. 6.
3. Walter, "Cloak and Dagger," p. 6.
4. Interview in the Toronto *Star*, 22 December 1944.
5. *Ibid.*
6. Walter, "Cloak and Dagger," p. 14.
7. Buckmaster quoted in Reader's Digest Association, *Canadians at War*, p. 231.
8. Cosgrove, *Evaders*, pp. 250-61.

CHAPTER 9: D-DAY (pp. 105 – 115).

1. Foot, *S.O.E. in France*, p. 379.
2. Cookridge, *They Came from the Sky*, p. 232.
3. Braddon, *Nancy Wake*, p. 226.
4. Foot, *S.O.E. in France*, p. 288.
5. Millar, *Horned Pigeon*, p. 314.
6. From Veilleux' citation for the M.B.E.

CHAPTER 10: ASSIGNMENTS FROM ALGIERS (pp. 116 – 128).

1. Report of the "Etat Major, Forces françaises de l'interieur; Relève chronologique des operations effectuées en Ardèche du 15 au 31 août 1944," in the possession of Chassé.
2. Report by Major Cyrus Manierre in S.O.E. file.
3. Interview in the Toronto *Star*, 22 December 1944.
4. *Ibid.*
5. *Ibid.*
6. Foot, *S.O.E. in France*, p. 394.
7. From Hunter's citation for the M.C.

CHAPTER 11: YUGOSLAVIA (pp. 129 – 154).

1. Barker, *British Policy,* pp. 149 and 152.
2. Conversation of the author with Drew-Brook, 30 January 1976.
3. Letter of Stevan Serdar to the author, 14 July 1981.
4. Unpublished autobiography of Eric Curwain.
5. Deakin, *Embattled Mountain,* pp. 185-86.
6. Clissold, *Whirlwind,* p. 163.
7. Hamilton *Spectator,* 5 October 1968.
8. Deakin, *Embattled Mountain,* p. 1.
9. *Ibid.,* pp. 219-20.
10. Jones, *Twelve Months,* p. 141.
11. Maclean, *Eastern Approaches,* p. 320.
12. Quoted in Bayles, "Jones of Yugoslavia," p. 35.
13. Jones, *Twelve Months,* p. 28.
14. *Ibid.,* p. 122.
15. Hamilton *Spectator,* 5 October 1968.
16. Bayles, "Jones of Yugoslavia," p. 35.
17. Rogers, *Guerrilla Surgeon,* p. 153.
18. Letter of John Holmes to Hume Wrong, 11 September 1945, in the possession of John Holmes.
19. Davidson, *Partisan Picture,* pp. 66-67.
20. Private account of his wartime service by Dr. Dafoe written in 1946 and now in the possession of Michael Dafoe.
21. From the C.B.C. talk given by Dr. Dafoe on 13 August 1945.
22. Ibid.

CHAPTER 12: THE BALKANS AND ITALY (pp. 155 – 176).

1. Unpublished autobiography of Eric Curwain.
2. Letter from Peter Boughey to the author, 10 September 1979.
3. Conversation of the author with André Durovecz, 19 May 1980.
4. Stafford, *Britain and European Resistance,* pp. 193-194.
5. Undated postwar letter (1946?) from Vetere to Department of National Defence.
6. Quoted in the Toronto *Star,* 13 November 1945.

CHAPTER 13: ASIA (pp. 177 – 191).

1. See, for example, Spencer Chapman, *Jungle Is Neutral.*
2. Sweet-Escott, *Baker Street Irregular,* pp. 230-31.
3. Spencer Chapman, *Jungle Is Neutral,* p. 28.
4. William Slim, *Defeat into Victory* (London: Cassell, 1956), p. 340.
5. Sweet-Escott, *Baker Street Irregular,* p. 230.
6. For a few details on the escape of the M.T.B.s, see Benjamin Proulx, *Underground from Hong Kong* (New York: Dutton, 1943), pp. 121-22.

7. Transcript of interview by Victor Wilson with Hugh Legg, 28 May 1975.
8. Reginald H. Roy, *For Most Conspicuous Bravery* (Vancouver: University of British Columbia Press, 1977), p. 200.
9. S.O.E. report on Operation Oblivion.
10. Albert Wedemeyer, *Wedemeyer Reports* (New York: Holt, 1958), p. 281.

CHAPTER 14: SARAWAK (pp. 192 – 200).

1. Malcolm MacDonald, *Borneo People* (London: Hutchinson, 1956), p. 37.
2. *Ibid.*, p. 98.
3. *Ibid.*, p. 80.
4. Diary of Ray Wooler, in his possession.
5. Department of Defence, Canberra, Volumes of History of Inter Allied Services Department and Services Reconnaissance Department, Special Operations, CRS A3270, vol. 1, pt. 2, chapter 1, p. 9.
6. For a graphic description of the horrors of prison camp life in Kuching, see Agnes Newton Keith, *Three Came Home* (Toronto: McClelland and Stewart, 1946).
7. Diary of Ray Wooler.
8. S.O.E. report on the training of Chinese-Canadians.

CHAPTER 15: BURMA (pp. 201 – 220).

1. Walter, "Cloak and Dagger," p. 22.
2. Kermit Roosevelt, *The War Report of the O.S.S.* (New York: Walker, 1976).
3. Sweet-Escott, *Baker Street Irregular,* p. 247.
4. Beamish, *Burma Drop,* p. 43.
5. Sweet-Escott, *Baker Street Irregular,* p. 249.
6. Bowen, *Undercover in the Jungle,* p. 104.
7. Undated letter (1953?) from Thibeault to Fournier.
8. Letter from Lt.-Colonel H. W. Howell to Force 136 Headquarters, 2 June 1945, S.O.E. file.
9. Bowen, *Undercover in the Jungle,* p. 158.
10. Meunier, "Force 136 Burma," p. 16.
11. *Ibid.*, p. 17.
12. Conversation of the author with Cyril Dolly, 12 May 1980.
13. Foot and Langley, *M.I.9.,* pp. 282-83.

CHAPTER 16: MALAYA (pp. 221 – 241).

1. Quoted in Gerrard Tickell, *Moon Squadron* (London: Wingate, 1956), p. 199.
2. Conversation of the author with George Chin, 7 September 1979.
3. Letter from Colin Munro to the author, 11 March 1981.
4. S.O.E. report.

CHAPTER 17: ESCAPE AND EVASION (pp. 245 – 260).

1. Quoted in Barry Broadfoot, *Six War Years* (Toronto: Doubleday, 1974), pp. 97-99.
2. Quoted in Cosgrove, *Evaders*, p. 6.
3. E. H. Bates' introduction to Paul Brickhill, *Escape or Die* (London: Evans, 1952), p. 9.
4. Foot, *Resistance*, p. 40.
5. Cosgrove, *Evaders*, pp. 23-24.
6. Conversation of the author with LaBrosse, 3 September 1976.
7. Foot, *S.O.E. in France*, pp. 94-95.
8. Darling, *Secret Sunday*, pp. 108-9.
9. Conversation of the author with LaBrosse, 3 September 1976.
10. Langley, *Fight Another Day*, p. 193.
11. Conversation of the author with LaBrosse, 3 September 1976.
12. *Ibid.*

CHAPTER 18: DIEPPE AND BEYOND (pp. 261 – 271).

1. Conversations of the author with Vanier and LaFleur, 31 January and 27 February 1977.
2. Darling, *Secret Sunday*, p. 85.
3. Neave, *Saturday at M.I.9*, p. 227; a slightly different version from a wartime report by Airey Neave is in Appendix I of Dumais, *Man Who Went Back*, p. 209.
4. Conversation of the author with Vanier, 31 January 1977.
5. Huguen, *Par les Nuits les plus longues*, p. 160.
6. Picquet-Wicks, *Four in the Shadows*, p. 194.
7. Neave, *Saturday at M.I.9*, p. 242.

CHAPTER 19: THE CROSS-CHANNEL FERRY (pp. 272 – 286).

1. Conversation of the author with LaBrosse, 3 September 1976.
2. Dumais, *Man Who Went Back*, p. 117.
3. *Ibid.*, p. 123.
4. Quoted in the *New York Times*, 18 October 1976.
5. From a report by Airey Neave, quoted in Appendix I of Dumais, *Man Who Went Back*, p. 210.
6. Conversation of the author with LaBrosse, 3 September 1976.
7. Neave, *Saturday at M.I.9*, p. 237.
8. Quoted in the *New York Times*, 18 October 1976.
9. Cosgrove, *Evaders*, p. 297.
10. Dumais, *Man Who Went Back*, pp. 197-99.
11. Conversation of the author with LaBrosse, 27 February 1981.
12. Dumais, *Man Who Went Back*, p. 203.

CHAPTER 20: THE MEDITERRANEAN AND ASIA (pp. 287 – 299).

1. Derry, *Rome Escape Line*, p. 55.
2. *Ibid.*, p. 63.
3. *Ibid.*, p. 65.
4. Letter from Major R. C. Jackman in the possession of Robert Stewart, 22 May 1944.
5. Memorandum of 28 May 1946 by Stewart about his wartime service in the possession of Robert Stewart.
6. From Stewart's Citation for the O.B.E.
7. Letter of Bill Lee to the author, 6 January 1981.
8. Conversation of the author with Bill Lee, 31 October 1980.

APPENDIX: FROGMEN IN BURMA (pp. 302 – 307).

1. Wright, *Frogmen of Burma*, pp. 62-63.
2. *Ibid.*, pp. 95-100.
3. John Terraine, ed., *Life and Times of Lord Mountbatten* (London: Hutchinson, 1968), p. 129.
4. Joseph Schull, *The Far Distant Ships* (Ottawa: Queen's Printer, 1961), p. 421.
5. *Ibid.*, p. 422.

Bibliography

BOOKS

Amery, Julian. *Sons of the Eagle: A Study in Guerrilla Warfare.* London: Macmillan, 1948.
____. *Approach March: A Venture in Autobiography.* London: Hutchinson, 1973.
Astley, Joan. *The Inner Circle: A View of the War at the Top.* London: Hutchinson, 1971.
Auty, Phyllis, and Richard Clogg, eds. *British Policy towards Resistance in Yugoslavia and Greece.* London: Macmillan, 1975.
Barker, E. *British Policy in South-East Europe in the Second World War.* London: Macmillan, 1976.
Beamish, John. *Burma Drop.* London: Elek, 1958.
Bowen, John. *Undercover in the Jungle.* London: William Kimber, 1978.
Braddon, Russell. *Nancy Wake.* London: Cassell, 1956.
Buckmaster, Maurice. *Specially Employed: The Story of British Aid to French Patriots of the Resistance.* London: Batchworth, 1953.
____. *They Fought Alone: The Story of British Agents in France.* London: Odhams, 1958.
Chapman, F. Spencer. *The Jungle Is Neutral.* London: Chatto and Windus, 1949.
Clissold, Stephen. *Whirlwind.* New York: Philosophical Library, 1949.
Cookridge, E. H. [Edward Spiro]. *Inside S.O.E.: The Story of Special Operations in Western Europe 1940-1945.* London: Arthur Barker, 1966.
____. *They Came from the Sky.* London: Heinemann, 1965.

Cosgrove, Edmund. *The Evaders.* Toronto: Clarke, Irwin, 1970.

Cross, John. *Red Jungle.* London: Robert Hale, 1957.

Darling, Donald. *Secret Sunday.* London: William Kimber, 1976.

Davidson, Basil. *Partisan Picture.* Bedford: Bedford Books, 1946.

Deakin, F. W. *The Embattled Mountain.* London: Oxford University Press, 1971.

Derry, Sam. *The Rome Escape Line.* London: Harrap, 1960.

Dumais, Lucien. *The Man Who Went Back.* London: Leo Cooper, 1975.

_____. *Un Canadien français face à la Gestapo.* Montreal: Editions du Jour, 1969.

_____. *Un Canadien français à Dieppe.* Paris: Editions France-Empire, 1968.

Elliot-Bateman, N. R., ed. *The Fourth Dimension of War.* Manchester: Manchester University Press, 1970.

Foot, M. R. D. *S.O.E. in France: An Account of the British Special Operations Executive in France 1940-1944.* London: H.M.S.O., 1966.

_____. *Resistance: An Analysis of European Resistance to Nazism 1940-1945.* London: Eyre Methuen, 1978.

_____. *Six Faces of Courage.* London: Eyre Methuen, 1978.

_____, and J. M. Langley. *M.I.9 Escape and Evasion 1939-1945.* London: The Bodley Head, 1979.

Ford, George H., ed. *The Making of a Secret Agent: The Pickersgill Letters.* Toronto: McClelland and Stewart, 1978.

Hawes, Stephen, and Ralph White, eds. *Resistance in Europe, 1939-1945.* London: Allen Lane, 1975.

Heslop, Richard. *Xavier.* London: Rupert Hart Davis, 1970.

Hinsley, F. H., et al. *British Intelligence in the Second World War.* Vols. 1 and 2. London: H.M.S.O., 1979 and 1981.

Howarth, Patrick, ed. *Special Operations.* London: Routledge and Kegan Paul, 1955.

_____. *Undercover: The Men and Women of the Special Operations Executive.* London: Routledge and Kegan Paul, 1980.

Huguen, Roger. *Par les Nuits les plus longues.* Saint-Brieuc: Les Presses Bretonnes, 1976.

Hutton, Clayton. *Official Secret.* London: MacParrish, 1960.

Jones, W. M. *Twelve Months with Tito's Partisans.* Bedford: Bedford Books, 1946.

Kemp, Peter. *No Colours or Crest.* London: Cassell, 1958.

_____. *Alms for Oblivion.* London: Cassell, 1961.

Langley, J. M. *Fight Another Day.* London: Collins, 1974.

Lindsay, Oliver. *At the Going Down of the Sun.* London: Nelson, 1981.

Mackasey, Kenneth. *The Partisans of Europe in World War II.* London: Hart-Davis MacGibbon, 1975.

Maclean, Fitzroy. *Eastern Approaches.* London: Cape, 1949.

Marshall, Bruce. *The White Rabbit: From the Story Told to him by Wing Commander F. F. E. Yeo-Thomas, G.C., M.C.* London: Evans, 1952.

McCall, Gibb. *Flight Most Secret: Air Missions for SOE and SIS.* London: William Kimber, 1981.

Melnyk, T. W. *Canadian Flying Operations in South East Asia 1941-1945.* Ottawa: Department of National Defence, 1976.

Michel, Henri. *The Shadow War.* London: Deutsch, 1972.

Millar, George. *Horned Pigeon.* London: Heinemann, 1946.
———. *Road to Resistance, An Autobiography.* London: Heinemann, 1980.

Montagu, E. *Beyond Top Secret Ultra.* London: Peter Davies, 1977.

Neave, Airey. *Little Cyclone.* London: Hodder and Stoughton, 1954.
———. *Saturday at M.I.9.* London: Hodder and Stoughton, 1969.

Newnham, Maurice. *Prelude to Glory.* London: Sampson Low, Marston, n.d.

Pearson, Michael. *Tears of Glory.* London: Macmillan, 1979.

Picard, Henri. *Ceux de la Résistance.* Nevers: Editions Chassaing, 1949.

Piquet-Wicks, Eric. *Four in the Shadows.* Norwich: Jarrolds, 1970.

Reader's Digest Association Ltd. *The Canadians at War.* 2 vols. Montreal, 1969.

Rogers, Lindsay. *Guerilla Surgeon.* London: Collins, 1957.

Rootham, Jasper. *Miss Fire.* London: Chatto and Windus, 1946.

Stacey, C. P. *The Canadian Army.* Ottawa: King's Printer, 1946.

Stafford, David. *Britain and European Resistance 1940-1945.* London: Macmillan, 1980.

Stuart, Campbell. *Opportunity Knocks Once.* London: Collins, 1952.

Sweet-Escott, Bickham. *Baker Street Irregular.* London: Methuen, 1965.

Trenowden, Ian. *Operations Most Secret: S.O.E.: The Malayan Theatre.* London: William Kimber, 1978.

Verity, Hugh. *We Landed by Moonlight.* London: Allen, 1978.

Wighton, Charles. *Pin-Stripe Saboteur.* London: Odhams, 1959.

Windsor, John. *The Mouth of the Wolf.* Toronto: Totem, 1978.

Wright, Bruce S. *Frogmen of Burma*. Toronto: Clarke, Irwin, 1968.

Young, Gordon. *In Trust and Treason*. London: Studio Vista, 1959.

PERIODICALS

Alderman, Tom. "Father and Hero – But Who Were You?" *Canadian Magazine*, 14 February 1970.

Bayles, William D. "Jones of Yugoslavia." *Maclean's*, 1 December 1944.

Coulon, Jacques. "Le Reseau Shelburne," *Perspectives*, vol. 9, no. 38, 23 September 1967.

Gubbins, Sir Colin. "Resistance Movements in the War." *Journal of the Royal United Service Institution*, London, vol. 93, May 1948.

Hubbell, John G. "Good Evening to the House of Alphonse." *Reader's Digest*, September 1966.

MacKenzie, N. A. "The 'Lawrence of Yugoslavia' Who Refused to be Defeated." *Atlantic Advocate*, May 1970.

Meunier, P. C. M. "Force 136 Burma." *Springbok*, vol. 17, no. 2, Autumn 1947.

Morchain, G. "Under the Nose of the Gestapo." *Sentinel*, January 1970.

Porter, McKenzie. "Sonia Was a Spy." *Maclean's*, 15 February 1953.

———. "The Last Days of Frank Pickersgill." *Maclean's*, 2 December 1961.

Roy, Patricia E. "The Soldiers Canada Didn't Want: Her Chinese and Japanese Citizens." *Canadian Historical Review*, vol. 59, no. 3, September 1978.

Sirois, A. L. "Liaison Officer Reports." *The Rum Jar*, Regina, Royal Canadian Legion, Autumn 1954.

Sismey, Eric. "Commando Bay." (Victoria) *Daily Colonist*, 23 September 1975.

Trent, Bill. "How a Top-Secret Force Fought the Nazis." *Weekend Magazine*, vol. 12, nos. 6 and 7, 1962.

Index

"Actor" Circuit, 106
Alcock, Ian, 305–7
Algiers, 17, 116–17, 121–24, 126–27, 173, 285
Allier, 109
Alor Setar, 233
Ambérieu, 91
Amboise, 39
Amiens, 271
Andorra, 260
.Angers, 33
Angoulême, 82–83, 85
Arcachon, 107
Archambault, Jean-Paul, xiv, 90–93, 96, 100, 202, 203, 210, 212
Ardèche, 118–20
Argentan, 114
Arisaig, 15, 29
Atkins, Vera, xiv, 30–31
Auvergne, 108, 266
Avery, Harry, 303, 305
Avignon, 99

Bailey, William, 134–35, 137
Bairnsfather, Bruce, 293–94
Bali, 237

Bangkok, 235
Banska Bystrica, 166
Barcelona, 10, 249, 260
Bari, 17, 147, 152, 154, 160–63, 166, 168, 177, 290
Barker, Elizabeth, xiii, 130
Bassein, 219, 220
Batu Pahat, 240–41
Beaumont, Dr., 262, 263, 271
Beauregard, Alcide, 65–67, 74, 79, 91
Beauvais, 281
Beekman, Yolande Unternährer, 33–34, 68–70, 79, 278
Bégué, Georges, 81
Belgrade, 134, 151
Belsen, 55
Benoit, Joseph Henri Adelard, 90, 92–95, 100, 114, 202, 203, 210, 219, 222, 225, 239–41
Berlin, 64, 93
Berne, 175
Beyne, Colonel, 122–23
Bieler, Gustave, 27–31, 33–36, 38–39, 44, 65–70, 72, 74, 76, 78, 92, 117, 156
Bieler, René-Maurice, 31
Birmingham University, 169

Blois, 56
Bochereau, René, 82–83
Bodo, Gustav, 162–63, 165
Bollaert, Emile, 266–68
Bombay, 179, 185, 203, 218, 226, 241
Bordeaux, 85, 106–8, 233, 258
Borosh, Henri, 92–93
Bosnia, 134, 150, 153
Boughey, Peter, xiv, 158, 164–65
Bourg, 91
Boury, Camille, 68
Boxshall, E.G., xiv
Bozanich, Rudolph, 290
Brescia, 175
Brindisi, 160
Brisbane, 189
British Army Aid Group, 184
Broadhurst, "Duggie," 227–29
Brockville Officers' Training School, 94, 106
Brooks, Tony, 79–80
Brossolette, Pierre, 266–68
Broussine, Georges, 260, 265–66
Browne-Bartroli, Albert, 96–97
Brussels, 169, 269
Bucharest, 47, 168, 170
Buchenwald, 61, 63, 71–73, 82, 286
Buckmaster, Maurice, 12, 29, 70, 81, 82, 98, 114, 115
Budapest, 160, 163, 164–65, 166, 167, 168
Burr, Derek, 233–34, 235–36
"Butler" Circuit, 33, 40-41, 58
Butt, Sonia, 15, 96, 202
Byerly, Robert Bennett, 59–61, 65, 73–74
Byrnes, Henry "Barney," 288–89

Cairo, 130, 132–33, 136–39, 141, 143–45, 150, 157, 158, 160, 169–70
Calcutta, 179, 205, 206, 210, 213–15, 217–18, 222, 226, 234, 235, 236, 237, 305

Calgary, 140, 170
Canadian Armoured Corps School, 158
Canadian Grenadier Guards, 106
Canet, 263
Cap Finisterre, 267
Carcassonne, 124
Carleton and York Regiment, 127
Carlsen, Jens Peter, 155
Caskie, Donald, 254
Casselman, Ontario, 121
Cavelcoressi, Peter, 5
Caza, Roger Marc, 79–80, 202, 203, 222, 225, 239–40
"Celery," Operation, 294, 297
Chaklala, 292
Campinchi, Paul-François, 258, 275–77, 279, 281, 285
Chamberlain, Neville, 3
Chan, Roy, 196, 198
Changi, 296–97
Channel Islands, 13
"Character," Operation, 208, 210–11
Charolles, 97
Chartres, 58–59
Chartrand, Joseph Gabrielle, xv, 29, 38–43, 53, 54, 58, 65, 71, 76, 117
Chassé, Pierre Edouard, xv, 117–28, 122, 202, 203, 210, 219–20, 222, 225, 233, 234–36, 238
Château-du-Loir, 41
Chaudière, Régiment de la, 99, 115
Chaumont, 94
Chauny, 274
Cheng, Roger, xv, 186, 189, 191, 196–98
Chiang Kai-shek, 190–91, 206, 292
Chicago, University of, 59
Chilliwack, British Columbia, 225
Chin, George, xv, 231–32
Chindwin River, 207
Chittagong, 179
Chung, Charley, xv, 233
Chungking, 190, 204, 205, 292

Churchill, Winston, 1, 2, 4, 6, 10, 130, 144
Clough, Major, 295
Cluny, 97
Coates, John, 162–63, 167
Cobham, 81
Cognac, 82–83
Colombo, 179, 222, 237, 296–97, 299
Combined Operations Pilotage Parties, 302, 306
"Comet" Line, 270
Comilla, 210
Corbin, Charles, 83, 85
Cordelette, Eugène, 31, 33, 69
Corsica, 258, 285
Cosgrove, L.M., 191
Critchley, Alfred, 140
Croatia, 135, 138–39, 141, 143, 145
Crockatt, Norman, 10
Culioli, Pierre, 54–55, 71
Curwain, Eric, 158–61

Dachau, 70
Dafoe, Colin Scott, 151–54
Dale, Madeleine, 30
Dalhousie University, 140
Dalton, Hugh, 3
Dansey, Claude Marjoribanks, 10, 257
Darling, Donald, 249, 254–55, 260
Dartmouth, England, 43, 277, 278, 282
d'Artois, Lionel Guy, xv, 15–16, 91, 95–99, 202–3
Darwin, Australia, 193
Davidson, Basil, 157
Davis, John, 221–22, 227, 228
Deakin, Sir William, xiv, 141–43, 145
Debrecen, 167
de Chastelain, Alfred Gardyne, 169–70
Dedijer, Vladimir, 148
"Deerhurst," Operation, 164
Defendini, Alphonse, 61, 71

de Gaulle, Charles, 107, 118, 119, 204, 206, 266
Dehler, John Harold McDougal, xv, 124
de Jongh family, 270
de Mauduit, Count and Countess, 258, 260
Deniset, François Adolphe, 60, 65, 71, 73–74, 76
Dent, Irving, 42
Déricourt, Henri, 53
Derna, 17, 138, 141
Derry, Sam, 287–89
Dhuison, 54–56
Diclic, George, 139, 149–50
Dieppe, 256, 261–64, 269, 271
Dignam, Mary, 190
di Lucia, John, 173–74
"Diplomat" Circuit, 100
"Ditcher" Circuit, 66, 91
di Vantro, Angelo, 172
Dolly, Cyril Carlton Mohammad, xv, 217–18
Domodossola, 176
d'Oultremont, Georges, 270–71, 285
"Dracula," Operation, 219–20
Drava River, 162–63
Drew-Brook, Tommy, xv, 88–89, 135
Druzic, Milan, 139, 149
Duchalard, Charles Joseph, 36–38, 44, 76, 100, 126
Duclos, Gustave, xv, 101, 104, 203
Dugi Otok, 291
Dumais, Lucien, xv, 100, 261, 264, 268, 272–85
Dupont, Maurice, 100–102
Durocher, Lucien Joseph, 121, 124
Durovecz, Andre, xv, 159, 166–68

Edinburgh, University of, 174, 176
Edmonton, Alberta, 154
Epernay, 93
Erba, 175

Erdeljac, Peter, 138–39, 141, 146
"Eureka" Beacon, 37, 193

Farmer, John, 108–9
Fismes, 270, 271
Flossenbürg, 69–70, 72–73
Foggia, 291
Fonsomme, 33
Foot, M.R.D., xii, xiii, xiv, 3, 72, 220, 251–52
Fort Garry Horse, 115
Fournier, Joseph Ernest, 125–27, 202, 203, 210, 212–14
Fraser, Hugh, 230
"Freelance" Circuit, 108–9
Fresnes, 56
Fung, Henry, xv, 226–27
Funkspiel (Dutch), 58–59, 64
Funkspiel (French), 58–59, 62, 64
Fusco, Frank, 172
Fusiliers Mont-Royal, 61, 100, 106, 261, 264, 268

Gander, Newfoundland, 189
Garel, François, 40–42, 71
Gelleny, Joseph, 162–63, 165, 167
Geneva, 126
Genoa, 175
Georgescu, George Eugene Stephane, 169–70
Gibraltar, 38, 108, 135, 158, 160, 254, 260, 263, 264
Godmanchester, 257
Gordon, Laurence Laing, 204–5
Goring, Hermann, 64
Goss, Peter, 218
Grandclement, André, 106–7
Grant, Alison, 52–53, 56
Green, D.E.F., 126–27
Greenock, 159, 264
Grenoble, 48, 101
Gross Rosen, 60, 73

Gubbins, Colin, 19
Guelph, 51
Guingamp, 255
Guyotville, 116, 118, 124, 126–27

Haifa, 137
Hainan, 184
Haiphong, 205
Hanna, John Elmore, 239–40
Hanoi, 204, 205, 206, 207
Harrington, John, 214–17
"Helford Flotilla," 253
Helford, 278
Herend, 164
Herter, Adam, 161
Heslop, Richard, 110–11
Hicks, George, 91
Himmler, Heinrich, 64
Hinchfield, 114
Hine, Robert, 203–31
Hiroshima, 197, 223, 239
Hitler, Adolf, 4, 6, 64, 67, 73, 128, 129, 300
Ho Chi Minh, 206
Ho, Harry, xv, 233
Holmes, Ronald, 184, 186, 189, 190, 191
Hong Kong, 184, 186, 191, 199, 201, 292
Horana, 179, 203, 226, 237, 239
Howell, H.W., 212–14
Humboldt, Saskatchewan, 99, 101
Hunter, Anthony, 141, 143
Hunter, Bentley Cameron, 125–27, 202, 210, 219
Hydra Wireless Station, 89
"Hyena" Operation, 212, 214

Imphal, 293–94
Irish Fusiliers, 292
Irrawaddy River, 219, 303–5
Istanbul, 130
Izernore, 112

Java, 298
Jephson, Ronald, 141, 143
Jedburghs, 117
Jessore, 210, 226, 237
Johore, 223, 239, 240, 295
Johore Bahru, 296
Joly, Guy, 261–65
Jones, William, 139–41, 143–49
Juvigny, 103–4

Kajang, 227
Kangar, 235–36, 238
Karachi, 292
Kedah, 234, 235, 237
Kehl, 46
Kelowna, British Columbia, 174
Kendall, Francis Woodley, 184–87,
    188, 189, 191, 203
Kerambrun, François, 277, 279
King City, Ontario, 168n
King, Lewis, 196, 198
King, Prime Minister W.L.
    Mackenzie, 48, 185, 201n
Kingston, 186
Kingsville, Ontario, 162
Kluang, 240
Kombol, Nikola, 150–51
Kuala Kubu Bahru, 232
Kuala Lumpur, 178, 226, 229, 231–33,
    299
Kuala Pilah, 232
Kuching, 197
Kunming, 205
Kwantung, 185
Kweilin, 185

Labelle, Paul-Emile, xv, 117, 121–24,
    202, 203
LaBrosse, Raymond, xv, 24, 251,
    255–60, 272, 274–85

Labuan, 196, 197, 198
LaFleur, Conrad, xv, 261–65, 269–71,
    285
Landes, Roger, xiv, 81, 85, 106–7, 233,
    234, 235
Langley, British Columbia, 288
Langley, James xiii, 257, 269
La Pointe, Ferdinand Joseph,
    127–28
Larossé, James, 101, 103–4
Lavigne, Marianne, 92, 93
Le Cheylard, 119
Le Cornec, François, 255, 268, 276
Lee, Bill, xv, 226, 295–99
Lee, Bing, xv, 226, 228–30
Legg, Hugh John, 188–89, 191n, 198,
    225
Le Henaff, Yves, 265–68
"Le Legionnaire," "Roger," 259
Le Mans, 96, 114
Lesage, J.E., 66
Lethbridge, Alberta, 115
Lethbridge, R.F., 158
Letpadan, 216–17
Levy, Mike, 227
Lew, Bob, xv, 230–31
Leyburn, 190, 193
Liewer, Charles, 39–40, 42
Lille, 28, 31, 33, 34, 67
Lillooet, British Columbia, 186
Limoges, 79
Lisbon, 49, 249
L'Italien, "Tintin," 96–97
Liverpool, 203
Lizza, Peter, 172–73
Lock, Tom, 188
Loire, 48
London, 47, 49, 79, 83, 85, 94, 108, 112,
    124, 132, 138, 143, 157, 169, 186, 201,
    237, 239, 246, 250, 251, 254, 255,
    256, 258, 273, 275, 278, 281, 290
Louie, Ernie, 232, 239–41
Louie, Victor, xv, 232–33, 239
Lowe, Norman, 196, 198n

Lunding, Capt., 70
Lungchou, 205
Lyon, 48, 66, 73, 79–80, 91, 97, 113,
    120, 123

Macalister, Jeannine, 51
Macalister, John Kenneth, 44, 50–56,
    57–58, 70–73, 74, 286
Macdonald, Ian, 226–28
MacArthur, Douglas, 189
McGill University, 28, 92, 126, 140,
    186, 217, 236
MacLean, Angus, 248
Maclean, Fitzroy, xiv, 145
McNaughton, Andrew, 14

Macedonia, 150
Madoc, Ontario, 151
Madras, 179, 236n, 238
Madrid, 10, 38, 249
Magyar, Adam, 159–60
Mainguy, Joseph, 282
Maisonneuve, Régiment de, 29–30,
    39, 52, 65, 121
Malayan People's Anti-Japanese
    Army (M.P.A.J.A.), 221–40, 295,
    305, 307
Malraux, André, 40, 42
Manchester, 17
Mandalay, 207, 215, 219, 303–5
Manitoba, University of, 45, 47, 60
Manzo, Peter, 172
Mao, Tse-tung, 191
Maple Creek, Saskatchewan, 225
"Marathon," Operation, 269
Markos, Steve, 156–58, 168
"Marksman" Circuit, 111–12
Marsan, 81
Marseille, 48, 79, 80, 99, 122, 123,
    178, 253, 254, 258, 263–64
Massey, Vincent, 147
Massingham, 116–17, 127, 173
Mate, Steve, 158, 164
Maxwell, W., 231

Meerut, 189, 190n, 226
Meiktela, 208–9, 304
Melbourne, 189, 190, 198
Menzies, Sir Stewart, 10
Meunier, Pierre Charles, xv, 105–9,
    202, 203, 210, 214–17, 222, 233,
    251n
Michel, Henri, 35
Mihailovic, Draza, 6, 132, 137–38
Milan, 173, 175–76
Mirepoix, 124
Misercordia, Frank, 172n
Miskolc, 167
Moldovan, Victor, 170
Montargis, 31
Montauban, 80
"Montcalm," "Commandant," 103
Montceau-les-Mines, 98
Montelimar, 122
Montenegro, 139, 141
Montreal, 19, 28, 38, 43, 61, 68, 70, 71,
    88, 90, 92, 95, 99, 101, 105–6, 110,
    117, 125, 172, 199, 202, 236–39, 261,
    285
Montreal, University of, 29, 95
Montreuil-Bellay, 49
Moore, Kay, xiv, 45, 47, 49, 51, 53
Mormont, 107
Morotai Island, 196–97
Morrison, Alistair, 228–29
Morvillars, 102
Moulins, 109
Mountbatten, Louis, xii, 179, 208,
    210, 219, 222, 229, 291, 303–5
Mount Durmitor, 141
Mount Plakho, 214
Mount Voltore, 174
Muar, 241
Munich, 70
Munro, Colin xv, 236–38

Nagasaki, 223
Naidenoff, Toncho, 170–71

Nantes, 41
Naples, 117
Nardi, Vincent, 172
Neave, Airey, xiv, 269, 277, 281
New Brunswick, University of, 302
New Delhi, 179, 189, 218, 239, 291
Newmarket, 17
New York City, 88, 134, 135, 218, 239
New York University, 217
Niagara Falls, 172, 173, 174
Niagara-on-the-Lake, Ontario, 169
Nipissing, Ontario, 230
Nürnberg, 46

"Oaktree" Line, 255–58, 260, 276
"Oblivion," Operation, 186, 189,
    190–91
Office of Strategic Services (O.S.S.),
    20, 89, 121, 158, 160, 206
O'Flaherty, Monsignor, 287, 289
O'Leary, Pat (A. Guérisse), 254, 259
Orléans, 58
Ortona, 173
Osborne, Sir Francis D'Arcy
    Godolphin, 287–89
Ottawa, 59, 79, 86, 121, 124, 159, 172,
    185, 189, 199, 239
Ottawa, University of, 79
Oxford, University of, 45, 51

Pahang, 223
Paoshan, 293
Paray-le-Monial, 98
Paris, 31, 47, 71, 73, 85, 92, 93, 104, 109,
    124, 178, 250, 255, 257–58, 262,
    267, 268, 269, 274, 276, 278, 281,
    282, 283, 285
Paterson, George Robert, 174–76
Pau, 48, 259, 263
Pavicich, Marko, 151
Pavicich, Mica, 151
Pavlic, Paul, 138–39, 141, 146

Pearkes, George, 187–88
Pécs, 162–63
Pegu Yoma Mountains, 209, 214–15
Penticton, British Columbia, 188
Perlis, 234–35, 238
Perpignan, 263
Pertschuk, Maurice, 37–38
Petit Rocher, New Brunswick, 125
Pickersgill, Frank Herbert Dedrick,
    xiv, 44–58, 60–63, 70–71, 73–74,
    76, 286
Pickersgill, Jack, xv, 45, 47, 48
"Pimento" Circuit, 79–80
Placke, Josef, 57, 60–62
Plelo, 284–85
Plogoff, 267
Plouha, 254, 255, 268, 276, 281–84
Political Warfare Executive, 90, 105,
    113–15, 178
Pont d'Ain, 91
Poona, 179, 185, 203, 226
Port Swettenham, 238n
Portal, Charles, 5
Privas, 120
"Prosper" Circuit, 33, 41, 53–56
Protville, 17, 117
"Prunus" Circuit, 37–38
Pyrenees, 10, 38, 82, 108, 249, 253,
    270, 281
Putra, Syed, 235–36, 238

Quebec City, 202
Queen's Own Rifles, 172
Queen's University, 151
Queen's York Rangers, 170
Quimper, 47, 265

Rabinowitch, Alec, 61
Rake, Dennis, 108
Ramat, David, 137, 141
Rambouillet, 257–58

Rangoon, 183, 208–10, 213–17,
   219–20, 222, 233, 303–5
Ravitsch (Rawicz), 41, 56, 60, 62
Rawalpindi, 239
Rechenmann, Charles, 81–83
Recife, 136
Red Deer, Alberta, 225
Reims, 93, 270–71
Rejang River, 193–97, 199
Relief of Allied Prisoners of War and
   Internees, (R.A.P.W.I.), 225
Rennes, 43, 259, 279
Revigny, 102–3
Rhône, 66, 120, 123
Richmond, Quebec, 95
Ride, Leslie, 184
Rilly-de-Montagne, 94
Ringway, 17, 19–21, 29, 39, 65, 81, 100,
   116, 164, 174, 265, 273
Rivière-du-Loup, Quebec, 101
Robertson, Norman, 148
Rochester, University of, 173
Rodrigues, Georges, 71, 285–86
Romas-Petit, Henri, 112
Rome, 287–89
Romorantin, 54
Roosevelt, Franklin, 138, 150, 190,
   206
Ross, Captain, 295
Rouen, 34, 40, 262
Rousset, M.J.L., 41
Royal Army Medical Corps, 112, 151
Royal Artillery, 126
Royal Canadian Army Medical
   Corps, 163, 217
Royal Canadian Artillery, 60, 236,
   299
Royal Canadian Corps of Signals,
   (R.C.C.S.), 59, 65, 75, 76, 79, 80,
   110, 121, 124, 125, 127, 186, 202,
   255, 285
Royal Canadian Engineers, 188
Royal Canadian Ordnance Corps, 110
Royal Hamilton Light Infantry, 156

Royal Montreal Regiment, 38
Royal 22nd Regiment, 117, 121, 236
Rudellat, Yvonne, 54–55

Sabourin, Romeo, xiv, 61–62, 65, 71,
   73–74, 80, 278, 286
Saigon, 205, 206
Saint-Brieuc, 276, 279, 282–83, 285
St. Catharines, Ontario, 163
St. Denis, 48, 245
St. Génie Laval, 66
St. Jean d'Iberville, Quebec, 261
St. Michel-en-Maurienne, 127
St. Perpetué, Quebec, 110
St. Quentin, 28, 31, 33–34, 44, 65,
   67–69
St. Rambert, 91
Salween River, 209
San Francisco, 189, 205
San Sebastian, 249, 271
San Vito dei Normanni, 160–61
Sarnia, 169
Saskatchewan, University of, 216
Saskatoon, 80, 202n
Sault, 122, 123
Saumur, 48
"Savannah," Operation, 157
Schwerin, 286
Sea Reconnaisance Units, 304–5
Seaford, 237
Searle, Robert, 117
Sedan, 54, 62
Sées, 114
Selangor, 228–29
Serbia, 150, 152
Serdar, Stevan, xv, 139, 151
Seremban, 229
Services Reconnaisance Department,
   183, 193, 196
Seymour, John, 166–67
Seyne, 126
Shan State, 218–19
Sharic, Joe, 151

Shaw, Allen, 232–33
Shawinigan Falls, Quebec, 110
"Shelburne" Line, 274, 279–81, 283
Sherk, Ray, 247
"Shetland Bus," 188
Shiu, Jimmy, 196, 198
Sibu, 197, 199
Simic, Alexandre, 138–39, 141, 146
Singapore, 178, 180–82, 199, 204,
    221–23, 227, 229, 237, 241, 294–99,
    305–6
Sirois, Allyre Louis Joseph, xv, 80, 85,
    96, 106, 202, 233
Sittang River, 209–10, 214, 219
Slovenia, 147
Smrke, Janez, 151
Sochon, William, 193
Special Air Service, 285
Special Boat Section, 304–5
Special Training School 101, 87,
    180–82
Special Training School 102, 137
Special Training School 103, 87, 89,
    92, 95, 99, 136, 155–56, 159,
    169–70, 173, 188
S-Phone, 18, 62, 193
Stafford, David, xiii, 171
Stalin, Josef, 130
Starcevic, Ivan, 143
Stefano, Joseph, 172
Stephenson, William, 88
Stewart, Arthur, 292–99
Stichman, Paul, 151
Stradishall, 17
Strange, Burton, 303, 305
Strasbourg, 114
Stuart, Sir Campbell, 2
Stuart, William Yull, 134–35, 137,
    141–43
Stuki, Walter, 109
Sumatra, 298
Sungei Patani, 235
Suttill, Alfred Francis, 53–56
Sweet-Escott, Bickham, xiii, 208

Swift Current, Saskatchewan, 225
Sydney, 191
Szenttamáspuszta, 157

Taiwan, 184
Tampin, 232
Taranto, 289
Tarbes, 83
Taschereau, Leonard Jacques, 99–104,
    202, 203, 210–12
Tempsford, 17, 30, 116, 257
Tenay, 91
Thame, 81
Tharrawaddy, 217
Thibeault, Paul-Emile, xv, 99–104,
    202, 203, 210, 212–14
Three Bridges, 256
Thunder Bay, Ontario, 158
"Tideway Green," Operation, 239–41
Tientsin, 292
Tito, 6, 132, 134, 135, 138–39, 141–42,
    148, 157–58, 161–62
Tokai, 162
Toronto, 52, 80, 87, 88, 97, 125, 133,
    135, 140, 145, 156, 158–59, 163,
    168n, 170, 172, 186, 202, 271n, 290
Toronto, University of, 45, 47, 51, 140
Toulouse, 37, 79–81, 259, 260, 262–63
Toungoo, 209–10, 215, 229
Tourcoing, 34
Tours, 40, 47
Transylvania, 156
Trepca, 134
Trincomalee, 179
Trotobas, Michael, 28, 67
Troyes, 100, 104
Turk, Michael, 162–63, 165, 167

Unionville, Ontario, 168

Valencay, 53

Vancouver, 47, 135, 188, 189, 191, 199, 226, 228, 232, 233
Vanier, Georges, 47, 118
Vanier, Robert, xv, 261–69
Vass, Alexander, 163–65
Vaucluse, 122–23
Veilleux, Marcel, 110-13
Ventoux, 122
Vernon, British Columbia, 204
Vernonvillers, 104
Verona, 173
Veszprém, 164
Vetere, Ralph, 172–73
Vichy, 9, 27, 47–48, 106, 108–10, 204, 206, 264
Victoria, British Columbia, 305
Vienna, 165
Vining, Charles, 88
Vis, 290
Vonda, Saskatchewan, 80

Wake, Nancy, 108–9
Walter, Felix, 12, 30, 76, 90, 97, 201–2
Wanborough, Manor, 29
Wedemeyer, Albert, 190–91
Wellandport, Ontario, 149

Western Ontario, University of, 173
Wetaskiwin, Alberta, 225
Wetzlar, 165
Whitby, Ontario, 87–88, 136
Wickey, John Hippolyte, xv, 113–15
Williams, Val (Bouryschkine, Vladimir), 254–55, 257–60, 273, 279
Windsor, Ontario, 161n, 170
Winnipeg, 44–45, 47, 60, 133, 156
Wong, Ted, xv, 228
Wooler, John Raymond, xv, 19, 116–17, 161, 193–96, 199
Wright, Bruce, 302–5
Wright, Richard, 164–65
Wuppertal, 115

Yaritch, A.D., 290
Yeo-Thomas, F.F.E., 49–50, 70–71
Yunnan, 293–94

Zagreb, 134
"Zipper," Operation, 222–24, 229, 232, 240, 294, 306